Advances in Information Security

Volume 78

Series editor
Sushil Jajodia, George Mason University, Fairfax, VA, USA

More information about this series at http://www.springer.com/series/5576

Saed Alrabaee • Mourad Debbabi • Paria Shirani
Lingyu Wang • Amr Youssef • Ashkan Rahimian
Lina Nouh • Djedjiga Mouheb • He Huang
Aiman Hanna

Binary Code Fingerprinting for Cybersecurity

Application to Malicious Code Fingerprinting

 Springer

Saed Alrabaee
Information Systems & Security (CIT)
United Arab Emirates University
Al Ain, United Arab Emirates

Paria Shirani
Gina Cody School of Engineering
and Computer Science
Concordia University
Montreal, QC, Canada

Amr Youssef
Gina Cody School of Engineering
and Computer Science
Concordia University
Montreal, QC, Canada

Lina Nouh
Deloitte Middle East
Riyadh, Saudi Arabia

He Huang
Moody's Analytics
Toronto, ON, Canada

Mourad Debbabi
Gina Cody School of Engineering
and Computer Science
Concordia University
Montreal, QC, Canada

Lingyu Wang
Gina Cody School of Engineering
and Computer Science
Concordia University
Montreal, QC, Canada

Ashkan Rahimian
East Tower
Bay Adelaide Centre Deloitte Canada
Toronto, ON, Canada

Djedjiga Mouheb
Department of Computer Science
University of Sharjah
Sharjah, United Arab Emirates

Aiman Hanna
Gina Cody School of Engineering
and Computer Science
Concordia University
Montreal, QC, Canada

ISSN 1568-2633   ISSN 2512-2193   (electronic)
Advances in Information Security
ISBN 978-3-030-34240-1   ISBN 978-3-030-34238-8   (eBook)
https://doi.org/10.1007/978-3-030-34238-8

This Springer imprint is published by the registered company Springer Nature Switzerland AG.
The registered company address is: Gewerbestrasse 11, 6330 Cham, Switzerland

Preface

Today's industries, government agencies, and individuals heavily rely on information and communication technologies, which make them vulnerable to cyber-attacks targeting their digital and critical infrastructure. Furthermore, millions of malware strains are detected on a daily basis that might have significant security and privacy consequences on these systems and their users. Furthermore, many developers reuse libraries without performing an in-depth security analysis to find potential vulnerabilities in the borrowed code. As such, designing and implementing automatic and/or systematic techniques to detect and fingerprint these security threats in binary code is a highly desired capability in the cybersecurity domain.

Binary analysis is an essential capability with extensive applications, such as reverse engineering, threat and vulnerability analysis, malware analysis, digital forensics, software infringement, and code reuse detection. Binary code fingerprinting is a challenging problem that requires an in-depth analysis of the code and its components in order to derive canonical signatures and patterns, termed as fingerprints. Binary code fingerprinting can be precious to several analyses and use cases of paramount importance, such as compiler provenance, library function identification, code reuse detection, vulnerability search, patch analysis, malware detection and malware clustering, and authorship attribution. Indeed, automatically recognizing reused functions in a binary code is a critical requirement in binary code fingerprinting, especially considering the fact that many modern pieces of malware typically contain a significant amount of library functions, or functions borrowed from free and open-source software packages. Besides, with the large influx of malware samples and binary code to be analyzed on a daily basis, special care should be dedicated to the efficiency and the scalability of binary code fingerprinting. Providing such a capability will dramatically reduce the workload of reverse engineers and will greatly improve the efficiency as well as the accuracy of binary code fingerprinting. Furthermore, this capability is extremely useful for security researchers and reverse engineers, since it can provide important insights about a given binary code, such as revealing its functionality, attribution to its author(s), identifying reused libraries, and detecting vulnerabilities. Nevertheless, automated binary code fingerprinting is inherently a challenging undertaking, since a substantial amount of important information available in the source code does not survive the compilation process.

This book is the result of numerous years of research on binary code fingerprinting. It addresses several major challenges in this domain and presents novel, automatic, accurate, efficient, and scalable binary analysis techniques. In terms of book structure, the authors first tackle compiler provenance attribution to identify the compiler family, version, and optimization settings. Next, the authors propose different function identification methods for (a) addressing the need of efficiently identifying standard library functions, (b) providing solutions for identifying reused functions, (c) addressing the identification of reused free open-source software packages, and (d) identifying similar functions between two binary code samples or a given code and a database of already analyzed functions. Finally, authorship attribution addresses the problem of inferring information related to the authorship of a given binary code. The book illustrates the application of the aforementioned solutions to malware samples and vulnerable binary code and demonstrate the efficiency, scalability, and accuracy of the proposed approaches in real-world scenarios.

This book provides a comprehensive state-of-the-art knowledge on binary code fingerprinting, covering a wide range of binary analysis applications along with their challenges, and proposes innovative solutions to address these challenges. It offers key insights and critical knowledge to security engineers, researchers, graduate students, professors, and subject matter experts who are involved in reverse engineering, malware analysis, and binary code fingerprinting.

Al Ain, United Arab Emirates   Saed Alrabaee
Montreal, QC, Canada   Mourad Debbabi
Montreal, QC, Canada   Paria Shirani
Montreal, QC, Canada   Lingyu Wang
Montreal, QC, Canada   Amr Youssef
Toronto, ON, Canada   Ashkan Rahimian
Riyadh, Saudi Arabia   Lina Nouh
Sharjah, United Arab Emirates   Djedjiga Mouheb
Toronto, ON, Canada   He Huang
Montreal, QC, Canada   Aiman Hanna
November 20, 2019

Acknowledgments

We would like to express our gratitude to our collaborators who have enabled us to develop a great understanding of the challenges and the techniques underlying malware defence and binary code fingerprinting research. In this regard, Dr. Debbabi would like to pay tribute and express his gratitude to one of the very first pioneers of cybersecurity R&D in Canada, namely Robert Charpenter, a retired national defence scientist who had a major positive impact on this important and strategic field since the mid-1990s. It was a privilege and an honor to co-lead with him a series of impactful and successful research collaborations and to train a generation of successful and highly qualified cybersecurity experts. Later, we have had the pleasure to collaborate with Philippe Charland, Thomas Dullien, Martin Salois, and Benjamin Fung under the National Defence (DND) and Natural Sciences and Engineering Research Council of Canada (NSERC) research partnership program. At the successful completion of this great collaborative R&D project, we pursued research on this topic with support from the NSERC Discovery Grant, Concordia University Research Chair Tier 1 in Information Systems Security, Faculty Research Support program of the Gina Cody School of Engineering and Computer Science as well as the National Defence NSERC Discovery Accelerator Supplement Program. A special thanks as well to Dr. Andrei Soeanu for his valuable feedback and suggestions.

Contents

1	**Introduction**	1
	1.1 Motivations	2
	1.2 Binary Fingerprinting for Cybersecurity	3
	1.3 Outline	4
2	**Binary Analysis Overview**	7
	2.1 The Importance of Binary Analysis	7
	2.1.1 Evading Techniques of Malware Detection	9
	2.1.2 Binary Analysis Challenges	10
	2.2 Software Fingerprinting Applications	11
	2.2.1 Authorship Attribution	12
	2.2.2 Clone Detection	14
	2.2.3 Library Function Fingerprinting	16
	2.2.4 Binary Software Evolution	18
	2.2.5 Vulnerability Analysis	20
	2.2.6 Program Provenance Analysis	21
	2.3 Methodology	22
	2.3.1 Nature of Binary Analysis	23
	2.3.2 Binary Analysis Strategies	25
	2.3.3 Binary Analysis Approaches	25
	2.3.4 Feature Taxonomy	25
	2.4 Implementation	28
	2.4.1 Disassembling Tools	28
	2.4.2 Feature Ranking	30
	2.4.3 Machine Learning Techniques	31
	2.4.4 Distance Between Features	33
	2.5 Code Transformation	34
	2.5.1 Obfuscation Techniques	34
	2.5.2 Refactoring Techniques	35
	2.5.3 The Impact of Compilers	35

2.6   Binary Frameworks for Software Fingerprints 36
       2.6.1   BitBlaze 36
       2.6.2   BAP 36
       2.6.3   BinNavi 36
       2.6.4   iBinHunt 36
       2.6.5   BitShred 37
       2.6.6   BinSlayer 37
       2.6.7   BinJuice 37
       2.6.8   BinCoa 37
       2.6.9   BINSEC 38
       2.6.10   BinGraph 38
       2.6.11   MAYHEM 38
       2.6.12   Exposé 39
       2.6.13   REWARDS 39
       2.6.14   Helium 39
       2.6.15   Hercules 40
       2.6.16   Malheur 40
       2.6.17   MARD 40
       2.6.18   BinGold 40
       2.6.19   BinGo 41
       2.6.20   BinConvex 41
       2.6.21   BinCross 41
       2.6.22   BARF 42
       2.6.23   Aligot 42
       2.6.24   Howard 42
2.7   Learned Lessons and Concluding Remarks 43

3 Compiler Provenance Attribution 45
3.1   Introduction 45
       3.1.1   Objectives 46
       3.1.2   Motivating Example 47
       3.1.3   Approach Overview 50
3.2   Compiler Provenance 51
       3.2.1   Tier 1: Compiler Family Identification 52
       3.2.2   Tier 2: Compiler Functions Labeling 56
       3.2.3   Tier 3: Version and Optimization Recognition 63
3.3   ECP Approach 69
       3.3.1   ECP Overview 69
       3.3.2   Dataset Generation 70
       3.3.3   ECP Evaluation Results 70
       3.3.4   Discussion 72
3.4   BINCOMP Evaluation 73
       3.4.1   Dataset Preparation 73
       3.4.2   Evaluation Results 73
       3.4.3   Comparison 76
3.5   Limitations and Concluding Remarks 77

4 Library Function Identification 79
   4.1 Introduction 80
      4.1.1 Motivating Example 81
      4.1.2 Threat Model 82
      4.1.3 Approach Overview... 82
   4.2 Feature Extraction 83
      4.2.1 Graph Feature Metrics 84
      4.2.2 Instruction-Level Features 85
      4.2.3 Statistical Features 86
      4.2.4 Function-Call Graph 87
      4.2.5 Feature Selection.. 88
   4.3 Detection 89
      4.3.1 B^{++}tree Data Structure 89
      4.3.2 Filtering 91
   4.4 Evaluation.. 92
      4.4.1 Experimental Setup 92
      4.4.2 Dataset Preparation 92
      4.4.3 Function Identification Accuracy Results.................... 94
      4.4.4 Impact of Compilers 95
      4.4.5 Impact of Feature Selection 95
      4.4.6 Impact of Filtering 97
      4.4.7 Scalability Study 97
   4.5 Limitations and Concluding Remarks 98

5 Identifying Reused Functions in Binary Code 101
   5.1 Existing Representations of Binary Code 101
      5.1.1 Control Flow Graph.. 102
      5.1.2 Register Flow Graph 103
      5.1.3 Function-Call Graph 106
   5.2 Reused Function Identification.................................. 107
      5.2.1 Overview 107
      5.2.2 Building *SIG* Blocks 108
      5.2.3 *SIG*: Semantic Integrated Graph 112
      5.2.4 Graph Edit Distance 115
   5.3 Evaluation.. 116
      5.3.1 Dataset.. 117
      5.3.2 Accuracy Results of Sorting and Encryption Algorithms.. 118
      5.3.3 Impact of Compilers and Compilation Settings 120
      5.3.4 Impact of Obfuscation and Refactoring Techniques 121
   5.4 Limitations and Concluding Remarks 122

6 Function Fingerprinting 123
   6.1 Introduction 123
      6.1.1 Overview 124
      6.1.2 Threat Model 125

6.2   Function Fingerprinting 126
      6.2.1   Feature Extraction... 126
      6.2.2   Fingerprint Generation....................................... 131
      6.2.3   Fingerprint Matching 135
6.3   Evaluation 140
      6.3.1   Dataset Preparation 141
      6.3.2   Comparison with Existing Tools 142
      6.3.3   Function Reuse Detection 143
      6.3.4   Scalability Evaluation.. 146
      6.3.5   Resilience to Different Compiler Optimization Levels 147
      6.3.6   Library Function Detection.................................. 149
      6.3.7   Malware Similarity Analysis 151
      6.3.8   Resilience to Obfuscation 152
6.4   Limitations and Concluding Remarks 155

7   Free Open-Source Software Fingerprinting 157
7.1   Introduction 157
      7.1.1   Approach Overview.. 159
      7.1.2   Threat Model 160
7.2   Identifying FOSS Functions 160
      7.2.1   Normalization 160
      7.2.2   Feature Extraction... 161
      7.2.3   Feature Analysis 161
      7.2.4   Feature Selection.. 162
      7.2.5   Detection Method 165
7.3   Evaluation 172
      7.3.1   Experiment Setup 172
      7.3.2   Dataset Preparation 172
      7.3.3   Evaluation Metrics 173
      7.3.4   FOSSIL Accuracy.. 174
      7.3.5   Comparison 174
      7.3.6   Scalability Study 176
      7.3.7   The Confidence Estimation of a Bayesian Network........ 176
      7.3.8   The Impact of Evading Techniques 177
      7.3.9   The Impact of Compilers 180
      7.3.10 Applying FOSSIL to Real Malware Binaries............... 181
7.4   Limitations and Concluding Remarks 185

8   Clone Detection 187
8.1   Introduction 187
      8.1.1   Motivating Example 188
      8.1.2   Overview 190
8.2   Function Clone Detection 190
      8.2.1   Normalization 190
      8.2.2   Basic Block Comparison 192
      8.2.3   Fuzzy Matching Detection Engine 193
      8.2.4   Fingerprint-Based Detection Engine 197

8.3 Evaluation... 198
    8.3.1 Clone Detection 198
    8.3.2 Compiler Optimization 201
    8.3.3 Code Obfuscation 202
    8.3.4 Recovering Patch Information................. 204
    8.3.5 Searching Malware and Vulnerability Functions 207
    8.3.6 Comparison with Other Tools 208
8.4 Limitations and Concluding Remarks 209

9 Authorship Attribution 211
9.1 Approach Overview 211
9.2 Authorship Attribution 212
    9.2.1 Filtering 213
    9.2.2 Canonicalization 214
    9.2.3 Choice Categorization 215
    9.2.4 Classification 220
9.3 Evaluation... 221
    9.3.1 Experimental Setup 222
    9.3.2 Dataset....................................... 222
    9.3.3 Evaluation Metrics 222
    9.3.4 Accuracy 223
    9.3.5 Scalability 225
    9.3.6 Impact of Code Transformation Techniques................ 226
    9.3.7 Impact of Obfuscation 227
    9.3.8 Impact of Compilers and Compilation Settings 227
    9.3.9 Applying BINAUTHOR to Real Malware Binaries........ 227
9.4 Limitations and Concluding Remarks 230

10 Conclusion.. 231

References... 235

List of Figures

Fig. 2.1   The applications of fingerprints in binary code 12
Fig. 2.2   A taxonomy of authorship attribution approaches 14
Fig. 2.3   A taxonomy of clone detection approaches 15
Fig. 2.4   A categorization of binary analysis topics.......................... 23
Fig. 2.5   A taxonomy of binary features 26

Fig. 3.1   BINCOMP multi-tiered framework 51
Fig. 3.2   Supervised compilation steps and produced artifacts 52
Fig. 3.3   Statement transformation example in MSVC, GCC, and Clang.... 54
Fig. 3.4   Intersecting programs to obtain common compiler functions 57
Fig. 3.5   Clustering and heatmap of syntactical/structural features 62
Fig. 3.6   ACFG construction of __do_global_ctors() function....... 67
Fig. 3.7   Fingerprint of __do_global_ctors() function 68
Fig. 3.8   Sample of GCC compiler constructor and terminator.............. 69
Fig. 3.9   Accuracy results 71
Fig. 3.10   Impact of the threshold value 71
Fig. 3.11   Diversity in datasets 72
Fig. 3.12   Time efficiency... 72
Fig. 3.13   The accuracy against different compilers........................... 75
Fig. 3.14   Time efficiency... 76
Fig. 3.15   Accuracy comparison of BINCOMP, XIDA PRO, and IDA PRO ... 77

Fig. 4.1   Control flow graph of three library functions 81
Fig. 4.2   Approach overview 83
Fig. 4.3   Indexing and detection structure 90
Fig. 4.4   ROC curve for BINSHAPE features 94
Fig. 4.5   Impact of top-ranked features 96
Fig. 4.6   Impact of best features 96

Fig. 4.7   Impact of filtering 97
Fig. 4.8   Scalability study 98

Fig. 5.1   Control flow graph for bubble sort function 102
Fig. 5.2   Register flow graph construction.................................... 105
Fig. 5.3   Register flow graph for bubble sort function 106
Fig. 5.4   Function-call graph for bubble sort function 106
Fig. 5.5   SIGMA approach overview 107
Fig. 5.6   iCFG for bubble sort function 110
Fig. 5.7   mRFG for bubble sort function 111
Fig. 5.8   cFCG for bubble sort function 112
Fig. 5.9   Simple example of *SIG* 113
Fig. 5.10   *SIG* for bubble sort 114
Fig. 5.11   Statistics of function variants similarities 118

Fig. 6.1   BINSIGN system 125
Fig. 6.2   Fingerprint generation process 131
Fig. 6.3   Example of tracelet generation..................................... 132
Fig. 6.4   Sample of a function CFG... 136
Fig. 6.5   Fingerprint matching process 138
Fig. 6.6   Example of candidate selection 139
Fig. 6.7   Number of target functions vs. number of candidate functions 144
Fig. 6.8   Impact of number of basic blocks on the matching time........... 145
Fig. 6.9   Architecture of the distribution process 147
Fig. 6.10   Matching different optimization levels 148
Fig. 6.11   CFG of different versions of _memcmp function 150
Fig. 6.12   CFG of different versions of _memcpy_s function............... 151
Fig. 6.13   CFG of RC4 function in (**a**) Zeus and (**b**) Citadel 152
Fig. 6.14   Effects of obfuscation techniques on a CFG 153
Fig. 6.15   Examples of instruction substitution in basic blocks.............. 154

Fig. 7.1   Approach overview 159
Fig. 7.2   Random walks between BB_0 and BB_7 nodes 163
Fig. 7.3   Neighborhood subgraph hash labels computation example 169
Fig. 7.4   The performance of FOSSIL against a large set of functions 177
Fig. 7.5   Confidence estimation: precision vs. recall 177
Fig. 7.6   Obtained FOSS packages in malware families 183
Fig. 7.7   The relationship between FOSS packages and malware evolution . 185

Fig. 8.1   Examples of control structures and corresponding CFGs........... 189
Fig. 8.2   Examples of nested control structures and corresponding CFGs... 189
Fig. 8.3   Workflow of BINSEQUENCE 190
Fig. 8.4   Basic block normalization... 191
Fig. 8.5   Basic block comparison 193

Fig. 8.6   Two versions of the same function 195
Fig. 8.7   The memoization table of path exploration 196
Fig. 8.8   An example of neighborhood exploration 197
Fig. 8.9   Accuracy of different optimization levels 202
Fig. 8.10   `UlpParseRange` function before and after patch 205
Fig. 8.11   `UlpDuplicateChunkRange` before and after patch 206
Fig. 8.12   One of the patched parts of the *UlpDuplicateChunkRange* 207

Fig. 9.1   BINAUTHOR architecture 213
Fig. 9.2   Precision results of authorship attribution 224
Fig. 9.3   Large-scale author attribution precision 226

List of Tables

Table 2.1   A comparison between different authorship attribution systems .   13
Table 2.2   A comparison between different binary clone detection systems.   17
Table 2.3   A comparison of static library function identification systems ...   19
Table 2.4   Software evaluation recovery systems comparison................   20
Table 2.5   Bug search and vulnerability detection systems comparison   21
Table 2.6   Program provenances discovery systems comparison............   22
Table 2.7   Comparison of disassembler tools   31

Table 3.1   List of disassembly functions (MSVCP binary)..................   49
Table 3.2   Mnemonic groups and operand types used in normalization   55
Table 3.3   Clustering based on numerical and symbolic features   59
Table 3.4   Instruction patterns for annotation   64
Table 3.5   Utilized compilers and compilation settings for dataset
            generation   73
Table 3.6 F-measure results..   74
Table 3.7   Accuracy results for variations of compiler versions   76
Table 3.8   Accuracy for variations of compiler optimization levels   76

Table 4.1   Examples of graph metrics   84
Table 4.2   Comparing graph features of _memcpy_s and _strcpy_s   85
Table 4.3   Example of instruction-level features   85
Table 4.4   Example of mnemonic groups   86
Table 4.5   An excerpt of the projects included in our the dataset   93
Table 4.6   Impact of compilers and optimization settings   95

Table 5.1   Original classes of register access   103
Table 5.2   Structural information categories..................................   109
Table 5.3   Color classes for iCFG   109
Table 5.4   Updated register classes for Table 5.1   111
Table 5.5   Part of traces for SIG bubble sort function   115
Table 5.6   Graph features for exact matching   115
Table 5.7   Programs used in our system evaluation   117

Table 5.8   Similarity between sort function variants 119
Table 5.9   Similarity between encryption function variants 119
Table 5.10   Dissimilarity between sort and encryption functions 120
Table 5.11   Accuracy in determining the similarity between binaries 120
Table 5.12   Impact of light obfuscation and refactoring techniques 121

Table 6.1   Tracelet features 127
Table 6.2   Global features 128
Table 6.3   Mnemonic groups 129
Table 6.4   Examples of API categories 130
Table 6.5   Example of signature hash generation 134
Table 6.6   Example of a function fingerprint illustrated in Fig. 6.4 137
Table 6.7   Feature weights 140
Table 6.8   Dataset details 141
Table 6.9   Function matching comparison 142
Table 6.10   Results of function reuse detection 144
Table 6.11   Impact of different optimization levels on accuracy 148
Table 6.12   Library function identification in `Putty.exe` 149
Table 6.13   Library function identification in `Heap.exe` 149
Table 6.14   Candidates of RC4 Function from `Citadel` 151

Table 7.1   Top-ranked opcode distributions of sorting algorithms 165
Table 7.2   Instruction frequencies in function x 166
Table 7.3   Instruction frequencies in function y 167
Table 7.4   Top-ranked opcode frequencies and corresponding z-scores 170
Table 7.5   Example of the functionality of collected FOSS packages 173
Table 7.6   Accuracy results without BN model 174
Table 7.7   Accuracy results with BN model 174
Table 7.8   Accuracy results of different versions of FOSS packages 175
Table 7.9   Comparison results on 160 projects 175
Table 7.10   Evading techniques and their effect on FOSSIL component...... 179
Table 7.11   Impact of compilers and compilation settings 180
Table 7.12   FOSS functions found in malware binaries 181
Table 7.13   Results comparsion with exisiting technical reports 182

Table 8.1   The memoization table of the LCS of `ABCAE` and `BAE` strings .. 192
Table 8.2   Clone detection results using open-source projects as noise 199
Table 8.3   Clone detection results using dynamic link libraries as noise 200
Table 8.4   Clone detection results between `zlib` and `libpng` 200
Table 8.5   Results for function reuse detection 203
Table 8.6   Patched analysis for `HTTP.sys` 204
Table 8.7   Comparison with other tools 208

Table 9.1   An example of computing (μ_i, ν_i) 214
Table 9.2   Features extracted from the `main` function....................... 216

Table 9.3	Examples of actions taken in terminating a function	216
Table 9.4	Logistic regression weights for choices	221
Table 9.5	Dataset statistics for BINAUTHOR evaluation	222
Table 9.6	Characteristics of malware dataset	228
Table 9.7	Statistics of applying BINAUTHOR to malware binaries	228

Chapter 1
Introduction

Binary code fingerprinting is essential to many security use cases and applications; examples include reverse engineering, digital forensics, malware detection and analysis, threat and vulnerability analysis, patch analysis, and software license infringement. More specifically, in the context of security, such a capability is highly required to analyze large amount of malware and applications in order to uncover their malicious behaviors, characterize their network footprints, and consequently derive timely, relevant, and actionable cyber intelligence that could be used for detection, prevention, mitigation, and attribution purposes. Indeed, everyday, a deluge of cyberattacks is launched against the cyber infrastructure of corporations, governmental agencies, and individuals, with unprecedented sophistication, speed, intensity, volume, inflicted damage, and audacity. Besides, the threat landscape is shifting towards more stealthy, mercurial, and targeted advanced persistent threats and attacks against industrial control systems, Internet of things (IoT) devices, social networks, software defined network (SDN) and cloud infrastructure, mobile devices and related core networks, which exacerbates even more the security challenges. These attacks emanate from a wide spectrum of perpetrators such as criminals, cyber-terrorists, and foreign intelligence/military services. The damage can be even more significant when the target involves critical infrastructure components. In this context, there is an acute desideratum towards binary code fingerprinting techniques and technologies in order to subject the aforementioned threats to an in-depth analysis and correlation to derive timely and relevant cyber threat intelligence that can enable detection, prevention, mitigation, and attribution of related cyberattacks.

This book addresses some of the most important aspects of binary code fingerprinting such as compiler provenance, reused binary code discovery, fingerprinting of free open-source software packages, and authorship attribution.

© Springer Nature Switzerland AG 2020
S. Alrabaee et al., *Binary Code Fingerprinting for Cybersecurity*, Advances in
Information Security 78, https://doi.org/10.1007/978-3-030-34238-8_1

1.1 Motivations

Reverse engineering [126] is a primary step towards understanding the functionality and the behavior of a software when its source code is unavailable. The objective of reverse engineering often involves understanding both the control and data flow structures of the functions in a given binary code. However, reverse engineering is a tedious and time-consuming process, as binary code inherently lacks structure due to the use of jumps and symbolic addresses, highly optimized control flow, varying registers and memory locations based on the processor architecture and compiler, and the possibility of interruptions [70], and thus its success depends heavily on the experience and knowledge of the reverse engineering team. Moreover, when the software to be analyzed is large in size, this task becomes tedious and overwhelming.

Binary code fingerprinting is extremely useful for reverse engineers and security experts, since it allows for the extraction of fingerprints that capture the needed semantics for a target application. However, fingerprint extraction is a challenging task since a substantial amount of important information is lost during the compilation process, notably, typing information, variable and function naming, original control and data flows, etc.

Binary code fingerprinting for code reuse detection is of great interest to reverse engineers. For example, given a binary and a repository of already analyzed and commented code, one can speed up the analysis by applying code reuse detection on a given unknown binary. This allows to identify identical or similar code in the repository, and to subsequently focus only on the new functionality or distinct components of the binary. This is especially important in the context of malware analysis, since modern malware are known to contain a significant amount of reused code [81]. Moreover, a typical goal of malware analysts is to discover clues that lead to identifying the parties that are the originators or developers of the malicious code. Such clues should be able to discriminate among code produced by different authors, which could also be used to detect stylistic similarities between several malicious programs, or to track the sharing of program components and programmer expertise within the malware community. Additionally, binary code fingerprinting is of high interest to software maintainers and consumers. In many software development environments, it is common practice to copy and paste existing source code, as this can significantly reduce programming effort and time. However, if the reused code contains a bug or a vulnerability, and the developers copied the code without fixing the bug, they may bring the bug into their own project. Library reuse is a special case in which developers either include the source code of a certain library into their projects, or statically link to the library. Either way, the bug contained in the copied code will be brought into the new project. Thus, code reuse detection can help identifying such bugs resulting from source code sharing.

Last but not least, binary code fingerprinting can be applied in numerous scenarios, such as software plagiarism detection, open-source project license violation detection, and binary diffing. In essence, code reuse detection can be typically achieved by calculating the similarity percentage of two code regions. The higher the similarity, the more likely they are from the same source code base.

1.2 Binary Fingerprinting for Cybersecurity

In order to assist reverse engineers and security analysts in their challenging pursuits, automatic and efficient techniques together with the underlying tools are needed to extract fingerprints from binary code in order to support various use cases and applications. We detail hereafter some of these analyses that are extremely relevant in reverse engineering especially when it comes to the security investigation of a target binary code.

Compiler Provenance Attribution: Compiler provenance comprises numerous pieces of information, including compiler family and version, compiler-related functions, and compiler optimization level. Obtaining this information is essential for many binary analysis applications, such as clone detection, function fingerprinting, and authorship attribution. Consequently, it is important to elaborate an efficient and automated approach for ascertaining compiler provenance.

Function Fingerprinting: Binary code fingerprinting represents a challenging undertaking which requires an in-depth analysis of binary components in order to derive signatures that can be used for identification purposes. Fingerprints are useful in automating reverse engineering tasks, such as clone detection, library identification, authorship attribution, malware analysis, patch and vulnerability analysis, etc.

Function Reuse Identification: Modern software programs binaries usually contain a significant amount of third-party library functions reused from standard libraries or Free Open-Source Software packages (FOSS). When the source code is unavailable, it is important for security applications (e.g., malware detection, software license infringement, and digital forensics) to be able to identify the use of FOSS packages in a target binary. This capability also enhances the effectiveness and efficiency of reverse engineering tasks since it reduces false library correlations with otherwise unrelated code bases. Specifically, during the analysis of malware binaries, reverse engineers often pay special attention to reused functions and free open-source packages for several reasons. First, recent reports from anti-virus and anti-malware companies indicate that finding the similarity between malware codes attributable to reused third-party libraries can aid in developing profiles for malware families [186]. For instance, Flame [81] and other malware in its family [80] all contain code packages that are publicly available, including SQLite and LUA [186]. Second, a significant proportion of most modern malware leverages third-party libraries. As such, identifying reused libraries is a critical preliminary step in the process of extracting information about the functionality of a malware binary. This could also help during malware triage in order to identify common types of malware and to determine their functionalities and threat levels. Third, in more challenging situations, where obfuscation techniques (semantically equivalent code alterations to make it difficult to understand) might have been applied and binaries of reused third-party libraries may differ from those of their original source files, it is still desirable to determine which parts of the malware binary are borrowed from which third-party libraries. Finally, in addition to identifying third-party library reuse, clustering third-party libraries based on their common origin may help reverse engineers to identify new malware from a known family or to decompose a malware binary based on the origin of its functions.

Binary Authorship Identification: Binary authorship attribution refers to the process of identifying the author(s) of a given anonymous binary code based on stylistic characteristics. It aims to automate the laborious and often error-prone reverse engineering task of discovering information related to the author(s) of a binary code. Therefore, segregating features related to program functionality from those of related to authorship (e.g., authors' coding habits) is essential. This feature segregation is crucial for an effective authorship attribution because what is unique in a particular binary may be attributed to either the author style, the utilized compiler, or the program functionality. Moreover, a reliable approach in the case of multiple authors, the ability to handle binaries generated after the application of refactoring techniques or simple obfuscation methods, and validation against real malware samples need to be considered.

1.3   Outline

The remainder of the book is organized as follows:

- Chapter 2 provides an overview of binary analysis in relation to the underlying challenges, fingerprinting applications, existing methodologies, and related implementations. It then details the impact of code transformation involving obfuscation, refactoring, and compiler optimization before discussing a number of noteworthy binary frameworks for software fingerprinting.
- Chapter 3 details a practical approach called BINCOMP [240], which can be used to analyze the syntax, structure, and semantics of disassembled functions in order to ascertain compiler provenance. In this context, it elaborates on each component of the three-layer stratified architecture of BINCOMP. This involves the derivation of default compiler code transformation, the disassembling of functions across compiled binaries in order to extract statistical features and to label compiler-related functions as well as the extraction of semantic features from the labelled functions to identify the compiler version and the optimization level. Experimental results are also presented to demonstrate the effectiveness and the performance of BINCOMP.
- Chapter 4 describes a scalable and robust system called BINSHAPE [264], which provides an automated framework suitable for identifying library functions. In

essence, BINSHAPE derives a robust library function signature based on hetero-geneous features covering control flow graphs, instruction-level and statistical characteristics, as well as function-call graphs. In addition, a tailored data structure is employed to store such signatures in a manner that facilitates an efficient matching against a target function. The chapter also details the experimental evaluation of BINSHAPE over a diverse set of C/C++ binaries. The experimental results indicate the ability of BINSHAPE to efficiently and accurately identify library functions in real binaries obtained from different compilers along with the ability to handle slight modifications and some obfuscation techniques.

- Chapter 5 presents SIGMA [61], a technique for identifying reused functions in binary code by matching traces of a novel representation of binary code, namely, the semantic integrated graph (SIG). The SIGs enhance and merge several existing concepts from classical program analysis into a joint data structure. This allows to capture in a unified manner different semantic descriptors of common functionalities in a given binary code in order to identify reused functions, actions, or open-source software packages. This chapter also presents the results of the experimental evaluation that indicate the promising potential of the described technique.

- Chapter 6 describes a binary function fingerprinting framework called BIN-SIGN [226]. This framework aims at providing an accurate and scalable solution to binary code fingerprinting by computing and matching syntactic and structural code profiles for disassembled binaries. This chapter details the underlying methodology as well as the employed performance evaluation, which is emphasized on several use cases, including function reuse and malware analysis. In addition, experimental results are provided for a database of about 6 million functions.

- Chapter 7 elaborates on the design and implementation of a resilient and efficient system called FOSSIL [62] that allows identifying FOSS packages in real-world binaries. This system incorporates three components that are employed, respectively, for extracting statistically derived syntactical features of functions, for extracting the semantics of the functions, and for applying the Z-score in order to extract the behavior of the instructions in a function. The system is evaluated on three datasets: real-world projects with known FOSS packages, malware binaries for which there are security and reverse engineering reports on their use of FOSS, and a large repository of malware binaries.

- Chapter 8 presents a fuzzy graph matching approach called BINSEQUENCE [163] that allows to compare two functions based on their corresponding binary sequences. The approach employs an initial mapping between assembly basic blocks, which is then extended using neighborhood exploration. An effective filtering process using min-hashing is also employed to make the approach scalable. Experimental results illustrate the efficiency of BINSEQUENCE, which can attain high-quality similarity ranking of assembly functions, given a large assembly code repository with millions of functions. In addition, several practical use cases are presented, including patch analysis, malware analysis, and bug search.

- Chapter 9 details BINAUTHOR [63], which represents a system capable of decoupling program functionality from authors' coding habits in binary code. In order to capture coding habits, BINAUTHOR leverages a set of features based on collections of functionality-independent choices that are made by authors during coding. The experimental evaluation demonstrates the superior performance of BINAUTHOR in several areas. As such, it allows to successfully attribute a larger number of authors with a very good accuracy based on large datasets extracted from selected open-source C++ projects. Moreover, it is quite robust with no significant accuracy drop when the initial source code is subjected to refactoring techniques, simple obfuscation, and different compilers. Furthermore, by decoupling authorship from functionality, it can be used on real-world malware binaries (`Citadel`, `Zeus`, `Stuxnet`, `Flame`, `Bunny`, and `Babar`) in order to automatically generate evidence on similar coding habits.
- Chapter 10 serves as a conclusion for this book. It summarizes the material presented in the foregoing chapters together with related concluding remarks. In addition, it provides a discussion of topics that are worth exploring in the area of binary code fingerprinting with a special emphasis on applications and use cases that are extremely relevant to cybersecurity.

Chapter 2
Binary Analysis Overview

When the source code is unavailable, it is important for security applications, such as malware detection, software license infringement, vulnerability analysis, and digital forensics to be able to efficiently extract meaningful fingerprints from the binary code. Such fingerprints will enhance the effectiveness and efficiency of reverse engineering tasks as they can provide a range of insights into the program binaries. However, a great deal of important information will likely be lost during the compilation process, including variable and function names, the original control and data flow structures, comments, and layout. In this chapter, we provide a comprehensive review of existing binary code fingerprinting frameworks. As such, we systematize the study of binary code fingerprints based on the most important dimensions: the applications that motivate it, the approaches used and their implementations, the specific aspects of the fingerprinting framework, and how the results are evaluated.

The chapter is organized as follows. We explain the importance of binary analysis, the evading techniques from the detection methods, and the binary analysis challenges in Sect. 2.1. Then, in Sect. 2.2, we describe the applications that motivate binary code fingerprinting. In Sect. 2.3, we systematize binary code fingerprints according to their generation approaches while in Sect. 2.4, we systematize the fingerprint domains. Thereafter, we discuss the effects of different code transformations in binary fingerprinting in Sect. 2.5. The selected set of binary frameworks for software fingerprinting is detailed in Sect. 2.6. Finally, we conclude the chapter in Sect. 2.7.

2.1 The Importance of Binary Analysis

Binary analysis is of paramount importance for many security applications, including performance analysis [54, 107, 214], debugging [66], software reverse engineering [88, 129], software reliability [201], digital forensics, and security analysis [132,

© Springer Nature Switzerland AG 2020
S. Alrabaee et al., *Binary Code Fingerprinting for Cybersecurity*, Advances in Information Security 78, https://doi.org/10.1007/978-3-030-34238-8_2

164, 227]. The analysis of binary code represents a critical capability for the aforementioned applications since it does not require the availability of the source code and it targets the actual software artifact being executed. Even in the case where the source code is available, experience has shown that the semantics of the binary code that is executed may differ from the source code [69].

Binary code fingerprint analysis is quite important for many security applications. As such, it assists in the tedious and error-prone task of manual malware reverse engineering. In this pursuit, it enables the application of suitable security tools on binary code, including tools for authorship attribution [59, 90, 212, 213, 251], clone detection [103, 133, 159, 256], library function identification [165, 235, 283], compiler provenance extraction [240, 252], binary similarities [64, 84, 110], vulnerability and bug detection [130, 231, 232], code reuse discovery [61, 103, 255], and the assignment of a fingerprint to each function for subsequent use by a binary search engine [98, 112, 118, 179, 223]. Typically, when malware attacks a computer system, there is an urgent need to determine its author and its characteristics. Such analysis requires reverse engineering, which represents a manual process that is typically laborious, costly, and time-consuming [69].

Reverse engineering is a common approach for recovering abstractions at the design level from an unknown (target) code or system in order to gain an understanding, as thorough as possible, of its functionality, architecture, and its internal components (e.g., functions). However, the analysis of program binaries is challenging [265] given that a great deal of semantic information is lost during the compilation process, including function prototype, buffer characteristics, and the original data and control flow graphs (CFGs).

A binary code consists of a set of modules, function sequences, basic blocks, instructions, and data. When analyzing such sequences, reverse engineers follow a series of interleaved steps. Thus, in the initial phase, they attempt to obtain essential information about the capabilities and objectives of the binary code. Such information plays a significant role in the efforts to identify the objective of a suspicious piece of code. Moreover, it can assist in detecting and mitigating the malicious behavior of infected systems [69].

We examine over 150 research contributions in this area and we systematically classify fingerprints extracted from binary code according to their applications. Our analysis shows that existing binary code fingerprint extraction techniques differ significantly. For instance, the employed analysis methods can employ static analysis, dynamic analysis, or a combination of both. Existing techniques can extract fingerprints based on semantic, structural, and syntactic features from different types and sources of information, such as a set of modules, instructions, basic blocks, or data and code sequences.

Our analysis reveals that the existing approaches also differ significantly in terms of detection techniques. These include exact and inexact matching, the use of probabilistic models, and machine learning models. Even the fingerprints themselves vary in relation to the scalability, efficiency, and robustness against obfuscation techniques. Moreover, we show that the field of binary code fingerprint analysis is multidisciplinary, with various research works published in many areas, including security, systems, software engineering, and programming languages. As such, the systematic discussion of binary code fingerprint analysis presented in this chapter is motivated by the variety of fingerprint approaches and detection methods as well as by the interdisciplinary nature of this research area.

2.1.1   Evading Techniques of Malware Detection

Binary analysis is very important both for the malware authors and for the anti-virus vendors and researchers, although each group performs different operations on the binaries according to their goals. For instance, such operations can include:

- *Binary modification*: This operation is essential as it allows a malware author to alter existing code or to inject new code into programs in order to execute malicious activities without needing the source code or debug information.
- *Binary comparison*: This operation is very important for the researchers as a way to automatically classifying new malware samples by assuming that unknown malware is often derived or grown from known malware.
- *Signature matching*: Usually anti-virus vendors search for the presence of a virus signature inside a given binary. If the signature is found, it is likely that the program is infected. While the signature method to detect known malware is quite effective, it fails to detect unknown malware. Moreover, a malware author may obfuscate the binary code to avoid such techniques.

One can note that malware authors and malware researchers are engaged in a "detected-undetected" game. The researchers undertake maximum efforts and incur notable costs when searching for efficient methods to detect malware, especially unknown malware. In contrast, malware authors develop the best evading techniques to thwart anti-virus and anti-malware software. For example, the `Chernobyl` virus can be detected by checking for a hexadecimal sequence [289]:

```
E800 0000 005B 8D4B 4251 5050
0F01 4C24 FE5B 83C3 1CFA 8B2B
```

However, in the context of aforementioned example, a little modification would render the anti-virus software ineffective.

The evading techniques can be summarized as follows:

- *Compression*: This involves the compression of a binary code and the embedding of a decompression algorithm that allows the execution of compressed program.
- *Polymorphic*: The polymorphic malware changes its code at every execution time while keeping its main functionality and semantics in order to evade detection.
- *Obfuscation*: Malware authors usually obfuscate their malicious code in order to evade detection. In this context, the ability of code obfuscation to thwart most of the existing detection techniques (e.g., misuse detection) relies on their purely syntactic nature that sensitizes malware detection with respect to slight syntactic modifications in the program.

- *Packing*: This is a strategy used by malware authors to mask the meaning of their malicious software in an attempt to fool signature-based analysis. It is proven to be relatively effective.
- *Encryption*: This strategy is used to perform simple encoding while others utilize complex encryption or download instructions from a remote host.

Irrespective of the means, in essence, the goal of each strategy is as follows: modify the external appearance of the binary code without changing its semantics, usually to hide malicious intent.

2.1.2   Binary Analysis Challenges

There are significantly more challenges when analyzing binary code compared to analyzing source code. We summarize these challenges as follows:

C1 *Compiler effects*: Compilers may have forged significant intricacies into binary code, which complicates analysis. Such intricacies tend to markedly impact the abilities of binary analysis frameworks, most probably resulting in the generation of factual errors by the frameworks and inaccurate reporting results. Moreover, such binary code intricacies affect the analytical aptitudes relative to comprehending the process and objective of a binary program as well as the capacity of a binary analysis framework to appropriately instrument binary programs.

C2 *Lack of semantic information*: In essence, binary code lacks a lot of semantic information compared to the source code. Such information may be related to the structure of the code, buffer characteristics, and the function prototypes that are to be exploited at binary level. Thus, this lack of information makes binary analysis notably more difficult.

C3 *Disassembly difficulty*: Prior to any kind of binary analysis, disassembling binaries is the first step since assembly files may provide more information compared to binary files. However, both program entry point and function boundary discovery represent challenging tasks.

C4 *Loose data and code segment allotment*: For the x86 processor architecture, the widely familiar formats of today are the ELF (executable and linking format) and the PE (portable executable), as employed in Linux and Windows, respectively. The two forenamed formats separate the file into segments (i.e., data and control), which can be allocated to store data, executable code, or both, and can be marked as being writeable, readable, or/and executable at runtime. However, there is no strict policy regarding the allotment with respect to data and code, with the code sections frequently incorporating data, such as strings, constants, or jump tables.

C5 *Lack of established segment layout*: Inside the segments (e.g., code or data), it is not necessary that the code follows a certain layout. Also, the processes are not equally obligated towards adhering to subsequent queuing, but may be connected to each other, connecting different process fragments via jumps. This kind of twisted layouts can be generated as a result of post-processing tools that switch the binary to a final stage after completing the compilation and linking processes. Moreover, binaries built directly from assembly language, which have not been compiled from a high level language, have no need of adhering to any function or procedure concept.

C6 *Function boundary*: The starting address of a function is used to highlight the boundary of the function. For this purpose, the *symbol table* is utilized for function boundary identification and control flow construction. However, in the absence of *symbol table* or being inaccurate, function boundary detection becomes challenging.

C7 *Symbol information*: In binary code, symbol information comes in two forms, each with a specific function. First, the identification of global variables and exported procedures is done using addresses and names. Second, during the software development, debuggers employ debug symbols in order to provide developers with simple yet comprehensible information that usually maps back to the source code. As part of the final compilation of a released software product, the stripping of all symbols is performed, excluding the public symbols of dynamic libraries. If the symbol information is available, its significance lies in offering assistance to the binary assessment procedure by identifying procedure boundaries, variables, and variable types.

C8 *Return instructions*: For the x86 processor architecture, a `ret` instruction can equally be employed in an indirect jump, such as `jmp eax`, which operates an identical jump to the instruction progression `push eax, ret`. As a result, return and call instructions generally fail to be handled consistently in relation to procedure gathering and return in high level languages. This behavior of return instructions in vulnerability exploits is generally employed to generate chains of program code that mutually make up a vulnerable code sequence. Deliberately concealed, hand-written assembly code is rampant in elaborated malware or any reverse-engineering-protected program, although these approaches can be employed to prevent manual and/or automated analysis.

2.2 Software Fingerprinting Applications

Generally, the users leave fingerprints on the Internet when they share any textual data or when they perform certain activities, such as sending emails or connecting to various Internet accessible services. Malware authors involved in cybercrime generally perform their illegal activities on vulnerable networks, Internet telephony, emails, accessible files and software usage, etc. Taking this into consideration, an important step in fighting cybercrime is to track the perpetrators and to discover their fingerprints. In this pursuit, it is desirable to have an automated set of techniques that can be used to uniquely identify a given binary from a large dataset of fingerprints, which are constructed based on the various types of data involving network traffic patterns, voice, emails, binaries, etc. Such fingerprint features could be used either by exact matching algorithms, such as those involving signature

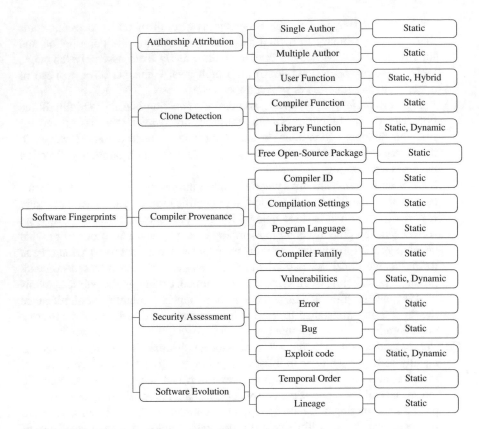

Fig. 2.1 The applications of fingerprints in binary code

matching and misuse detection, or by inexact matching algorithms, such as those employing edit distance methods and anomaly detection. Fingerprinting is used as well in the context of various binary analysis applications. Fingerprint applications can be classified as presented in Fig. 2.1. As can be seen, fingerprints can be used in different domains, such as authorship attribution, clone detection, compiler provenance, security assessment, and software evolution.

2.2.1 Authorship Attribution

Authorship attribution represents the study of identifying the actual author of a given anonymous artifact (typically a file) based on content such as text, linguistic stylometry, and other features. However, in the case of binary authorship attribution, most of the existing research is focusing on the authorship attribution accuracy for source code [90], with just a few research initiatives aimed at binary authorship analysis. More recently, research in binary authorship attribution has grown at a slower pace, given that elaborating reliable authorship attribution technology is quite difficult and challenging. These approaches can be classified into two groups: (1) identifying the author of a binary code [59, 90, 251] and (2) identifying multiple authors of a binary code [212, 213]. In [59, 90, 251], it is shown that certain stylistic features can actually survive the compilation process and remain intact in the binary code, thereby showing that authorship attribution for binary code should be feasible.

The methodology developed by Rosenblum et al. [251] represents the first attempt to automatically identify authors of software binaries. The main concept employed involves the extraction of syntactic features by using predefined templates such as idioms (sequences of three consecutive instructions), n-grams as well as graphlets. A subsequent approach to automatically identify the authorship of software binaries is proposed by Alrabaee et al. [59]. The main concept employed involves the extraction of a sequence of instructions with specific semantics and the construction of a register flow graph that is based on the register manipulation. A more recent approach that allows to automatically identify the authorship of software binaries is proposed by Caliskan-Islam et al. [90]. The approach involves the extraction of syntactic features present in the source code obtained from decompiling the executable binaries. In [212, 213], a new fine-grained technique is introduced to address the problem of identifying multiple authors of binary code by determining the author of each basic block. This involves the extraction of syntactic and semantic features at a basic block level, down to constant values in instructions, width and depth of a function CFG, backward slices of variables, etc.

Table 2.1 provides a comparison of the existing binary authorship research works in terms of extracted features, implantation setup as well as the availability of their code. The extracted features include structural, syntactic, and semantic features. In addition, most of the approaches are compatible with the Linux binaries (e.g., ELF), and the binaries that they are dealing with are originally written in C or C++. Each of the approaches requires a training dataset, with the exception of Meng's approach [212, 213]. Finally, we indicate if the tool is available for researchers, and we mention the use of private repositories, general repositories (e.g., GitHub), and public repositories (i.e., the code is available but not in general repositories). Furthermore, the existing approaches are categorized in Fig. 2.2. The extracted features are at different levels; for example, Meng extracts the features encountered at the basic block level [212, 213]. The machine learning algorithm used also varies; for instance, Rosenblum et al. [251] employ support vector machine (SVM), while Caliskan et al. [90] utilize a random forest classifier.

Table 2.1 A comparison between different systems that identify the authors of program binaries

| Approach | Features | | | Implementation | | | |
	Syntactic	Semantic	Structure	Language	Platform(s)	Dataset	Availability
[59]	•	•		C++	Windows	•	Private
[90]	•		•	C	Windows/Linux	•	GitHub
[251]	•	•	•	C++	Linux	•	Public
[212]		•	•	C++	Linux		Private

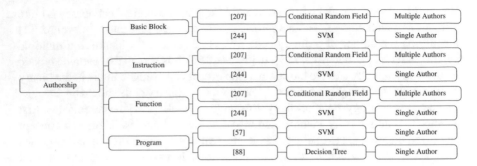

Fig. 2.2 A taxonomy of authorship attribution approaches

2.2.2 Clone Detection

Clone detection can be defined as the process of identifying code fragments that have high similarity, with respect to a large code base. The major challenge is that the clone detector does not usually know beforehand which code fragments may be repeated. Consequently, a naive clone detection approach may have to compare every pair of code fragments. Such comparison is prohibitively expensive in terms of computation and infeasible in many real-life situations. However, given a collection of assembly files that have been previously analyzed and a target assembly code fragment, as in the case of malware analysis, the objective is not to identify every duplicate code fragment but rather to only identify all code fragments in the previously analyzed assembly files that are similar to the target fragment. This problem is known as the assembly code clone search. In this setting, a code fragment represents any sequence of code lines, with or without comments, at any level of granularity (e.g., code block, function) [254]. A code fragment is a clone of another code fragment if they are similar based on a given similarity score [254]. A similar notion to the source code clone detection has been used in order to define the following four types of clones for binary code clone detection [254]:

- *Type I*: Identical code fragments, except for variations in layout, whitespace, and comments.
- *Type II*: Structurally and syntactically identical fragments, except for variations in terms of memory references, constant values, registers, layouts, whitespace, and comments.
- *Type III*: Copied fragments with additional modifications. Statements can be added, changed, or removed, in addition to variations in terms of memory references, constant values, registers, layout, whitespace, and comments.
- *Type IV*: Code fragments that perform the same functionality while being implemented using different syntactic constructs.

In this context, the problem of code clone search can be described as follows. Given a large repository of previously analyzed code along with a new target code sample, identify all code fragments in the repository that are syntactically

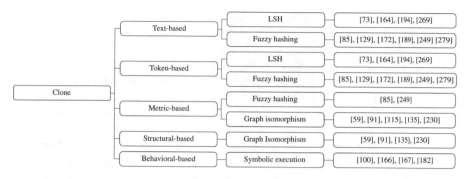

Fig. 2.3 A taxonomy of clone detection approaches

or semantically similar to the code fragments in the target sample (typically a malware). According to the employed approach, clone detection can be categorized into five groups as follows: *Text-based* approach [168], *Token-based* approach [133, 177, 286], *Metric-based* approach [87, 256], *Structure-based* approach [61, 139], and *Behavior-based* approach [103, 171].

Moreover, the development of specific methods for finding similar clones in software represents a long-standing topic in the field of security research that includes a wide range of approaches and techniques. The methods can be classified based on their underlying methodology, as shown in Fig. 2.3:

- *Locality sensitive hashing (LSH)*: This is a widely used method that has been studied for decades in order to solve the approximated similarity problem, since deriving exact similarities over multiple code features is not scalable to high-dimensional data. Among the prevalent problems of LSH is the issue of handling uneven data distribution, given that LSH involves partitioning the data space equally. Certain methods have been proposed to address this issue, including the LSH-Forest [75], LSB-Forest [276], C2LSH [143], and SK-LSH [199]. However, LSH-Forest, C2LSH, and SKLSH are not robust against various compiler settings, while LSB-Forest dynamically and unequally partitions the data space in addition to having scalability issues [277].
- *Fuzzy hashing*: The fuzzy hashing algorithms, which are also known as similarity digest, are a type of compression function for computing the similarity between individual files [194]. In this context, a well-known tool for similarity detection [258] employs *n*-tokens. It represents a fuzzy hashing technique that actually selects a subset of *n*-tokens in order to find similar code. A new system, known as REDEBUG [167], employs feature hashing in order to encode *n*-tokens into a bit vector, which allows REDEBUG to perform similarity checking in a cache-efficient manner. According to Jang et al. [168], REDEBUG swaps out winnowing[1] for feature hashing for improved speed. Furthermore, a binary-

---

[1]Fingerprint generation based on a sequence of hash values that allows to make sure that at least part of any sufficiently long match is detected.

oriented, obfuscation-resilient method that is based on the longest common subsequence of semantically equivalent basic blocks has been introduced for plagiarism similarity detection [202]. It actually combines rigorous program semantics with fuzzy matching based on longest common subsequence.

- *Graph isomorphism*: This represents another frequently used method. The first graph isomorphism algorithm suitable for small graphs was proposed in 1976 [282]. Later on, many methods have been introduced for large-scale graph data, such as TURBOISO [155] and STWIG [274]. More recently, graph isomorphism methods have been employed in order to compare data flow graphs [93, 193, 236]. Moreover, it was shown that the subgraph isomorphism problem can be solved within reasonable time. However, the application of graph isomorphism matching for assembly clone detection involves the subgraph identification, where subgraphs are isomorphic to the graphs in the repository, which can significantly increase the complexity of the task.

- *Symbolic execution*: This represents a set of techniques to analyze a program in order to determine what inputs cause each part of a program to execute. SYMDIFF [187] is a language-agnostic semantic diff tool conceived for imperative programs. It provides differential symbolic execution that allows to analyze behavioral differences between different versions of a program. Another research work carried out by Homan et al. [170] compares the execution traces using the longest common subsequence. More recently, a method to automatically find vulnerabilities and generate related exploits has been proposed [67]. This involves preconditioned symbolic execution, which represents a new technique for targeting symbolic execution. Another method for mutating well-formed program inputs or simply fuzzing has become a highly effective and widely used strategy to find bugs in software [245]. Moreover, in [245], a mathematical formalism is introduced on how to reason about one critical aspect in fuzzing: how to pick seed files in the best way to maximize the total number of bugs found during a fuzz campaign.

A comparison between existing clone detection works in terms of methodology, feature types, and detection methods is provided in Table 2.2.

2.2.3 Library Function Fingerprinting

There are various approaches for performing library function identification. The best-known, FLIRT [46] derives signatures from the first byte sequence of the function. However, its main drawback is the potential signature collision. In contrast, UNSTRIP [165] employs pattern matching to identify wrapper functions based on their interactions with system calls, using a flexible fingerprint pattern matching algorithm. In order to capture the semantics of functions, UNSTRIP defines a semantic descriptor based on the name and concrete parameter values of any system calls invoked as the fingerprint is generated. Subsequently, a

Table 2.2 A comparison between different binary clone detection systems

Approach	Analysis			Features			Detection		Clone level			
	Static	Dynamic	Hybrid	Syntactic	Structural	Semantic	Exact	Inexact	Instruction	Basic block	Region	Function
[61]	•			•		•	•		•			•
[87]	•					•		•	✓	✓		✓
[93]	✓	✓			✓							✓
[103]	✓				✓	✓		✓				✓
[118]	✓			✓	✓	✓		✓	✓	✓		✓
[133]	✓						✓				✓	
[139]	✓			✓	✓	✓		✓	✓			✓
[168]			✓	✓		✓		✓				✓
[171]	✓	✓				✓			✓			✓
[193]	✓					✓		✓	✓			✓
[236]	✓					✓		✓				✓
[256]	✓			✓				✓				✓

pattern matching algorithm is used to identify the wrapper functions based on the library fingerprints. In LIBV [236], a graph isomorphism algorithm is employed on execution-dependence graphs (EDGs) in order to identify both full and inline functions. The more recently developed BINSHAPE [264] extracts other feature types, such as function-call graphs or strings, which are not affected by the compiler optimization settings. In another approach, BINHASH [171], each function is represented using a set of features defined as the input and output of a basic block, and then min-hashing [65] is applied for efficient detection.

A number of cross-architecture approaches have been proposed for finding known bugs in firmware images. A noteworthy example is DISCOVRE [130], which extracts the structural features and then applies the maximum common subgraph (MCS) isomorphism to the CFGs in order to find functions that are similar. To employ subgraph isomorphism efficiently, the aforementioned approach employs pre-filtering based on statistical features. In contrast, GENIUS [136] evaluates the effectiveness of pre-filtering and demonstrates that it can lead to significant increase in accuracy. Inspired by DISCOVRE, GENIUS [136] extracts statistical and structural features, then generates codebooks from annotated CFGs, and then converts the codebooks into high-level numerical feature vectors (feature encoding). Subsequently, it compares the encoded features via locality sensitive hashing (LSH) to address the scalability issues. However, the codebook generation procedure may be expensive, and some structural CFG changes may also affect the accuracy of GENIUS. Moreover, signature collision might be an issue given that similar, especially small, functions are highly susceptible to have similar hash values. Pewny et al. [231] were the first researchers to solve the cross-architecture problem by employing input/output (I/O) pairs in order to discover basic block semantics. The discovered semantics are not suitable to determine the vulnerabilities in a given code; however, many other studies provide appropriate techniques for discovering unknown vulnerabilities, such as the fuzzing techniques. Carefully selected fuzzing seeds have been shown to effectively trigger unknown vulnerabilities [95, 245].

The aforementioned proposals are compared in Table 2.3.

2.2.4 Binary Software Evolution

Software evolution or software lineage refers to the presence of an evolutionary relationship among a collection of software. It represents temporal ordering as well as derivative relations by including branching and merging histories. Software lineage can be the subject of inference, the goal of which is to recover the lineage given a set of program binaries. Moreover, software lineage can provide very useful information in many security scenarios, including malware triage and software vulnerability tracking, as highlighted by Jang et al. [169]. Initially, Belady and Lehman studied the software evolution of IBM OS/360 [78]. Then, Lehman and Ramil formulated eight laws that describe the software evolution process [191]. In [153], the authors investigated malware metadata collected by

Table 2.3 A comparison of static library function identification systems

Approaches	Features				Methods	Architectures			Compilers			
	Syntactic	Semantic	Structural	Statistical		x86-64	ARM	MIPS	VS	GCC	ICC	Clang
[46]	•				PM	•			•	•		
[112]		•	•		LCS, DFA	•	•	•		•		
[130]			•	•	MCS, JD	•	•	•				
[136]			•	•	ML, LSH, JD	•	•	•		•		•
[165]		•			PM, SE	•				•		
[179]	•		•		GI	•				•		
[202]		•	•		LCS, SE	•				•	•	
[236]		•	•		GI, DFA	•			•	•		
[264]	•	•	•	•	B⁺tree	•			•	•		

The presence of the (•) symbol indicates that a proposal is offering the corresponding feature, otherwise it is empty. The following abbreviations are used for different methods

PM Pattern matching, *GI* Graph isomorphism, *GED* Graph edit distance, *LSH* Locality sensitive hashing, *LCS* Longest common subsequence, *MCS* Maximum common subgraph isomorphism, *SPP* Small primes product, *SE* Symbolic execution, *DFA* Data flow analysis, *JD* Jaccard distance, and *ML* Machine learning

Table 2.4 A comparison between different software evolution recovery systems

	[78]	[121]	[153]	[169]	[177]
Language	C++	C	C	C	C/C++
Platform(s)	Linux	Linux/Windows	Linux	Linux	Linux
Pseudo timestamp	✗	✓	✗	✗	✓
Tool chain	✓	✗	✗	✗	✓
Lehman's rules	✗	✗	✓	✓	✓
Error recovery	✗	✓	✗	✓	✗

an anti-virus vendor in order to describe the evolutionary relationships among malware. Furthermore, in [121], the authors studied malware evolution with the intent to discover new variants of well-known malware. The phylogeny models based on code similarity have been elaborated in order to understand how new malware relates to previously seen malware [177]. Table 2.4 provides a comparison of existing works in terms of language, platform, and methodology.

2.2.5   Vulnerability Analysis

Detecting the presence of security vulnerabilities in binary code represents a difficult and time-consuming task. While notable progress has been made toward the development of automated solutions for vulnerability detection, the tedious process of manual analysis still remains necessary for any binary auditing task. In this context, vulnerability analysis typically includes discovering standard errors, finding bugs, detecting vulnerabilities, and identifying exploit code. Different tools have been proposed for the analysis of such vulnerabilities. Primary works propose binary specific automated solutions for bug finding [106, 147, 152, 288, 291]. Other works have been focused on manual exploit generation [67, 156]. Automatic tools for exploit generation have also been presented [67, 100, 148, 157, 207, 302]. Moreover, Yamaguchi et al. [293] model vulnerable code with a definition graph for vulnerability pattern generation. This definition graph allows to capture the definition of function arguments and their data sanitization checks. Actually, this work shares a similar idea of how to characterize the pattern of vulnerable code.

In order to more accurately identify bugs in binary code, different semantic-based approaches have been investigated as well. The approach proposed by David et al. [110] captures the semantics of execution sequences to circumvent control flow graph changes while the TEDEM [232] approach captures the semantics by using the expression tree corresponding to a basic block. The latter approach is basic block-level matching and provides only a similarity score. BLANKET-EXECUTION [125] (BLEX) employs the dynamic runtime environment of the program as a feature in order to conduct the code search. This semantic feature resides at the function or component level, and can be used only on a single platform,

Table 2.5 A comparison of different systems to discover standard errors, vulnerabilities, and bugs

Approach	Analysis			Reasonable cost			Discovery		
	Static	Dynamic	Hybrid	Manual	Time	Space	Standard error	Vulnerability	Bug
[67]	✗	✓	✗	✗	✗	✓	✗	✓	✓
[89]	✓	✗	✗	✗	✓	✗	✓	✓	✗
[95]	✓	✗	✗	✗	✓	✗	✓	✓	✗
[106]	✗	✗	✓	✗	✓	✗	✓	✗	✗
[110]	✗	✓	✗	✗	✗	✓	✓	✗	✓
[125]	✓	✗	✗	✗	✓	✗	✓	✓	✗
[147]	✗	✓	✗	✓	✗	✗	✓	✗	✗
[148]	✗	✓	✗	✗	✗	✓	✓	✗	✓
[152]	✗	✓	✗	✗	✗	✓	✓	✓	✗
[156]	✗	✓	✗	✗	✓	✗	✗	✗	✓
[157]	✗	✗	✓	✓	✗	✗	✓	✗	✗
[207]	✗	✓	✗	✗	✓	✗	✗	✗	✓
[232]	✓	✗	✗	✗	✓	✗	✓	✓	✗
[245]	✗	✓	✗	✗	✗	✓	✓	✗	✓
[291]	✓	✗	✗	✗	✓	✗	✗	✓	✗
[293]	✓	✗	✗	✗	✓	✗	✓	✓	✗
[302]	✓	✗	✗	✗	✓	✗	✓	✓	✗

with no ability to reason about the vulnerabilities in the code. As previously mentioned (in Sect. 2.2.3), Pewny et al. [231] provide the first work to address the cross-architecture problem. Their approach employs I/O pairs in order to capture the semantics at the level of basic blocks. However, their approach is unable to reason about the vulnerabilities in the target code. Symbolic execution is another technique for vulnerability discovery. The symbolic execution of a program explores all possible execution paths throughout that program and determines whether any combination of inputs could cause the program to crash [89, 244]. A comparison between aforementioned works is presented in Table 2.5.

2.2.6 Program Provenance Analysis

Program binaries are generated in different phases, starting from the source code and ending with the binary code in the form of a byte string. The language, compiler, and build options are typically selected by the programmer before code generation. Binary provenance is defined as the information derived from the process of transforming the source code into binary code. Such information may include the choice of compiler, the compiler version, the speed related optimization, the program source language, and the debug information. Forensic analysis can acquire information about system crashes, the compiler's impact on performance issues, the information gained through decompilation, or the code susceptibility

Table 2.6 A comparison between different approaches that discover binary provenances

	Features			Compiler				Provenance		
Tool	Syntactic	Semantic	Structural	ICC	Clang	VS	GCC	Source compiler	Source language	Compiler version
[96]	✓	✓	✓	✗	✗	✓	✓	✗	✗	✗
[240]	✓	✓	✓	✓	✓	✓	✓	✓	✗	✓
[250]	✗	✓	✗	✓	✓	✓	✓	✓	✓	✓
[252]	✓	✓	✗	✓	✓	✓	✓	✓	✗	✗

to reverse engineering. Although binary code has characteristics that reveal how it was created, the process of identification and determining its origin is difficult. Determining the origin of a program requires knowledge of the source languages, compiler optimization options, version, and compiler family involved in binary creation.

A modest amount of research has been conducted in this area; there are few works proposed [96, 240, 250, 252] to identify compiler provenance from program binaries. For instance, Chaki et al. [96] detect the similarity based on provenance (whether the binaries were compiled using the same or similar compilers). The authors propose a set of semantic and syntactic features related to the functions. The semantic attribute represents the effect of executing a function in a particular hardware state, whereas the syntactic attributes represent n-grams and n-perms. Rahimian et al. [240] present a stratified system, which extracts various syntactic and semantic features from the assembly functions, such as annotated CFGs, call graphs, strings, and instruction sequences. Rosenblum et al. [252] propose an approach for extracting binary provenance, based on wildcard-idiom features (a sequence of instructions which ignores some details such as literal arguments as well as memory offsets) and deals with compiler provenance extraction as a structured classification problem. Mutual information (MI) is used to filter out redundant features and an automatic technique is proposed to recover toolchain provenance [250], including the source language, compiler, and compilation options that define the transformation process used to produce the binary. Other elaborated tools, such as EXEINFO [43], RDG [49], and IDA PRO [46], are currently employed in practice. A comparative summary of the available methodologies, source compiler identification, and the type of extracted binary provenance is provided in Table 2.6.

2.3 Methodology

In this section, we further discuss the nature of binary analysis, the strategies, and the relevant approaches used for binary analysis. The proposed classification of binary analysis is shown in Fig. 2.4, which is explained in more details as next. We further propose a taxonomy for the employed binary features.

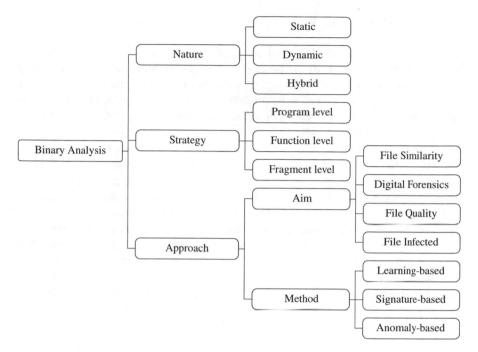

Fig. 2.4 A categorization of binary analysis topics

2.3.1   Nature of Binary Analysis

Binary analysis can be first classified based on its nature: whether the analysis is performed statically, dynamically, or in a hybrid manner. In this section, we present these types of analysis and discuss their advantages and limitations.

2.3.1.1   Static Analysis

Static analysis is the process of handling binary files without executing them. Static analysis of binaries is a difficult process [180]. From a theoretical viewpoint, the absence of types and structure means that much of the original information present in source code is lost and cannot be used for analysis. From a practical viewpoint, a great amount of technical detail must be dealt with diligently, such as dynamic linking, function pointers, or the large number of specialized instructions [68]. However, the required theoretical and engineering effort is a worthwhile investment for several reasons and opens up multiple avenues of application, which will be outlined in this section. The information gathered by static analysis on binaries can assist in the largely manual process of reverse engineering, i.e., in recovering information about the functionality, dependencies, and interfaces of a program. Moreover, static analysis on binaries allows the verification of software for bugs or possible hazards, such as backdoors, time bombs, or the presence of a malware [195].

2.3.1.2 Dynamic Analysis

Analyzing the behaviors exhibited by a program while it is being executed is called dynamic analysis. In the process of code analysis, input/output pairs help to obtain an overview of the program behavior. One possibility to monitor the specific functions that are called by a program involves the interception of function calls. This process of interception is termed as hooking [124]. The program being analyzed is manipulated such that, along with the intended function, a so-called hook function is also invoked. The hook function is delegated to implement the required functionality analysis (e.g., analyzing the input parameters or logging its invocation into a file). In static analysis, function parameter analysis aims at inferring the set of possible parameter values or their types statically. In contrast, dynamic function parameter analysis is focusing on the actual passed values at the time of function invocation. For an analyst, a valuable information source to understand the behavior of a sample code is represented by the instruction trace (the sequence of machine code instructions executed by the sample during dynamic analysis). While usually difficult to read and interpret, such traces may contain valuable information that is not represented at a higher level of abstraction such as the analysis report of function calls and system calls.

2.3.1.3 Hybrid Analysis

Hybrid analysis represents a combination of static analysis and dynamic analysis techniques. As part of hybrid analysis, static analysis is performed before executing the program, while dynamic analysis is subsequently performed in a selective manner, based on the information gathered during the static analysis [253]. In [101], a novel framework is proposed for classifying malware using both static analysis and dynamic analysis. The authors define features or characteristics of malware as Mal-DNA (Malware DNA). Mal-DNA combines static, dynamic as well as hybrid characteristics. The framework contains three components. The first component, START (STatic Analyzer using vaRious Techniques), extracts the static characteristics of malware. The second component, DeBON (Debugging-based Behavior mOnitor and aNalyzer), extracts hybrid and dynamic characteristics of the malware. The third component, CLAM (CLassifier using Mal-DNA), classifies malware based on the Mal-DNA extracted from the first two components using machine learning algorithms. Very little research has been conducted on dynamic analysis prior to static analysis; for instance, starting from an execution trace (dynamic) and subsequently using control-flow traversal parsing techniques (static) to find malicious code [203].

2.3.2 Binary Analysis Strategies

Binary analysis frameworks can be defined based on which strategies they adopt. We can define those strategies at three levels: program level, function level, and fragment level. The function level takes into consideration the boundaries of a specific function and defines the starting-ending addresses of the function. This process is a challenging task [262]. The other levels do not require such a process.

2.3.3 Binary Analysis Approaches

The third classification of binary analysis, as shown in Fig. 2.4, is based on the approaches, which are composed of their aims and methods. The aims specify what is being targeted, while the methods state how the binary analysis is performed. Typically, there could be different goals, such as clone detection, search engine, function fingerprinting, and binary function categorization, all of which have been discussed in previous sections. Digital forensics encompasses authorship attribution, binary analysis verification, and author characterization. File quality is related to the quality of a binary and covers different aspects, such as bugs, vulnerabilities, etc. In the aforementioned domains, three methods could be used: signature matching, learning-based classifier, and a distance metric based method, which measures the distance between feature vectors.

2.3.4 Feature Taxonomy

The structure of features applicable for binary analysis and malware detection is depicted in Fig. 2.5. This can be categorized into three distinctive feature groups:

1. *Syntactic features*, with respect to a file object, for instance, n-grams;
2. *Semantic features*, which consist of different kinds of meaningful features, such as statistics of opcodes;
3. *Structural features*, which deal with the structure of a program; for instance, the characteristics of a function control flow graph (i.e., the number of nodes).

Various features are shown in Fig. 2.5. We briefly describe them as follows. A *mnemonic* of an instruction represents the operations, and typically an *opcode* is the hexadecimal encoding of the instruction. An *opcode* is a textual description, while multiple opcodes may map to the same *mnemonic*; for instance, opcodes 0x8b and 0x89 have the same mnemonic mov. *N-grams* are substrings of length n from a larger string. For instance, the string "MALWARE" can be segmented into the following 4-grams: "MALW," "ALWA," "LWAR," and "WARE." *Constants* are

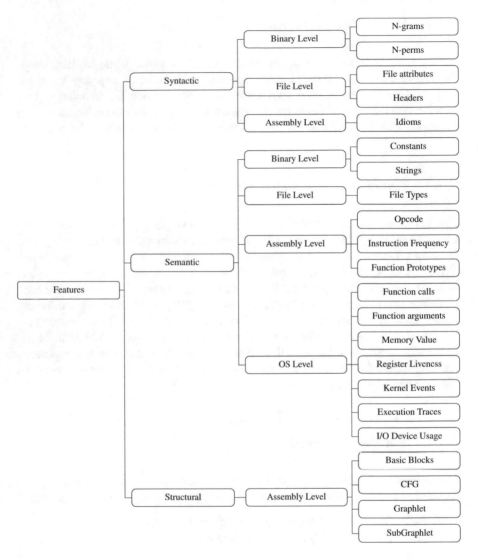

Fig. 2.5 A taxonomy of binary features

integer, float, or double values that can be used for computation as well as to specify pointer offsets. *Strings* could be ANSI single-byte null-terminated strings [179]. *File header* content includes subgroups of generic headers, module dependency tables, resources, file size, file name, and file types (e.g., ELF). *Idioms* are the low-level details of the program instruction that are used to recognize specific code patterns. *Idioms* are essentially short sequences of instructions intended to capture the stylistic characteristics that are embedded in the assembly files converted using disassembling tools.

A control flow graph (CFG) is a standard code representation that reflects both the structure and semantics of a function. It describes the order of statements to be executed as well as the conditions that need to be met for a particular path of execution. The *basic blocks* are represented by nodes which are connected by directed *edges* to indicate the transfer of control. A *graphlet* is an intermediary representation between the assembly instructions and the CFG. Each three-node subgraph of the CFG is considered as a graphlet. Each node of a graph/graphlet is actually a *basic block* with a list of neighbors (i.e., a basic block linked with other basic blocks via a branch instruction). *Supergraphlets* are obtained by collapsing and merging neighbor nodes of the CFG. A *tracelet* is a partial execution trace that represents a single partial flow through the program. A *register flow graph* captures the flow and dependencies between the registers, which represents an important semantic aspect about the behavior of a program. *Register liveness* measures how variables are controlled during execution, and whether local or global variables have been used.

Call graphlets are graphlets containing only nodes with a call instruction. Libcalls are function names of imported libraries, e.g., call ds: printf. A *system call* represents a request for a service, placed by a program to the kernel of an operating system. This may include services that are hardware-related (e.g., disk drive access), the creation/execution of new processes as well as communication with integral kernel services (e.g., process scheduling). *System calls* provide an essential interface between the executing process and the hosting operating system. Behavioral n-grams are generated by passing through the system services call sequence using a sliding window [189].

A *data flow graph* (DFG) is a directed graph that shows the data dependencies between a number of functions. The header data of binary files consists of different information including the data of import tables, which has information regarding the user-mode system functions that are used by applications [259], import-export and resource table data [210], and analysis of the header ELF structures that represent the binaries' structure for UNIX-originated operating systems [260]. The *program dependence graph* (PDG) [137, 228] was the first and the most classical data structure used for slicing. It was meant to represent imperative programs in Pascal-like languages and is essentially a pseudograph with edges representing control and data dependencies. Its creation is also an imperatively formulated algorithm that builds a control flow graph, a data dependence graph, a data dominator tree, etc. A *system dependence graph* (SDG) [161] is a generalization of a PDG that is capable of expressing inter-procedural relations and therefore capable of facilitating more global analyses and detection of inter-procedural code clones. A *dynamic dependence graph* [55] (DDG) is a variant more suitable for debugging and similar tasks that can benefit from representing runtime information. From this point of view, both PDGs and SDGs, as well as any of their extensions, are called *static dependence graphs*. A *value dependence graph* [290] (VDG) is an efficient structure similar to data flow/dependence graphs, but it is demand-driven. It does not require a full control flow graph, but a control flow graph can be generated from it.

2.4   Implementation

In this section, we first introduce the most common methods for binary file disassembly, which is considered the first step in binary analysis. We then describe the methods that have been followed in the literature to rank the extracted features. Subsequently, we describe the classification and clustering process. Finally, we briefly describe the manner by which features are extracted.

2.4.1   Disassembling Tools

The disassembler tool is important for studying the features of binary files (e.g., executables). In this subsection, we introduce the most commonly used tools as part of research activities. For the dynamic tools, the reader is referred to [124].

2.4.1.1   Interactive Disassembler (IDA)

IDA PRO [45] is a Windows, Linux, and Mac OS X hosted multiprocessor disassembler and debugger. IDA provides various features, such as function names, import API calls, export API calls, and compiler recognition. This tool is user-friendly, allowing researchers to add their code (e.g., python) as a plugin of IDA PRO.

2.4.1.2   Objdump

OBJDUMP is utilized for displaying various types of information about object files. It can also be used as a disassembler. Actually, it is part of the GNU Binutils for fine-grained control over executable and other binary data. For instance, in order to disassemble a binary file, the command objdump -Dslx *file* is used. OBJDUMP uses the Binary File Descriptor (BFD) library to read the contents of object files.

2.4.1.3   Portable Executable Explorer

PE EXPLORER [48] allows to reduce the time needed to understand complex malware. It unfolds each header, section, and table that is found in an executable file thereby revealing the values stored inside the malware. It also allows to reduce many internal information sources that are binary file specific, into a format that is more convenient for viewing. Thus, it provides the user with easy-to-read information about the functions of the executable. Moreover, it supports the Intel x86 instruction sets with the MMX, 3D Now!, SSE, SSE2, and SSE3 extensions. It also uses a qualitative algorithm that is designed to rebuild the assembly language source code of target binary win32 PE files with the highest possible accuracy.

2.4.1.4 Paradyn

PARADYN [50] is a tool that is used to parse and convert binary code into a machine code representation of a program. In this respect, PARADYN converts code snippets into abstractions, such as the instructions, basic blocks, and functions. The code and data represented by an address space is broken up into function and variable abstractions. Functions contain points that specify locations to insert instrumentation. Functions also contain a control flow graph abstraction, which contains information about basic blocks, edges, loops, and instructions.

2.4.1.5 Jakstab

JAKSTAB [181] represents an abstract interpretation-based disassembly and static analysis framework that allows for analyzing executables and for recovering reliable control flow graphs. It is conceived to support multiple hardware platforms using customized instruction decoding as well as similar processor architectures. It is written in Java and currently supports x86 processor architecture and 32-bit Windows PE or Linux ELF executables. Moreover, it translates machine code into low-level intermediate language as it simultaneously performs data flow analysis over the growing control flow graph. Also, data flow information is used to resolve branch targets as well as to discover new code locations. Other analyses can also be implemented in JAKSTAB in order to jointly execute alongside the main control flow reconstruction, aiming at improving the precision of disassembly, or alternatively conducted on the resulting preprocessed control flow graph.

2.4.1.6 OllyDbg

OLLYDBG [47] is a 32-bit assembly level analyzing debugger for Microsoft Windows. It is a shareware that can be downloaded and used for free. The following points can be highlighted about OLLYDBG:

- It provides code analysis, such as trace registers, recognizing procedures, API calls, loops, switches, tables, constants, and strings.
- It allows for user-defined comments, labels, and function descriptions.
- It is a configurable disassembler that supports both MASM and IDEAL formats.
- It can dynamically recognize ASCII and UNICODE strings and can recognize complex code constructs, such as call to jump procedures, and decodes calls to more than 1900 standard API as well as 400 C functions.

2.4.1.7   Angr

ANGR [265] is a framework for automatic binary code analysis, which is available for the research community. This framework has several capabilities compared to other frameworks. For instance, it is compatible with different CPU architectures including x86, MIPS, ARM, and PowerPC [99]. The disassembly of the binaries employs recursive traversal. Also, it supports both Windows and Linux binaries. ANGR focuses more on symbolic execution and for this purpose, a separate engine is included in the framework. Furthermore, it employs VEX-IR (Valgrind) to perform the analysis on intermediate representation.

2.4.1.8   ByteWeight

BYTEWEIGHT [72] employs machine learning models in order to label each byte of a binary code as representing a function starting point. Instead of pattern collection, it defines weighted prefix trees of function start [117], then recursive disassembly is employed combined with value set analysis [285] in order to discover the remaining bytes of the functions [117].

Table 2.7 provides a comparison among the aforementioned disassembler tools to provide the reader a better understanding of the capability of each tool.

2.4.2   Feature Ranking

In binary code analysis, the extracted features are typically quite large. Thus, it is needed to propose techniques, which are scalable, especially when dealing with malware binaries. Feature ranking is a solution that is proposed in the literature in order to consider the more relevant features. In this subsection, we pick the authorship attribution problem and demonstrate how feature ranking can be performed using mutual information.

The task of feature ranking algorithm consists in associating the identity of the most likely author of a feature. The features are extracted from the program binaries associated with a specific program. Various features exist in most programs, irrespective of the number of authors. The features exhibiting no specific correlation among the programs related to the same author should be ranked low. Mutual information measures the information that is shared by a feature and an author. Therefore, features can be ranked by employing mutual information (MI) between the feature and the actual (true) author as follows [224]:

$$MI(X, Y) = \sum \sum p(x, y) log_2 \frac{p(x, y)}{p(x)p(y)}, \qquad (2.1)$$

where $p(x, y)$ is the joint probability distribution function of a feature and an author, and $p(x)$ and $p(y)$ represent the marginal probability distribution functions

Table 2.7 Comparison of disassembler tools

	IDA PRO	OBJDUMP	PE	PARADYN	JACKSTAB	OLLYDBG	ANGR	BYTEWEIGHT
Free	✗	✓	✗	✓	✓	✓	✓	NA
Windows	✓	✗	✓	✗	✓	✓	✓	✓
Linux	✓	✓	✗	✓	✗	✓	✓	✓
Actively maintained	✓	✗	✗	✓	✓	✓	✓	✗
Static	✓	✓	✓	✓	✓	✓	✓	✓
Dynamic	✗	✗	✗	✗	✗	✓	✗	✗
Symbolic execution	✗	✗	✗	✗	✗	✗	✓	✗
Compiler identification	✓	✗	✓	✗	✗	✗	✗	✗
Library recognition	✓	✗	✗	✓	✗	✗	✓	✗
Trace registers	✗	✗	✗	✗	✗	✓	✗	✗
Function descriptions	✓	✗	✗	✗	✗	✓	✓	✓
Function boundary identification	✓	✗	✗	✓	✗	✓	✓	✓
Cross-platform architecture	✓	✗	✗	✗	✗	✗	✓	✗

NA stands for information not available

of a feature and an author, respectively. Mutual information allows to measure the extent to which knowing one of these variables reduces the uncertainty on the other. For instance, if feature x and author y are independent, knowing this feature does not provide any information about the author, and consequently their mutual information is zero.

2.4.3 Machine Learning Techniques

In this subsection, we introduce specific examples of fingerprint classification and fingerprint clustering.

2.4.3.1 Fingerprint Classification

Classification techniques assume the availability of a known set of classes (e.g., authors) along with their related program samples. Then, the classifier is built based on a selected set of features (e.g., top-ranked features), and provides a decision function to assign a label (e.g., authorship) to any new program based on the given set of known classes (e.g., authors). For instance, the LIBLINEAR support vector machine (SVM) [131, 275] implementation is an example for the actual classification. More specifically, the typical steps for authorship classification are as follows:

1. Each program is initially represented using an integer-valued feature vector describing the features present in the program.
2. These features are also ordered by using the aforementioned ranking algorithm that leverages the mutual information between each feature and the known author labels. A given number of the top-ranked features are selected while others are discarded to reduce both the training cost and the risk of overfitting.
3. A cross-validation is then performed on the top-ranked features. These features would jointly provide a good input to the decision function for the authorship classifier.

2.4.3.2 Fingerprint Clustering

Since training data with known labels (e.g., authorship) may not be always available, especially for malware binaries, it was more desirable to form clusters of malware programs based on a common factor (e.g., authorship). Thus, unsupervised learning algorithms are employed to perform the clustering tasks. There exist various clustering techniques, such as k-means [166] algorithm, which can be used for authorship clustering. For instance, author clustering can be performed by carrying out the following steps:

1. The clustering algorithm generates program clusters based on relative distances in a d-dimensional space. Specifically, a $d \times d$ distance metric A is defined whereby the mahalanobis distance [97, 115] between two feature vectors is measured as follows [251]:

$$D_A(X_a, X_b) = \sqrt{(X_a - X_b)^T A(X_a - X_b)}. \tag{2.2}$$

2. In order to ensure that the clustering is based on author styles instead of other properties, such as functionality, a two-part algorithm can be elaborated for transferring the knowledge learned from labelled dataset to unlabelled dataset.

2.4.4   Distance Between Features

One way to compare and measure the similarity between two given fingerprints is to calculate the distance between their feature vectors. This similarity metric can be evaluated by using a set of distance metrics. In this subsection, we introduce some of them as follows. Let f_1 and f_2 denote the two feature sets that are extracted from two functions F_1 and F_2, respectively.

The *symmetric distance* [51] between f_1 and f_2 is defined as follows:

$$SD(f_1, f_2) = \mid f_1 \setminus f_2 \mid \tag{2.3}$$

which denotes the cardinality of the set of features that are present in f_1 or f_2 but not in both. The symmetric distance essentially measures the number of features that are unique between the two functions of F_1 and F_2.

The *dice coefficient distance* [172] is defined as follows:

$$DC(f_1, f_2) = 1 - \frac{2(\mid f_1 \cap f_2 \mid)}{(\mid f_1 \mid + \mid f_2 \mid)}. \tag{2.4}$$

The *Jaccard distance* [172] is defined as follows:

$$JD(f_1, f_2) = 1 - \frac{\mid f_1 \cap f_2 \mid}{\mid f_1 \cup f_2 \mid}. \tag{2.5}$$

The *Jaccard containment distance* [56] is defined as follows:

$$JC(f_1, f_2) = 1 - \frac{\mid f_1 \cap f_2 \mid}{\min(\mid f_1 \mid, \mid f_2 \mid)}. \tag{2.6}$$

In addition to the aforementioned four distance measures, which are all symmetric (i.e., distance(f_1, f_2) = distance(f_2, f_1)), there is also an asymmetric distance measure which can evaluate the dissimilarity between two sets. This is referred to as the *weighted symmetric distance* [218], defined as follows:

$$WSD(f_1, f_2) = \mid f_1 \setminus f_2 \mid \cdot C_{del} + \mid f_2 \setminus f_1 \mid \cdot C_{add}, \tag{2.7}$$

where C_{del} and C_{add} denote the cost for, respectively, deleting and adding a feature. Note that $WSD(f_1; f_2) = SD(f_1; f_2)$ when $C_{del} = C_{add} = 1$.

The *Cosine similarity* [172] is defined as follows:

$$CS(f_1, f_2) = \frac{f_1 \cdot f_2}{\parallel f_1 \parallel \parallel f_2 \parallel}. \tag{2.8}$$

The resulting similarity is ranging from -1 (exactly dissimilar) to 1 (exactly the same) where a similarity value of 0 typically indicates independence, while the values departing from 0 indicate more or less similarity or dissimilarity. The cosine of two vectors can be obtained using the *Euclidean dot product* formula as follows:

$$f_1 \cdot f_2 = \parallel f_1 \parallel \parallel f_2 \parallel cos\Theta. \tag{2.9}$$

The *hamming distance* [249] is defined between two strings that are of equal length, and it is given by the number of positions where the corresponding symbols are different. More specifically, it measures the minimum number of substitutions that are needed to transform one string into another, or alternatively, the minimum number of errors that could have modified one string into another. For instance, the hamming distance between the strings "coral" and "carol" is 2.

2.5 Code Transformation

In this section, we discuss the code transformation that affects the accuracy of fingerprints in identifying the authors, functions, etc. Such transformations affect the accuracy of the systems and should be addressed in order to obtain high accuracy.

2.5.1 Obfuscation Techniques

Typically, binaries are converted to assembly files by using a disassembler. The code may then be subjected to obfuscation using an obfuscator. Generally, obfuscation techniques may be applied on three types of binary analysis platforms: disassemblers, debuggers, and virtual machines [298]. In the context of static analysis, the anti-disassembler category, which includes a variety of techniques (e.g., dead-code insertion, instruction aliasing, control flow obfuscation, binary code compression, encryption) will be discussed next.

DALIN [196] generator applies the following light obfuscation:

- *Register renaming* (RR), which represents one of the oldest and simplest techniques used in metamorphic generators;
- *Instruction reordering* (IR), which transposes the instructions that do not depend on the output of previous instructions;
- *Dead-code insertion* (DCI), which injects some code that has no effect on the program execution (i.e., may not be executed or may execute with no effect);
- *Equivalent instruction replacement* (EIR), which replaces the instruction(s) with equivalent instruction(s).

Another obfuscator, OBFUSCATOR-LLVM [173] can be used to apply the following obfuscations:

- *Equivalent instruction replacement* (EIR), which replaces instructions with other ones that are semantically equivalent instructions;
- *Bogus control flow* (BCF), which adds opaque predicates to a basic block;
- *Control flow graph flattening* (FLA), which flattens, even completely, the control flow graph.

Another tool, called TRIGRESS [52] is employed to obfuscate the source code by employing the following methods:

- *Virtualization* (VZ), which transforms a function into an interpreter whose bytecode language is specific for the function;
- *Jitting*, which transforms a function into one that can generate at runtime its actual machine code;
- *Dynamic*, which transforms a function into one that is continuously modifying its machine code at runtime.

2.5.2 Refactoring Techniques

The fingerprints that are used in the identification section may be affected if an adversary applies C++ refactoring techniques [30, 41]; an in-depth explanation of these techniques is provided in [140]. For instance, some examples of these techniques are as follows:

- Renaming a variable (RV);
- Moving a given method from a superclass to one of its subclasses (MM);
- Extracting a number of statements and placing them into a new method (NM).

2.5.3 The Impact of Compilers

With the presence of different compilers the binary analysis task becomes more challenging. Employing different compilers, compiler versions, and optimization settings results in significant variations in the binary representations of the same source code compiled with different compilation settings. In general, the Visual Studio (VS), GNU Compiler Collection (GCC), Intel C++ Compiler (ICC), and Clang are the most commonly used compilers with different optimization settings of: Od (no optimization), O2, and Ox (full speed). All of which affect the binary representation and consequently the binary analysis task. On the other hand, software is cross-compiled or deployed on a variety of CPU architectures (e.g., x86 or ARM), where instruction sets, calling conventions, register sets, function offsets, and memory access strategies differ. Therefore, the analysis of binaries compiled for different CPU architectures becomes more complicated and challenging.

2.6   Binary Frameworks for Software Fingerprints

In this section, we detail a selected set of binary frameworks that are suitable for the purpose of software fingerprinting. Due to space limitations, we select only the most used frameworks and consider the use cases of each framework. We briefly describe a set of noteworthy frameworks.

2.6.1   BitBlaze

BITBLAZE [269] represents a binary analysis platform which can automatically extract security-related properties from binary code (both vulnerable programs and malicious code) for effective defense. It provides an intermediate language suitable for operating on machine code as well as a number of analysis algorithms that can work on that language. This approach may be helpful in: (1) commercial off-the-shelf (COTS) vulnerability analysis and defense and (2) malicious code analysis and defense. The BITBLAZE architecture encompasses the following three components: (1) *Vine*, which is a static analysis component; (2) *TEMU*, which is a dynamic analysis component; and (3) *Rudder*, which is a hybrid analysis component.

2.6.2   BAP

BAP [86] is a publicly available platform for performing program verification and analysis on binary code. BAP can accept three kinds of inputs: x86 assembly, ARM assembly, and traces. These inputs are lifted to the BIL intermediate language in order to appen the side effects to the assembly instructions. Finally, program analysis and program verification are carried out on BIL.

2.6.3   BinNavi

BINNAVI [53] represents an integrated and platform-independent reverse engineering environment that allows to dissect and analyze binary files. It can be used as well to analyze the latest piece of malware found while tracking down a spearfishing attack, to discover new vulnerabilities in closed-source software, or to figure out whether a third-party embedded device poses a threat to a network.

2.6.4   iBinHunt

IBINHUNT [216] is a novel binary diffing technique that can cope with function obfuscation aimed at binary diffing tools that compare intra-procedural control flows. It actually discards all information on function boundary and compares the inter-procedural control flow of the binary programs. Moreover, it employs deep taint, which is a new dynamic taint analysis technique that assigns different taint tags to different parts of the program input and then traces the propagation of the tags in order to reduce the number of basic block matching candidates.

2.6.5   BitShred

BITSHRED [168] represents a framework for automatic code reuse detection in binary code. BITSHRED can be employed for identifying the amount of shared code based on the ability to calculate the similarity among binary code samples. Furthermore, BITSHRED can be applied to many security problems, such as bug finding and malware clustering. Experimental results indicate that BITSHRED may detect plagiarism among malware samples and can cluster them efficiently.

2.6.6   BinSlayer

BINSLAYER [221] combines the well-known BINDIFF algorithm [139] with the Hungarian algorithm for bi-partite graph matching, and employs a polynomial algorithm to find the similarity between executables [84]. More specifically, it can perform automated static comparison of binary files by combining the two aforementioned approaches.

2.6.7   BinJuice

BINJUICE [188] represents a tool for extracting the "juice" of a binary where the term "juice" stands for the abstraction of the semantics of the blocks of a binary. While the denotational semantics summarize the computation performed by a block, its juice represents a template of the relationships established by the block.

2.6.8   BinCoa

The BINary COde Analysis (BINCOA) framework [74] aims to facilitate the development of binary code analyzers. The framework is built around Dynamic Bitvector Automata (DBA) [73], which is a concise and generic formal model for low-level programs. The key design ideas of DBA are as follows: (1) focusing on a small set of instructions; (2) using a concise and natural modeling for common architectures; (3) using self-contained models, which have no requirement for a separate description of the memory model or architecture; and (4) employing a sufficiently low-level formalism, which allows DBA to serve as reference semantics of the executable file under analysis.

2.6.9   BINSEC

BINSEC [120] represents an open-source platform for binary-level code analysis. It is considered as a dynamic framework and the platform is actually based on an extension of the DBA [73, 74] intermediate representation (IR). The platform is composed of three main modules: (1) a front-end, which includes several syntactic disassembly algorithms in conjunction with a heavy simplification of the obtained IR; (2) a simulator for the recent low-level region-based memory model; and (3) a module dedicated for generic static analysis. However, this framework does not support ARM, PowerPC, and loaders (PE).

2.6.10   BinGraph

BINGRAPH [185] provides a new mechanism that allows to accurately discover metamorphic malware. In this respect, BINGRAPH leverages the semantics of a malware, as mutant malware can only manipulate their syntax. The authors first extract API calls from the malware. These are then converted into a hierarchical behavior graph. Subsequently, unique subgraphs are extracted from the hierarchical behavior graphs as semantic signatures that represent the common behaviors of a specific malware family.

2.6.11   MAYHEM

MAYHEM [94] is a system aimed at the automatic detection of exploitable bugs in binary (i.e., executable) programs. Every bug that is reported by MAYHEM is also accompanied by a functioning shell-spawning exploit. The functioning exploits assure the soundness and serve to confirm that each reported bug is security critical and actionable. MAYHEM actually works on raw binary code without the need for debug information. In order to make the exploit generation possible at the binary level, MAYHEM addresses two major technical issues: it is actively managing the execution paths in a memory efficient manner, and can reason about symbolic memory indices, where a load or a store address is depending on the user input. Moreover, it employs two novel techniques: (1) hybrid symbolic execution that allows for combining online and offline (concolic) execution in order to maximize the benefits provided by both techniques and (2) index-based memory modelling, a technique which allows MAYHEM to reason in an efficient manner on symbolic memory at binary level.

2.6.12 Exposé

EXPOSÉ [225] represents a tool that combining symbolic execution using theorem proving with function-level syntactic matching techniques in order to achieve elevated performance as well as high-quality rankings of applications. Higher rankings also indicate a higher likelihood of reusing the code of the library. EXPOSÉ is able to rank applications that use two libraries at the top or near the top. In addition, EXPOSÉ is able to rank applications correctly for different library versions as well as when different compiler options are used.

2.6.13 REWARDS

REWARDS [197] leverages dynamic analysis. More precisely, each memory location that is accessed by the program is tagged using a type specific time-stamped attribute. By following the runtime data flow of the program, this attribute is propagated to other memory locations and registers that are sharing the same type. During propagation, the type of a variable gets resolved if it partakes in a type-revealing execution point or a "type sink". In addition to the forward type propagation, REWARDS employs a backward type resolution procedure whereby the types of certain previously accessed variables get recursively resolved beginning from a given type sink. The procedure is constrained by the time stamps of relevant memory locations in order to disambiguate the variables that reuse the same memory location. Also, REWARDS can reconstruct in-memory data structure layouts that are based on the derived type information.

2.6.14 Helium

The HELIUM platform [211] allows for the automatic lifting of performance-critical stencil kernels from a stripped x86 binary and can generate the corresponding code in the high-level and domain-specific language called Halide [238]. In this context, HELIUM relies on dynamic traces in order to regenerate the kernels, after which a buffer structure reconstruction is performed to identify input, intermediate, and output buffer shapes. Subsequently, the platform abstracts from a forest of concrete dependency trees (containing absolute memory addresses) to symbolic trees that are suitable for high-level code generation.

2.6.15 Hercules

HERCULES [233] represents a framework for generating inputs aimed at reaching a given "potentially crashing" location. This type of crashing locations can be found via separate static analysis or alternatively, by analyzing crash reports provided by internal and/or external users. The test input generated by the framework serves as a crash witness. The framework is particularly well-suited for program binaries which take in complex structured inputs.

2.6.16 Malheur

MALHEUR [26, 246] is a tool for analyzing malware automatically, using both machine learning and dynamic analysis. MALHEUR has been designed in order to support the regular analysis of malicious programs and for the elaboration of detection capabilities and related defensive measures. It allows identifying previously unknown malware classes with similar behavior that can be clustered together and assigns the discovered classes to unknown malware in order to classify them. Moreover, MALHEUR leverages the concept of dynamic analysis: Malware binaries are collected in the wild and then executed in a sandbox, where their behavior is monitored during runtime. The execution of each malware binary results in a corresponding report of recorded behavior. MALHEUR then analyzes these reports via machine learning, for discovery and discrimination of malware classes.

2.6.17 MARD

MARD [58] is a novel framework that can analyze metamorphic malware. It provides real-time detection to provide protection to end points that often constitute the last defense against metamorphic malware. The capabilities of MARD include: (1) automation, (2) platform independence, (3) real-time performance optimization, and (4) modularity.

2.6.18 BinGold

BINGOLD [64] extracts the semantics of binary code in terms of both data and control flow. This allows for more robust binary analysis, since the extracted semantics of the binary code is generally immune to light obfuscation, refactoring, and the use of various compilers or compilation settings. More specifically, the authors employ data flow analysis in order to extract the semantic flow of the registers as well as the semantic components of the control flow graph, which are then synthesized into a novel representation called the semantic flow graph (SFG).

2.6.19   BinGo

BINGO [98] is a scalable and robust binary search engine. It supports different architectures and operating systems. The key contribution of BINGO resides in a selective inlining technique that allows capturing the complete function semantics by inlining relevant library and user-defined functions. The authors also introduce length varying partial traces in order to model binary functions in a fashion that is program structure agnostic.

2.6.20   BinConvex

BINCONVEX [208] represents a system for a non-convex abstract domain, suitable for analyzing executable binaries. The domain is actually based on binary decision diagrams (BDDs) that allow for an efficient representation of non-convex integer sets. Such sets are needed in order to represent the results of bitwise operations and jump table lookups, which are encountered more frequently in machine code rather than in high-level code, due to compiler optimization. The domain used by the authors allows to precisely compute abstract bitwise and arithmetic operations, losing precision only in the case of division and multiplication. Given that the operations are defined on the structure of the BDDs, they remain efficient even when executed on very large sets. In machine code, conditional jumps require the evaluation of expressions constructed with negation and conjunction. The authors implement a constraint solver that employs the fast intersection of BDD-based sets.

2.6.21   BinCross

BINCROSS is a system that derives bug signatures for known bugs [231]. The signatures are used in order to identify bugs in binaries that have been deployed on various CPU architectures (e.g., x86, MIPS). Different CPU architectures create plenty of challenges, including the incomparability of instruction sets between different CPU architectures. The authors of BINCROSS address this by first translating the binary code into an intermediate representation, which involves assignment formulas with input and output variables. Then, they sample concrete inputs in order to observe the input–output (I/O) behavior of basic blocks to grasp their semantics. Finally, they employ the I/O behavior to find parts of code that have similar behavior to the bug signature, effectively revealing those parts of code that contain the bug. The implemented tool allows for cross-architecture bug search in executables. The prototype currently supports three CPU architectures, namely x86, ARM, and MIPS, and can find binary code vulnerabilities in any of these architectures.

2.6.22   BARF

BARF [158] represents an open-source framework for binary analysis that targets a wide range of binary code analysis tasks that are common in the information security discipline. BARF is actually a scriptable platform that supports instruction lifting from multiple architectures. Moreover, it supports binary translation to an intermediate representation as well as an extensible framework for code analysis plugins and interoperation with external tools such as debuggers, SMT solvers [116], and instrumentation tools. The framework is primarily designed for human-assisted analysis, but also allows for full automation.

2.6.23   Aligot

ALIGOT [91] is a tool that uses input–output (I/O) relationships as a countermeasure to obfuscation. In this respect, it is more effective than many identification tools that require easily identifiable static features in the binary code. It leverages the fact that all obfuscated implementations still maintain the I/O relationship of the original function. ALIGOT allows the identification of cryptographic functions in obfuscated programs by retrieving their I/O parameters in an implementation independent manner followed by a comparison to those of known cryptographic functions. Cryptographic functions, such as TEA, RC4, AES, and MD5 can be identified, both in synthetic examples that are protected by a commercial-grade packer (ASPROTECT) as well as in several obfuscated malware samples (e.g., Sality, Waledac, Storm Worm, and SilentBanker). Furthermore, ALIGOT is able to recognize basic operations performed in asymmetric ciphers, such as RSA.

2.6.24   Howard

HOWARD provides a new solution to extracting data structures from C binaries without the need for symbol tables [267]. This way, debugging binaries becomes feasible and reverse engineering becomes simpler. HOWARD allows the recovery of most data structures in arbitrary binary code (GCC-generated) with high degree of precision. While it is still debatable that the problem of data structure identification has been solved, HOWARD still provides significant advances. For instance, HOWARD can extract precise data structures, such as nested arrays, from both the heap and stack.

2.7 Learned Lessons and Concluding Remarks

In this chapter, we presented a review of the literature relevant to binary analysis frameworks along with a detailed comparison thereof. We also studied their applicability in characterizing malware samples. It is quite clear that there are numerous features that can be potentially useful for determining malware characteristics. However, the difficult task is to verify their applicability via experimental studies. In the following, we discuss the learned lessons of binary analysis.

Feature Pre-processing: In order to fingerprint any types of functions (e.g., library or user functions), it is necessary to filter out irrelevant functions. For instance, the top-ranked features in a proposed authorship frameworks [251] are related to the compiler (e.g., stack frame setup operation) rather than the author style. Thus, it is very important to filter out the functions that are irrelevant (e.g., compiler functions) in order to better identify the author-related code portions. In order to avoid this issue, we suggest, as a prior step, to filter irrelevant functions by employing some existing approaches, such as FLIRT [151] mechanism or BINCOMP [240], for library function and compiler function filtering respectively. A successful discrimination between these groups of functions will provide considerable time saving while helping in shifting the focus of the analysis to more relevant functions.

Feature Extraction: While conducting the literature review, we observe that the features should be carefully selected in order to generate a precise fingerprint. For instance, for authorship fingerprinting, an indication is that features relate directly to the program size, which usually indicate functionality rather than style [59, 90, 251]. Therefore, the features should be selected based on the problem.

The Source of Features: When the binary code is ready for analysis, there are various suitable sources for extracting features relevant to the problem. For instance, one may decompile the binary file into a source file and then extract the features from the source code. Conversely, one could disassemble the binary file to an assembly file and then apply various existing reverse engineering tools, such as IDA PRO which can be used to extract hex bytes, the control flow graph, assembly instructions, etc. Apart from such static analysis methods, one may also execute the binary file in a sandbox environment which would allow to analyze the runtime behavior of the file. Notwithstanding, we observe that the accuracy of fingerprints heavily depends on the source of features that are used to generate the fingerprints.

Misleading Features: The names of many source code level functions are unidentified at the binary level, i.e., IDA PRO assigns a name that is prefixed with "sub" and postfixed with pseudo-random numbers generated by the compiler. This kind of functions with random numbers play an essential role for features to be highly ranked by calculating the entropy, such as mutual information. This discovery indicates that the techniques that extract features from such functions may select many features that are related not to user functions or author style but rather other properties, such as compiler-generated functions or reused code.

Function Inlining: In practice, compilers may inline small functions into the calling code as an optimization. Furthermore, function inlining significantly changes the program layout and introduces additional complexity to the code, which may bring more challenges for existing binary analysis approaches. Finding inlined code represents a challenging task [236]. The accuracy will undoubtedly decrease if the features are derived from a function that includes inlined functions. In this respect, the use of data flow analysis can provide the capability to find inlined code.

Leveraging Dynamic Analysis: Most of the existing fingerprint frameworks employ static analysis. However, when enhancing the existing frameworks with dynamic analysis, such as tainting or symbolic execution, generating the satisfiability conditions and providing proof-of-concept data become easier.

Binary Lifting: In order to unify the native code of different platforms, binary lifting is proposed to convert binary instructions into an intermediate representation (IR).

Chapter 3
Compiler Provenance Attribution

Compiler identification is an essential component of binary toolchain analysis with a multitude of applications in reverse engineering and malware analysis. Security investigators and cyber incident responders are often tasked with the analysis and attribution of binary files obtained from malicious campaigns which need to be inspected quickly and reliably. Such binaries can be a source of intelligence on adversary tactics, techniques, and procedures. Compiler provenance information can aid binary analysis by uncovering fingerprints of the development environment and related libraries, leading to an accelerated analysis. In this chapter, we present BINCOMP, which provides a practical approach for analyzing the syntax, structure, and semantics of disassembled functions to extract compiler provenance.

This chapter is organized as follows. The compiler provenance problem is introduced in Sect. 3.1. Sections 3.2 and 3.3 present two different approaches (BINCOMP and ECP) for the compiler identification problem. The evaluation results of BINCOMP are presented in Sect. 3.4. Then, Sect. 3.5 discusses its limitations before drawing the conclusions and hinting on future research directions.

3.1 Introduction

Contrary to open-source scenarios, program binaries often lack meaningful identifiers, function names, and code comments; all of which would have been relevant to understanding the context of program behavior. Furthermore, variations in compiler front-end languages, back-end transformation logic, and optimization heuristics complicate matters further. Compiler provenance can reveal information regarding the behavior, family, type, version, optimization, and functions of the originating binary compilers [69].

The primary key area of research on compiler provenance encompasses the core studies of function labeling, source compiler identification, and toolchain recovery [165, 250, 252]. Certain drawbacks can be identified in the current methods

© Springer Nature Switzerland AG 2020
S. Alrabaee et al., *Binary Code Fingerprinting for Cybersecurity*, Advances in Information Security 78, https://doi.org/10.1007/978-3-030-34238-8_3

and tools, particularly the usage of generic and rigid signatures (e.g., PEiD [40] and RDG [49]), extensive training set requirements, and computationally intensive feature ranking techniques that could limit practical applications of such methods. Alternative approaches adopt hidden Markov models (HMMs) to determine the most likely compiler [278], with an emphasis into malware detection as opposed to compiler property extraction (e.g., version and optimization level). Tools which employ heuristics (e.g., IDA PRO [45]) are also adept at identifying commonly known compilers, presuming the availability of type signatures.

The approach presented in this chapter builds on the existing approaches by applying new heuristics in feature selection and processing, based on domain-specific knowledge, leading to reduced computational complexity of the search processes along with increased accuracy and precision of detection results. Furthermore, the new approach aims to attain better robustness by leveraging more stable aspects of compiler behavior in place of byte-level classification.

3.1.1 Objectives

The main objective of this chapter is to provide a practical framework for characterizing compiler behavior using a set of perceptible feature profiles facilitating compiler comparability, identification, and property measurement. Through experiments with supervised compilation involving multiple toolchains, we have observed that certain compiler utility and helper functions are steadily preserved during the compilation and linkage processes, across distinct program contexts. At a low-level, such behavior can be determined by inspecting the code generation and emission mechanisms of source compilers [6] as well as the linked/runtime libraries. We assume that this property holds true for compilers/linkers in the scope of our analysis. Our approach pivots on such functions along with other compiler/linker characteristics to build plausible support for the most likely compiler/toolchain of target binaries. We are aiming to advance the following areas:

- Current approaches utilize generic signatures in conjunction with compiler attribute ranking and predefined templates [250, 252]. Such techniques may result in high detection accuracy despite being computationally expensive. However, drawbacks can be observed over the execution time and the extraneous number of features generated during processing, the majority of which are unrelated to compiler properties. Furthermore, the interesting features obtained as a result of feature selection and ranking may not distinctly describe compiler-specific functions, from a semantic or structural perspectives. Conversely, BINCOMP combines various engineered feature categories to capture structural, syntactic, and semantic aspects of compilers in support of provenance elucidation.
- Identifying compiler functions provides a significant support in program analysis applications such as binary authorship attribution [59, 251], function fingerprinting and recognition [61, 255, 272], and binary clone detection [123, 133]. In such applications, filtering out compiler or linker-specific functions can be considered as a pre-processing stage, which can assist analysts, channelizing their attention

towards user functions. The existing approaches have not considered defini-
tive function identification and labelling mechanisms [250, 252]. In contrast,
BINCOMP facilitates function analysis via identification of compiler/linker-
dependent functions.

3.1.2 Motivating Example

We analyze the compiled version of the minimal program shown in Listing 3.1 to
compare compiler emitted code under various compilation toolchains. This simple
program contains a `main` function that defines an integer variable and assigns a
value to it. Then, a stream I/O library call is made to print a string, followed by
an increment in the variable value. The program then terminates by returning an
integer. Listings 3.2, 3.3, and 3.4 show the disassembly of the compiled program
with MSVCP (Windows), GCC (Linux), and Clang, respectively. As can be seen,
the compilers generate different code sequences for an identical input.

Listing 3.1 Simple C++ Program

```
#include <iostream>
using namespace std;

int main() {
  int num = 110;
  cout << "hnum=" << num+1;
  num++;
  return num;
}
```

Listing 3.2 Compilation with MSVCP 14 on Windows, disassembly in IDA

```
var_4 = dword ptr -4
argc = dword ptr 8
argv = dword ptr 0Ch
envp = dword ptr 10h


push  ebp
mov   ebp, esp
push  ecx
mov   [ebp+var_4], 6Eh
mov   eax, [ebp+var_4]
add   eax, 1
push  eax
push  offset Str    ; "hnum="
mov   ecx, ds:std::basic_ostream<char,std::char_traits<char>> std::cout
push  ecx         ; int
call  std::operator<<<std::char_traits<char>>(std::basic_ostream<char,
std::char_traits<char>> &,char const *)
add   esp, 8
mov   ecx, eax
call  ds:std::basic_ostream<char,std::char_traits<char>>::operator<<(int)
mov   edx, [ebp+var_4]
add   edx, 1
mov   [ebp+var_4], edx
mov   eax, [ebp+var_4]
mov   esp, ebp
pop   ebp
retn
```

Listing 3.3 Compilation with GCC 8.1, disassembly with objdump

```
push    rbp
mov     rbp,rsp
sub     rsp,0x10
mov     DWORD PTR [rbp-0x4],0x6e
mov     esi,0x400825
mov     edi,0x601060
call    4005f0 <std::basic_ostream<char, std::char_traits<char> >&
std::operator<< <std::char_traits<char>>(std::basic_ostream<char,
std::char_traits<char> >&, char const*)@plt>
mov     rdx,rax
mov     eax,DWORD PTR [rbp-0x4]
add     eax,0x1
mov     esi,eax
mov     rdi,rdx
call    400610 <std::ostream::operator<<(int)@plt>
add     DWORD PTR [rbp-0x4],0x1
mov     eax,DWORD PTR [rbp-0x4]
leave
ret
```

Listing 3.4 Compilation with Clang 7.0, disassembly with objdump

```
push    rbp
mov     rbp,rsp
sub     rsp,0x10
mov     DWORD PTR [rbp-0x4],0x0
mov     DWORD PTR [rbp-0x8],0x6e
movabs  rdi,0x601060
movabs  rsi,0x400834
call    4005c0 <std::basic_ostream<char, std::char_traits<char>>&
std::operator<< <std::char_traits<char> >(std::basic_ostream<char,
std::char_traits<char> >&, char const*)@plt>
mov     ecx,DWORD PTR [rbp-0x8]
add     ecx,0x1
mov     rdi,rax
mov     esi,ecx
call    4005e0 <std::ostream::operator<<(int)@plt>
mov     ecx,DWORD PTR [rbp-0x8]
add     ecx,0x1
mov     DWORD PTR [rbp-0x8],ecx
mov     ecx,DWORD PTR [rbp-0x8]
mov     QWORD PTR [rbp-0x10],rax
mov     eax,ecx
add     rsp,0x10
pop     rbp
ret
```

Table 3.1 presents a subset of assembly functions extracted from the binary. When compiled with MSVCP14 and disassembled by IDA PRO (as presented in Listing 3.2), we obtain 90 assembly functions from the code segment, of which, 13 are library functions, 76 are related to compiler utility/helper functions and a single user function. The entry point of the program is _mainCRTStartup, which prepares the C runtime libraries and calls __scrt_common_main_seh. This is the function that handles the call to _main. It also manages the termination of _main before transitioning to the operating system.

When compiled with MSVC 2010, this program results in 37 assembly functions in fully optimized release mode. The disassembly includes 31 compiler utility/helper functions, five library, and one user function. Compilation and disassembly

Table 3.1 List of disassembly functions (MSVCP binary)

IsProcessorFeaturePresent(x)	__crt_debugger_hook
__RTC_Initialize	__except_handler4
__RTC_Terminate	__except_handler4_common
__SEH_epilog4	__exit
__SEH_prolog4	__get_entropy
___CxxFrameHandler3	__get_initial_narrow_environment
___isa_available_init	__get_startup_argv_mode
___local_stdio_printf_options	__get_startup_file_mode
___local_stdio_scanf_options	__initialize_default_precision
___p___argc	__initialize_narrow_environment
___p___argv	__initialize_onexit_table
___p__commode	__initterm
___raise_securityfailure	__initterm_e
___report_gsfailure	__onexit
___scrt_acquire_startup_lock	__register_onexit_function
___scrt_fastfail	__register_thread_local_exe_atexit_callback
___scrt_get_dyn_tls_dtor_callback	__scrt_common_main_seh
___scrt_get_dyn_tls_init_callback	__scrt_initialize_type_info(void)
___scrt_initialize_crt	__scrt_unhandled_exception_filter(x)
___scrt_initialize_default_local_stdio_options	__security_check_cookie(x)
___scrt_initialize_mta	__seh_filter_exe
___scrt_initialize_onexit_tabloo	__set_app_type
___scrt_initialize_winrt	__set_fmode
___scrt_is_managed_app	__set_new_mode
___scrt_is_nonwritable_in_current_image	_atexit
___scrt_is_ucrt_dll_in_use	_exit_0
___scrt_is_user_matherr_present	_guard_check_icall_nop(x)
___scrt_release_startup_lock	_main
___scrt_set_unhandled_exception_filter	_mainCRTStartup
___scrt_stub_for_acrt_initialize	_memset
___scrt_uninitialize_crt	_strlen
___security_init_cookie	_terminate
___setusermatherr	find_pe_section
__c_exit	post_pgo_initialization
__cexit	pre_c_initialization
__configthreadlocale	pre_cpp_initialization
__configure_narrow_argv	sub_4021E0
__controlfp_s	sub_402200
__crt_atexit	. . .

of the same program with MSVC 2012 generates 72 functions (with security checks enabled) of which 51 functions are related to the compiler, 18 are library functions, and three are user functions. While comparing the compiler-related functions, we notice that 25 functions have remained the same.

In our approach, given a list of disassembled functions, we explain how to identify the most likely build toolchain with which the input binary was compiled/linked. If we experiment with different program compilations, we observe that a subset of compiler-related functions remains intact. To extract the list of such functions, we intersect multiple sets of compiled programs and develop signature profiles. However, we do not rely on string-based function identifiers as the only feature for comparison. In stripped binaries as well as obfuscated files, such strings may not be available. Also, disassemblers often assign generic names to functions. Thus, we create numerical and symbolic representations of compiler/helper functions using multiple feature vectors as part of the compiler profiles. We also build compiler-specific behavioral profiles based on code transformations. These profiles describe compiler characteristics with respect to language structure transformation, source to assembly mappings, and code optimizations.

3.1.3 Approach Overview

We establish a hybrid architecture for BINCOMP comprising three main processes, each aimed at capturing a different set of compiler behavior properties. Collectively, these processes enable the solution to derive an accurate representation of source compiler behavior using syntactic, structural, and semantic profiles. Each process/tier builds upon a unique detection technique.

The new perspective of BINCOMP can be viewed as the continuous integration and learning of compiler code conversion profiles with a priori knowledge of their code transformations overlaid with statistical measures of the emitted code. Unique behavioral profiles can be built describing the sequence of compiler-specific function calls, function/library interdependencies, machine instruction categories, and the control flow graphs of initialization and terminator utility/helper code. Changes in compiler behavior (e.g., due to updates/new heuristics) are also captured and reflected in the respective profiles.

The main processes/tiers of the solution are depicted in Fig. 3.1.

- The initial process extracts syntactical features from the compiled code and generates two outputs, namely the compiler transformation profile (CTP) and compiler tags (CT). The detection method is based on pattern matching against predefined/incremental signatures.
- The subsequent process then identifies compiler functions (CF) by analyzing instruction-level features and building function profiles composed of numerical and symbolic feature vectors. This process aims to label helper and utility

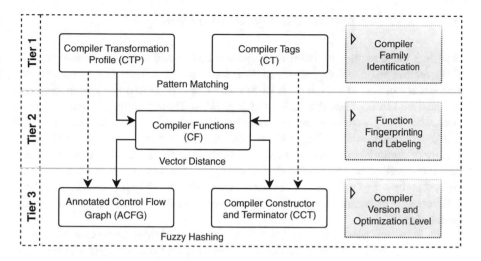

Fig. 3.1 BINCOMP multi-tiered framework

functions by measuring the similarity (calculating the distance) between known and target numerical vectors.

- The consecutive process elicits semantic features, which are captured using the annotated control flow graph (ACFG) and the compiler constructor and terminator (CCT) profiles. These semantic profiles are evaluated to infer the optimization heuristics, level, and version of the compiler in conjunction with the helper/utility feature vectors. Inexact matching using fuzzy hashing is performed on semantic graphs extracted during this phase.

Our experimental results indicate that the solution is pragmatic and effective in identifying the compiler of target binaries, and that the detection method is computationally efficient.

3.2   Compiler Provenance

This section presents a multi-tiered approach to compiler fingerprinting, identification, and behavioral profiling. The methodology is broken down into three tiers, namely compiler family identification, compiler function labelling, and optimization/version detection, as depicted in Fig. 3.1. Each tier consists of one or more processes that support the compiler detection heuristics.

3.2.1   Tier 1: Compiler Family Identification

Building the compiler transformation profile (CTP) and assigning compiler tags
(CT) are the main objectives of the Tier 1 processes. A supervised compilation
process is applied to a collection of known source code and the output binaries
are analyzed to populate the CTP and CT profiles. These profiles are subsequently
processed using pattern matching techniques to identify compiler families. The
BINCOMP behavioral profiles conform with standard compilation steps of C-based
family of compilers as shown in Fig. 3.2. In this figure, the labeled states indicate
feature extraction points (source F_S, binary F_B, exported library F_E) and the blocks
represent the set of artifacts that endure specific stages of the process. The marked
artifacts and respective feature vectors are used for data matching and signature
generation.

We have extended the assembly to source code matching technique presented
in [3, 239] combining syntactic features with structural and semantics features to
build and match the CTP profiles as follows:

1. **Define Pattern**: Input source code containing code and data patterns is defined
   during this step. The supervised compilation process yields compiler-specific
   transformation profiles that enable assembly to source code matching. This
   process is repeated using various combinations of chosen source components,
   which may include crafted excerpts of code and data patterns for control flow,
   branching statements, loops structures, memory access, calling conventions,
   system calls, and composite/abstract data types.
2. **Initialize**: The original source code (SRC) is the input of this step, resulting in an
   output which is a pre-processed source file that includes the contents of header
   files imported into the source code. As a result of this process, the symbolic
   constants are replaced with their values. The values of constants and the list of
   source-level functions including their prototypes are then extracted as part of the
   source features F_S to support the signature generation process.
3. **Compile**: The compilation step takes the target platform specifications and
   the expanded source file generated in previous step as inputs, and generates
   a platform-dependent assembly file (IAS) according to compilation settings,
   such as optimization level and code generation parameters. The list of assembly
   functions is then extracted in support of the signature generation process.

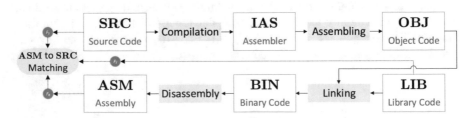

Fig. 3.2 Supervised compilation steps and produced artifacts

4. **Assemble**: The input assembly file is translated into machine object code (OBJ), which in turn gets disassembled for feature extraction. In support of signature generation, each assembly-level function is matched against the respective source-level function extracted during the first step. Subsequently, function-level transformation (mapping) profiles are created between assembly code patterns and source language statements. These profiles provide directives on syntactic styles and transformation rules of the source compiler.
5. **Link**: The output binary file (BIN) is built by linking the library object code (LIB) with the user object code (OBJ) generated in the preceding step. The produced file may include the code (statistically linked) or references (dynamically imported) of the library functions called in the source program.
6. **Disassemble**: The binary file gets disassembled into assembly (ASM) file listings. In addition to the assembly-level functions extracted from the object file (OBJ) in previous steps, the disassembly at this stage includes extra helper/utility functions inserted by the linker, which are used for signature generation. Furthermore, the disassembly is utilized to extract compiler tags.
7. **Match**: The code transformation profiles describe compiler behavior in translating code/data patterns to binary representations. These profiles are matched against target assembly functions to identify the most likely compiler based on binary features F_B.

3.2.1.1   Compiler Transformation Profile (CTP)

The CTP is a feature that captures syntactical aspects of compiler behavior. The code transformation profile for each compiler is obtained as an outcome of the supervised compilation process explained above. This feature describes how compilers reflect source-level code and data abstractions (e.g., control statements, object, queue, stack, list, array, calls, etc.) into assembly-level instructions. For example, a simple if-then-else statement can be represented as cmp|test then jcc (conditional jump) in MSVC binaries.

Figure 3.3 compares the output of three compilers given an identical input presented in Listing 3.5. The excerpt shows a C++ switch-case statement assembled and compiled with (1) MSVC, (2) GCC and (3) Clang, respectively. Despite the resemblance, it is clear that each compiler family made a specific choice on the selection and sequence of assembly mnemonics, operands, register utilization, memory access, and data transfer. Such variations (as a result of data/control flow analysis) allow to extract identifiable features and to generate signatures for each compiler family.

Switch Statement Transformations		
ASM code compiled with MSVC	**ASM code compiled with GCC**	**ASM code compiled with Clang**

```
lea eax, DWORD PTR _g$[ebp]     lea rax, [rbp-0x1]           mov eax, 0x601180
push eax                        mov rsi, rax                 mov edi, eax
mov ecx, DWORD PTR __imp_cin    mov edi, 0x601180            lea rsi, [rbp-0x5]
push ecx                        call 400670 std::char_traits call 400640 std::char_traits
call std::char_traits<char>
add esp, 8
                                                             movsx ecx, BYTEPTR [rbp-0x5]
mov dl, BYTE PTR _g$[ebp]       movzx eax, BYTEPTR [rbp-0x1] mov edx, ecx
mov BYTE PTR tv67[ebp], dl      movsx eax, al                sub edx, 0x41
cmp BYTE PTR tv67[ebp], 65      cmp eax, 0x41                mov QWORDPTR [rbp-0x10], rax
je SHORT $LN4@main              je4007b3 <main+0x2c>         mov DWORDPTR [rbp-0x14], ecx
cmp BYTE PTR tv67[ebp], 66      cmp eax, 0x42                mov DWORDPTR [rbp-0x18], edx
je SHORT $LN5@main              je 4007c4 <main+0x3d>        je 400811 <main+0x51>
jmp SHORT $LN6@main             jmp 4007d5 <main+0x4e>       jmp 4007fd <main+0x3d>
                                                             mov eax, DWORDPTR [rbp-0x14]
$LN4@main:                                                   sub eax, 0x42
push OFFSET $SG29712            mov esi, 0x4008c5            mov DWORDPTR [rbp-0x1c], eax
mov eax, DWORD PTR _imp_cout    mov edi, 0x601060            je 400833 <main+0x73>
push eax                        call 400660 std::char_traits jmp 400855 <main+0x95>
call std::char_traits<char>                                  movabs rdi, 0x601060
add esp, 8                      jmp 4007e5 <main+0x5e>       movabs rsi, 0x400904
jmp SHORT $LN2@main
                                                             call400630 std::char_traits
$LN5@main:
push OFFSET $SG29714            mov esi, 0x4008c7            mov QWORDPTR [rbp-0x28], rax
mov ecx, DWORD PTR _imp_cout    mov edi, 0x601060            jmp 400872 <main+0xb2>
push ecx                        call 400660 std::char_traits movabs rdi, 0x601060
call std::char_traits<char>                                  movabs rsi, 0x400906
add esp, 8                      jmp 4007e5 <main+0x5e>
jmp SHORT $LN2@main                                          call 400630 std::char_traits

$LN6@main:                                                   mov QWORDPTR [rbp-0x30], rax
push OFFSET $SG29716            mov esi, 0x4008c9            jmp 400872 <main+0xb2>
mov edx, DWORD PTR _imp_cout    mov edi, 0x601060            movabs rdi, 0x601060
push edx                        call 400660 std::char_traits movabs rsi, 0x400908
call std::char_traits<char>
add esp, 8                                                   call 400630 std::char_traits
$LN2@main:                      nop                          mov QWORDPTR [rbp-0x38], rax
                                                             xor eax, eax
```

Fig. 3.3 Statement transformation example in MSVC, GCC, and Clang

Listing 3.5 Simple `switch-case` statement

```
char g;
cin >> g;
switch (g) {
        case 'A':
                cout << "A";
                break;
        case 'B':
                cout << "B";
                break;
        default:
                cout << "?";
                break;
}
```

- **Binary Feature Extraction**: In order to facilitate effective CTP signature generation, a subset of assembly features should be selected which most appropriately
  captures the original code semantics. To this end, we extract binary features F_B

from the normalized versions of assembly instructions and perform statistical
frequency analysis on the compiler emitted code.

- **Instruction Normalization**: We split each assembly instruction into two parts,
  namely mnemonic and operands. The mnemonic identifier is compared against
  a platform-specific group of instructions and the identifier member is replaced
  with the respective group label. Instruction mnemonics are classified into 11
  groups according to their operation semantics. For instance, mnemonics such
  as xor, shl, ror are replaced with LGC indicating the Logical operations
  group. Similarly, the assembly operands are encoded numerically according to
  their types to distinguish between general-purpose registers reg, direct memory
  references mem, immediate values imm, control registers ctr, etc. We consider
  10 types of operands during normalization. The complete list of operand types
  and mnemonic groups used in BINCOMP is displayed in Table 3.2.
- **Opcode Frequency Analysis**: We use the normalized form of instructions for
  frequency analysis and signature generation. We evaluate function metrics such
  as the number of occurrences of each assembly instruction per group, number of
  calls to registers and memory addresses, number of utilized mnemonic groups,
  list of frequent mnemonics, number and size of identified variables/arguments
  (based on register data flow), number of basic blocks, cyclomatic complexity
  (CC), number and size of constants/strings, and the number of inbound/outbound
  call references.

Table 3.2 Mnemonic groups and operand types used in normalization

Assembly mnemonic groups	DTR	Data transfer
	DTO	Data address object
	FLG	Flag manipulation
	DTC	Data conversion
	ATH	Binary arithmetic
	LGC	Logical operation
	CTL	Control transfer
	INO	Input/output
	INT	Interrupt/system
	FLT	Floating
	MSC	Misc.
Instruction operand types	reg	General register
	mem	Direct memory reference
	bix	Indirect memory reference
	imm	Immediate value
	ifa	Immediate far address
	ina	Immediate near address
	trr	Trace register
	dbr	Debug register
	ctr	Control register
	otr	Others

3.2.1.2 Compiler Tags (CT)

Compilers may leave behind fingerprints in form of strings or constants in the produced binaries by default. As an example, binaries compiled with GCC contain a tag which survives the symbol stripping process. Likewise, MSVC inserts watermarks of compiler versions in style of xor-encoded values in the file header section. Such values can be considered indicators of compilers and/or versions. Using a parsing mechanism, we extract compiler tag values from PE, ELF, and COFF binaries.

3.2.1.3 Detection Method

Suppose program P disassembly is comprised of functions $F = \{f_1, \ldots, f_n\}$. The file-level CT features are represented as a list of strings. The function-level CTP features for each $f_i \in F$ are represented with a feature vector $\mathbf{v}_{f_i} \in \mathbf{V}$ that captures the available CTP features of f_i in form of key/value pairs, i.e., (k_j, val_j): $\mathbf{v}_{f_i} := \langle (k_1, val_1), \ldots, (k_n, val_n) \rangle$. These features capture the compiler transformation patterns based on predefined (chosen) data/code components (e.g., loops, branching, arrays, etc.). For each compiler c_i, we generate a signature Sig_{c_i} which represents the behavior profile. A combination of exact and threshold-based matching techniques is used to compare the extracted CTP and CT features from target P program against the Sig_{c_i} profiles, resulting in the identification of the most similar compiler family c_i.

3.2.2 Tier 2: Compiler Functions Labeling

The purpose of tier 2 is to identify compiler functions (CF). The approach is shown in Fig. 3.4 and it is based on pairwise comparison and intersection of program disassemblies to identify function groups. In this tier, we leverage the supervised compilation process with chosen components (as explained in Sect. 3.2.1) to compile a pair of programs $\langle P_1, P_2 \rangle$ using compiler c_i. Following the standard compilation, assembling, linking, and disassembly processes, we obtain a pair of disassembled program functions $\langle F_{P_1}, F_{P_2} \rangle$, as well as their respective symbolic ($\mathbf{V}_s$) and numerical ($\mathbf{V}_n$) feature vectors.

In the general case, we define the total set of disassembly functions of program P_i as the union of five types of assembly functions, i.e., $F_{P_i} := (F_{S_i} \cup F_{D_i} \cup F_{E_i} \cup F_{H_i} \cup F_{U_i})$, namely, the set of statically linked functions F_{S_i}, dynamically imported functions F_{D_i}, exported functions F_{E_i}, helper/utility functions F_{H_i}, and user functions F_{U_i}. The ability to determine the type of assembly functions has applications in authorship analysis, algorithm recognition, library identification, API tagging, dependency analysis, and compiler identification.

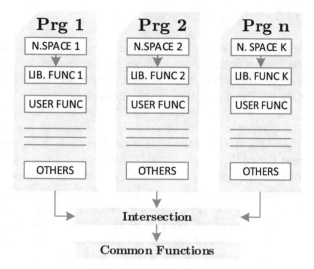

Fig. 3.4 Intersecting programs to obtain common compiler functions

Intersection

Common Functions

The helper/utility functions can be considered as a subset of the relative complement of the total set F_{P_i}, and the union of remaining functions, i.e., $F_{H_i} \subseteq F_{P_i} \backslash (F_{S_i} \cup F_{D_i} \cup F_{E_i} \cup F_{U_i})$. An effective function fingerprinting technique would be required to partition the set of F_{P_i} into five disjoint subsets, each representing a unique type of assembly functions. In practice, certain functions may serve multiple purposes resulting in non-pairwise disjoint sets of functions.

After intersecting the list of assembly functions $\langle F_{P_1}, F_{P_2} \rangle$ and computing the feature vectors, we use the numerical component of feature vectors ($\mathbf{V}_n$) to evaluate the pairwise similarity of assembly functions $Sim(f_i, f_j) \forall_i \in F_{P_1}, \forall_j \in F_{P_2}$ based on vector distance. The functions with similar attributes ($v_{n_1}, \dots, v_{n_z}$) are clustered using the k-means algorithm [135] into k clusters $C = C_1, \dots, C_k$ where ($k \leq |F_{P_1}| + |F_{P_2}|$) minimizing the intra-cluster sum of squares. The mean of the numerical feature values of each cluster is denoted by μ_i in the following equation:

$$\arg \min_C \sum_{i=1}^{k} \sum_{v_j \in C_i} \|v_j - \mu_i\|^2. \tag{3.1}$$

The initial number of clusters k can be estimated in k-means [135] or iteratively adjusted by dividing the clusters until reaching the target Gaussian distribution [154]. In our experiments, the final value of k was in range of ($(|F_{P_1}| + |F_{P_2}|)/2 \leq k < |F_{P_1}| + |F_{P_2}|$ due to the selected ratio of user (F_{U_i}) to non-user functions during the supervised compilation process.

The symbolic feature vector ($\mathbf{V}_s$) is used for cluster validation when function identifiers are available (e.g., debug binaries in supervised compilation). In such cases, the common identifiers can be used as the basis for function list intersections, i.e., we compute $list(set(\mathbf{V}_{P_1}.ids()) \cap set(\mathbf{V}_{P_2}.ids()))$, where the $list()$ function returns the list of disassembled functions and the $ids()$ method returns the name identifier of each function.

3.2.2.1 Compiler Functions (CF)

We extract features of compiler functions from program disassemblies, by following the intersection process explained in previous section. Two feature vectors V_s and V_n are built for each function to capture the symbolic and numerical aspects of the code. Given a target program P_t (unknown compiler), we build the disassembly $F_{P_t} = \{f_1, \ldots, f_m\}$, and leverage the CF function identification technique to determine the types of assembly functions $f_i \in F_{P_t}$ (from the set of $F_{P_t} := (F_{S_t} \cup F_{D_t} \cup F_{E_t} \cup F_{H_t} \cup F_{U_t}))$ based on the similarity calculations on $V_s = \{V_{s_1}, V_{s_2}, \ldots, V_{s_z}\}$ and $V_n = \{V_{n_1}, V_{n_2}, \ldots, V_{n_z}\}$. The vectors are compared against reference clusters of compiler profiles and the most similar functions are grouped together. Once the clusters are formed, the labels of the most similar compiler/linker function will be assigned to each cluster centroid. We use the code matching and function fingerprinting techniques presented in [226, 239] to encode structural, syntactic, and semantic features of assembly functions to facilitate binary comparison.

Table 3.3 provides an example of the computed features for two programs $prog1, prog2$ with distinct main functions, complied with GCC (O2) under Windows. The table lists the compiler functions as well as a subset of the feature vectors. The features were explained previously and summarized in Table 3.2. The three additional features, namely CC, BB, KX represent the cyclomatic complexity, number of basic blocks, and number of calls within functions, respectively. As can be seen, functions with similar numerical features are predominantly grouped together. The symbolic features show the program and function identifiers. As highlighted, certain functions with similar symbolic names pertaining to compiler/helper code exhibit small discrepancies in numerical values due to changes in structural information (e.g., basic blocks, calls). This observation indicates the importance of inexact function signatures (based on similarity calculation of numerical vectors) for CF detection and function labelling.

In order to validate our selection of features for compiler fingerprinting, we apply a hierarchical clustering technique based on principal component analysis (PCA) to rank the features of sample binaries presented in Table 3.3. Moreover, Fig. 3.5 shows the hierarchical clustering data applied to function feature vectors. This heatmap is created based on two principal components indicating the most important features for clustering numerical feature vectors. In addition, the features are sorted based on the order of importance. The first six features are the most impactful, namely REG, MEM, BB, CTL, CC, and IMM. The obtained results can be interpreted as follows. The CF compiler profile can be attributed based on the types of registers selected by the compiler and the method of memory access, followed by the structural complexity (basic blocks) which are identifiable to the compiler family's behavior.

3.2.2.2 Detection Method

In this section, we present a function fingerprinting approach for signature generation and detection from assembly functions. We define a feature extraction function

Table 3.3 Clustering based on numerical and symbolic features

Symbolic		Numerical																				
P_ID	FUNC_ID	DTR	DTO	FLG	DTC	ATH	LGC	CT_	INO	INT	FLT	MSC	CC	BB	KX	REG	MEM	BIX	BID	IMM	IFA	INA
prog1	_mainCRTStartup	1	0	0	0	1	0	1	0	0	0	0	1	1	2	1	1	1	0	2	0	1
prog1	_WinMainCRTStartup	1	0	0	0	1	0	1	0	0	0	0	1	1	2	1	1	1	0	2	0	1
prog2	_mainCRTStartup	1	0	0	0	1	0	1	0	0	0	0	1	1	2	1	1	1	0	2	0	1
prog2	_WinMainCRTStartup	1	0	0	0	1	0	1	0	0	0	0	1	1	2	1	1	1	0	2	0	1
prog1	__main	1	0	1	0	0	0	3	0	0	0	0	1	4	0	3	2	0	0	1	0	2
prog2	__main	1	0	1	0	0	0	3	0	0	0	0	1	4	0	3	2	0	0	1	0	2
prog1	__mingw_globfree	1	0	0	0	0	0	4	0	0	0	0	1	4	0	1	0	1	1	1	0	2
prog2	__mingw_globfree	1	0	0	0	0	0	4	0	0	0	0	1	4	0	1	0	1	1	1	0	2
prog1	_register_frame_ctor	3	0	0	0	1	0	2	0	0	0	0	1	1	2	4	0	1	0	2	0	2
prog2	_register_frame_ctor	3	0	0	0	1	0	2	0	0	0	0	1	1	2	4	0	1	0	2	0	2
prog1	__do_global_dtors	2	1	1	0	2	0	4	0	0	0	0	3	5	0	15	3	1	2	2	0	2
prog2	__do_global_dtors	2	1	1	0	2	0	4	0	0	0	0	3	5	0	15	3	1	2	2	0	2
prog1	_glob_store_entry.part.2	3	1	1	0	2	1	3	0	0	0	0	1	3	1	40	1	3	10	5	0	2
prog2	_glob_store_entry.part.2	3	1	1	0	2	1	3	0	0	0	0	1	3	1	40	1	3	10	5	0	2
prog1	__chkstk_ms	2	1	0	0	1	1	4	0	0	0	0	3	3	0	11	0	2	1	6	0	2
prog2	__chkstk_ms	2	1	0	0	1	1	4	0	0	0	0	3	3	0	11	0	2	1	6	0	2
prog1	_glob_store_entry	1	0	1	0	0	0	4	0	0	0	0	2	5	0	5	0	0	0	1	0	3
prog2	_glob_store_entry	1	0	1	0	0	0	4	0	0	0	0	2	5	0	5	0	0	0	1	0	3
prog2	_main	3	0	0	0	1	1	2	0	0	0	0	1	1	3	5	0	1	0	3	0	3
prog1	_telldir	1	1	0	0	2	0	4	0	0	0	0	2	4	1	7	0	1	2	4	0	3
prog2	_telldir	1	1	0	0	2	0	4	0	0	0	0	2	4	1	7	0	1	2	4	0	3
prog1	__report_error	2	1	0	0	1	0	1	0	0	0	0	1	1	3	11	1	2	8	4	0	3
prog2	__report_error	2	1	0	0	1	0	1	0	0	0	0	1	1	3	11	1	2	8	4	0	3
prog1	__dyn_tls_dtor@12	1	0	1	0	2	0	4	0	0	0	0	2	4	1	14	0	1	5	8	0	3

(continued)

Table 3.3 (continued)

	Symbolic	Numerical																				
P_ID	FUNC_ID	DTR	DTO	FLG	DTC	ATH	LGC	CTL	INO	INT	FLT	MSC	CC	BB	KX	REG	MEM	BIX	BID	IMM	IFA	INA
prog2	__dyn_tls_dtor@12	1	0	1	0	2	0	4	0	0	0	0	2	4	1	14	0	1	5	8	0	3
prog1	_glob_registry.part.1	3	1	1	0	2	1	5	0	0	0	0	3	4	2	27	1	3	6	5	0	4
prog2	_glob_registry.part.1	3	1	1	0	2	1	5	0	0	0	0	3	4	2	27	1	3	6	5	0	4
prog1	_main	3	1	0	0	2	1	2	0	0	0	0	1	1	4	17	0	3	9	6	0	4
prog2	__gcc_deregister_frame	3	0	1	0	1	0	3	0	0	0	0	3	5	2	15	0	3	1	7	0	4
prog1	__gcc_deregister_frame	3	0	1	0	1	0	3	0	0	0	0	3	5	4	15	0	3	1	7	0	4
prog1	_glob_store_collated_entries	3	0	1	0	2	0	3	0	0	0	0	5	5	4	22	0	2	2	2	0	6
prog2	_glob_store_collated_entries	3	0	1	0	2	0	3	0	0	0	0	5	5	4	22	0	2	2	2	0	6
prog1	_closedir	3	0	1	0	2	0	5	0	0	0	0	3	5	3	19	0	3	2	4	0	6
prog2	_closedir	3	0	1	0	2	0	5	0	0	0	0	3	5	3	19	1	3	2	4	0	6
prog1	_glob_initialise	3	1	1	0	2	1	6	0	0	0	0	5	8	1	34	1	2	6	7	0	6
prog2	_glob_initialise	3	1	1	0	2	1	6	0	0	0	0	5	8	1	34	1	2	6	7	0	6
prog2	__w64_mingwthr_add_key_dtor	3	1	1	0	1	1	5	0	0	0	0	2	5	3	37	3	4	7	8	0	6
prog1	__w64_mingwthr_add_key_dtor	3	1	1	0	1	1	5	0	0	0	0	2	5	5	37	3	4	7	8	0	6
prog1	_do_global_ctors	3	1	1	0	2	1	6	0	0	0	0	5	8	1	18	3	1	2	5	0	7
prog2	_do_global_ctors	3	1	1	0	2	1	6	0	0	0	0	5	8	1	18	3	1	2	5	0	7
prog2	__mingwthr_run_key_dtors.part.0	3	1	1	0	1	0	4	0	0	0	0	5	6	4	30	1	5	3	6	0	8
prog1	__mingwthr_run_key_dtors.part.0	3	1	1	0	1	0	4	0	0	0	0	5	6	8	30	1	5	3	6	0	8
prog1	_dyn_tls_init@12	3	0	1	0	2	2	7	0	0	0	0	6	12	1	32	3	1	5	16	0	8
prog2	_dyn_tls_init@12	3	0	1	0	2	2	7	0	0	0	0	6	12	1	32	3	1	5	16	0	8
prog2	__gcc_register_frame	3	0	1	0	1	0	3	0	0	0	0	6	10	4	29	1	6	3	14	0	9
prog1	__gcc_register_frame	3	0	1	0	1	0	3	0	0	0	0	6	10	8	29	1	6	3	14	0	9
prog2	_write_memory.part.0	3	1	1	0	1	0	5	0	0	0	0	4	9	6	61	0	6	29	12	0	11
prog1	_write_memory.part.0	3	1	1	0	1	0	5	0	0	0	0	4	9	9	61	0	6	29	12	0	11
prog2	__w64_mingwthr_remove_key_dtor	3	0	1	0	1	1	6	0	0	0	0	5	13	4	39	3	6	7	7	0	12
prog1	__w64_mingwthr_remove_key_dtor	3	0	1	0	1	1	6	0	0	0	0	5	13	7	39	3	6	7	7	0	12

prog	function																		
prog1	__mingw_glob	3	1	1	2	1	6	0	0	0	7	10	6	60	0	6	13	13	0	13
prog2	__mingw_glob	3	1	1	2	1	6	0	0	0	7	10	6	60	0	6	13	13	0	13
prog2	__mingw_TLScallback	3	1	0	1	0	7	0	0	0	7	13	4	23	6	2	2	12	0	15
prog1	__mingw_TLScallback	3	1	0	1	0	7	0	0	0	7	13	6	23	6	2	2	12	0	15
prog1	__cpu_features_init	3	0	3	0	3	7	0	0	0	15	25	0	30	10	0	0	25	0	15
prog2	__cpu_features_init	3	0	3	0	3	7	0	0	0	15	25	0	30	10	0	0	25	0	15
prog1	_rewinddir	3	1	0	2	4	6	0	0	0	7	15	4	70	0	6	30	23	0	16
prog2	_rewinddir	3	1	0	2	4	6	0	0	0	7	15	4	70	0	6	30	23	0	16
prog1	_seekdir	3	1	0	2	4	8	0	0	0	12	17	4	80	0	6	32	24	0	17
prog2	_seekdir	3	1	0	2	4	8	0	0	0	12	17	4	80	0	6	32	24	0	17
prog2	_readdir	3	1	0	2	4	7	0	0	0	11	20	7	91	0	8	34	25	0	22
prog1	_readdir	3	1	0	2	4	7	0	0	0	11	20	8	91	0	8	34	25	0	22
prog1	__pei386_runtime_relocator	3	1	1	2	1	9	0	0	0	15	27	6	106	5	6	23	32	0	25
prog2	__pei386_runtime_relocator	3	1	1	2	1	9	0	0	0	15	27	6	106	5	6	23	32	0	25
prog1	__gnu_exception_handler@4	3	1	1	2	2	8	0	0	0	18	25	7	42	0	11	10	35	0	28
prog2	__gnu_exception_handler@4	3	1	1	2	2	8	0	0	0	18	25	7	42	0	11	10	35	0	28
prog1	_opendir	3	1	1	3	5	6	0	0	0	13	21	11	135	0	19	39	36	0	28
prog2	_opendir	3	1	1	3	5	6	0	0	0	13	21	11	135	0	19	39	36	0	28
prog1	_glob_strcmp	4	1	2	2	4	6	0	0	0	32	53	5	154	0	9	30	34	0	50
prog2	_glob_strcmp	4	1	2	2	4	6	0	0	0	32	53	5	154	0	9	30	34	0	50
prog1	_glob_in_set	3	1	2	2	2	7	0	0	0	42	60	0	147	0	12	13	44	0	51
prog2	_glob_in_set	3	1	2	2	2	7	0	0	0	42	60	0	147	0	12	13	44	0	51
prog2	__mingw_CRTStartup	3	1	2	3	6	7	0	0	0	42	63	20	216	15	22	69	68	0	71
prog1	__mingw_CRTStartup	3	1	2	3	6	7	0	0	0	42	63	24	216	15	22	69	68	0	71
prog1	_dirname	3	1	1	2	3	10	0	0	0	44	68	17	215	5	31	90	57	0	73
prog2	_dirname	3	1	1	2	3	10	0	0	0	44	68	17	215	5	31	90	57	0	73
prog1	_glob_match	6	1	2	3	8	8	0	0	0	66	99	32	389	0	43	140	75	0	113
prog2	_glob_match	6	1	2	3	8	8	0	0	0	66	99	32	389	0	43	140	75	0	113

Light gray: Main functions in different programs. *Dark gray:* The same compiler functions in distinct programs may have slightly different numerical feature vectors due to changes in CFG and CG structures Fig3-ctp2

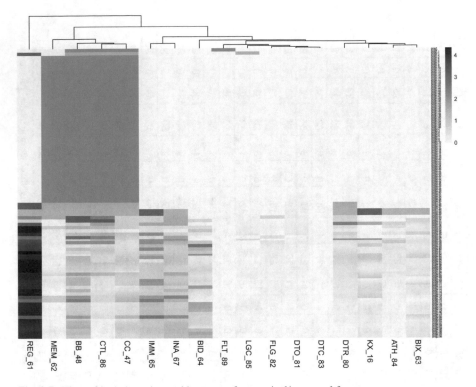

Fig. 3.5 Hierarchical clustering and heatmap of syntactical/structural features

as $X : F \rightarrow V$, where F is the set of helper/utility functions and V is the set of all possible features, i.e., $v_i = X(f_i)$. The input to this function is a program P comprised of a set of assembly functions $F = \{f_1, \ldots, f_m\}$, and the output is a set of features $v_i \in V$. The output feature vectors can be partitioned into two subsets of V_s and V_n.

A fingerprint computation function defined as $G : V \rightarrow T$ takes the set of features to generate the fingerprints. The encoded characteristics of function $f_i \in F$ are represented by each fingerprint $t_i \in T$:

$$t_i = G(v_i) = G(X(f_i)). \tag{3.2}$$

This function behaves similar to a hash function, compressing the variable-length input assembly vector into a fixed length signature digest. However, the output is based on a normalized version of assembly opcodes and types of operands. We interpret this function as a semantic hash that creates a bit vector of length n from the subset of features V from f_i. The hashing technique and sensitivity can be defined based on the feature space size and number of input bits.

$$t_i \in domain(V) \rightarrow \{0, 1\}^m. \tag{3.3}$$

Function fingerprinting depends on pairwise similarity comparisons for assembly functions. It also considers incremental clustering in which the similarity of a target function is calculated against a target group. Function M assigns a similarity score to a pair of candidate vectors, either at the level of fingerprints, i.e., $M : T \times T \rightarrow R^+$, or at the level of functions $M : V \times V \rightarrow R^+$.

Various similarity metrics can be considered for quantifying and measuring the distance between vectors (e.g., Cosine: $\cos \alpha = (\mathbf{v}_{f_i} \cdot \mathbf{v}_{f_j})/(\|v_{f_i}\| \cdot \|v_{f_j}\|)$, or Euclidean: $d_E = \sqrt{\sum(\mathbf{v}_{f_i} - \mathbf{v}_{f_j})^2}$). The Jaccard similarity of a candidate fingerprint pair (t_i, t_j) for functions (f_i, f_j) can be computed as follows [146]:

$$dist_J(t_i, t_j) = \frac{B(t_i \wedge t_j)}{B(t_i \vee t_j)}, \qquad (3.4)$$

where function B returns the number of set bits in the fingerprint vector.

The functionality of this tier can be abstracted using a labeling function C that takes the set of function fingerprints, for target T_t, and the reference T_r fingerprints and returns a label $l_i \in L$ based on the corresponding compiler, i.e., $C : T_t \times T_r \times N \rightarrow L$. In this relation, N is a mapping matrix that was learned during the supervised compilation process. This matrix links compilers to specific helper/utility function profiles based on similarity analysis. The labels obtained from this tier identify compiler-specific functions in target disassemblies.

3.2.3   Tier 3: Version and Optimization Recognition

The objective of tier 3 is to detect more refined compiler properties, such as optimization level and version. Similar to previous tiers, we leverage the supervised compilation process to generate features. However, this tier deals with graph-based structural and semantic features defined as annotated control flow graph (ACFG) and compiler constructor and terminator (CCT) profiles. Empirically, these two types of features are the most representative of optimization heuristics and differences in compiler versions. We use neighborhood [146] and fuzzy hashing, as well as graph encoding to adjust the granularity levels of binary components in support of fingerprint generation.

3.2.3.1   Annotated Control Flow Graph (ACFG)

We introduce a new graph-based representation, termed annotated control flow graph (ACFG), which represents a control flow graph extension. The purpose of this graph is to facilitate detection of compiler versions and optimization levels based on function compositions. We transform each disassembled compiler/linker function to graphs and build the ACFG profiles based on basic block opcodes types. Basic blocks

Table 3.4 Instruction patterns for annotation

Feature group	Description	Example
DTR & STK	Data Transfer and Stack	`push, mov, xchg`
ATH & LGC	Arithmetic and Logical	`add, xor`
CAL & TST	Call and Test	`call, cmp`
REG & MEM	Register and Memory	`esi, [esi+4]`
REG & CONST	Register and Constant	`esi, 30`
MEM & CONST	Memory and Constant	`[esi+8], 20`

are presented as nodes and edges show the execution path, i.e., if basic block B_j can directly follow B_i in execution, then there is edge from B_i to B_j.

The process of ACFG generation involves the following steps. For each function, starting with the CFG, we compute the operation code frequencies per assembly instruction groups. As shown in Table 3.2, each instruction can be grouped based on mnemonic semantics and operand types. We reduce the features according to Table 3.4 and categorize x86 instructions into six groups for graph encoding. We then complement the ACFG with encoded subgraph values and include it in the structural profiles of compilers. It should be noted that the conversion/annotation patterns are flexible and can be adjusted based on the use case and requirements of the target pattern.

Definition 3.1

1. An annotated control flow graph $ACFG$ is defined as an attributed graph (V, E, ζ, γ) where V denotes a set of vertices representing function basic blocks, $E \subseteq (V \times V)$ is a set of edges representing the control flow instruction, γ is an instruction clustering function, and ζ is a node coloring function based on operand types. Functions γ and ζ are used during the CFG normalization control flow graphs and subgraphs encoding.

3.2.3.2 ACFG Construction

In order to build the ACFG graph, we first normalize the input CFG according to the process presented in Algorithm 1. Each assembly instruction can be categorized according to the groups of mnemonic, types of operands, and the types of function calls, among others. The helper function `GetInstructionGroup()` in the normalization algorithm returns the groups of instructions for individual opcodes. The assembly instructions may have multiple operands and each operand may have a different type (e.g., immediate value, register, memory reference, etc.). The `NormalizeOperandType()` function returns the associated type of operands. Similarly, the destination of function calls could also be categorized according to their types. Call destinations can be local or external to the disassembly. System and API calls are grouped into multiple classes based on their side effects on the target

Algorithm 1: CFG normalization for ACFG generation

Input: $G = (BB, E)$: CFG of an assembly function.

Output: $G' = (BB', E')$: Norm-CFG, Lists A_CNT, G_CNT, C_CNT, and counts T, B.

1 **Initialization;**

2 $NCFG \leftarrow \text{init(graph)}$;

3 $A\_CNT \leftarrow \text{init(key, value)}$;   `// Instruction count`

4 $G\_CNT \leftarrow \text{init(key, value)}$;   `// Group count`

5 $C\_CNT \leftarrow \text{init(key, value)}$;   `// Call count`

6 $T \leftarrow 0$;   `// Number of instructions`

7 $B \leftarrow 0$;   `// Number of basic blocks`

8 **begin**

9   Perform flow-based breadth-first traversal (BFT) of the CFG basic blocks;

10   **foreach** *unvisited basic block* $bb \subseteq BB$ **do**

11   Create a node and add the corresponding basic block bb' to $Norm - CFG$;

12          $B \leftarrow B + 1$;

13   **foreach** *instruction* $INST \subseteq bb$ **do**

14              $T \leftarrow T + 1$;

15   Add a new instruction placeholder P to bb';

16   **foreach** *mnemonic* $M \in INST$ **do**

17   //Call the function to get the group label of M;

18                  $G_M \leftarrow \texttt{GetInstructionGroup}(M)$;

19   Place G_M in P as the group of mnemonic;

20   **if** $M \notin A\_CNT$ *list* **then**

21   Add M to the A_CNT list as key;

22                      $A\_CNT[M] \leftarrow 1$;

23   **else**

24                      $A\_CNT[M] \leftarrow A\_CNT[M] + 1$;

25   **if** $G \notin G\_CNT$ *list* **then**

26   Add G to the G_CNT list as key;

27                      $G\_CNT[G] \leftarrow 1$;

28   **else**

29                      $G\_CNT[G] \leftarrow G\_CNT[G] + 1$;

30   **foreach** *operand* $O \in INST$ **do**

31   **if** *mnemonic* $(M \in INST) \neq call$ **then**

32   //Call the function to get the type of O;

33                      $TP \leftarrow \texttt{NormalizeOperandType}(O)$;

34   Place TP in P as the operand of G;

35   **else**

36   //Call the function to get the category label;

37                      $FC \leftarrow \texttt{GetFunctionCategory}(O)$;

38   Place FC in P as the operand of G;

39   **if** $FC \notin C\_CNT$ *list* **then**

40   Add FC to the C_CNT list as key;

41   //Set the count value;

42                          $C\_CNT[FC] \leftarrow 1$;

43   **else**

44   //Increment the count value;

45                          $C\_CNT[FC] \leftarrow C\_CNT[FC] + 1$;

46   Flag the basic block bb as visited;

47   **foreach** *in/out edge* $(e_i^{bb}, e_o^{bb}) \subset E$ *in* CFG **do**

48   Create the corresponding in/out edge $(e_i^{bb'}, e_o^{bb'})$ to bb' in $NormCFG$;

49   Continue traversal to the next basic block bb;

50   **return** $Norm - CFG, A\_CNT, G\_CNT, C\_CNT, T, B$;

systems. The GetFunctionCategory() function returns the general context of functions and includes categories such as file, network, registry, crypto, service, and memory. Each category contains OS-specific API functions.

The next step involves encodings of subgraph components into canonical form to facilitate subgraph indexing and matching. Canonical encoding is a compact representation of a graph structure, in which the graph is split into smaller subgraphs (with K nodes) and each subgraph is associated with a canonical value. The graph adjacency matrix is required for the computation of K-graph values. Algorithm 2 presents the canonical graph encoding (CGE) generation process. The inputs to this algorithm are the normalized CFG of a function along with the parameter K. The objective of CGE is to compute the smallest hex value that can represent the adjacency matrix of the input CFG.

Algorithm 2: Canonical graph encoding for subgraph matching

Input: $G = (BB, E)$: CFG of an assembly function, K : Size of subtrees.
Output: SG : Encoded subgraph values list, A : Adjacency matrix.

1 **Initialization;**
2 SG := Empty(key, value) //Subgraph index and code;
3 **begin**
4 | Perform flow-based depth-first traversal of the CFG blocks;
5 | **foreach** *pair of basic blocks* $(bb_i, bb_j) \subset BB$ **do**
6 | | **if** $\{bb_i \mapsto bb_j\} \in E$ **then**
7 | | | $A[i, j] \leftarrow 1$;
8 | | **else**
9 | | | $A[i, j] \leftarrow 0$;
10 | $ST \leftarrow$ GenerateSpanningTree (CFG);
11 | $SubG \leftarrow$ GenerateSubgraphs (ST, K);
12 | **foreach** *subgraph* $g_n \in SubG$ **do**
13 | | rows $\leftarrow \emptyset$;
14 | | $id \leftarrow$ IndexOf (n);
15 | | **for** $i \leftarrow 1$ **to** K **do**
16 | | | rows $\leftarrow$ GetRow (A, i);
17 | | rows $\leftarrow$ ReverseBits $(rows)$;
18 | | code $\leftarrow$ ConvertToHex $(rows)$;
19 | | Add id to SG as key.;
20 | | $SG[id] \leftarrow$ code;
21 | **return** SG, A;

The control flow semantics and encoded instructions are captured by ACFG, which carries the required information for precise compiler function identification. Similar compiler functions are translated into equivalent ACFG profiles. In contrast, a CFG only accounts for the structure of functions (unrelated functions may have a similar structure), which can result in high false positive rates if it is used as the only detection criteria for function fingerprinting.

Figure 3.6 shows an example of the __do_global_ctors() GCC compiler function in CFG and normalized ACFG representations. Each basic block is

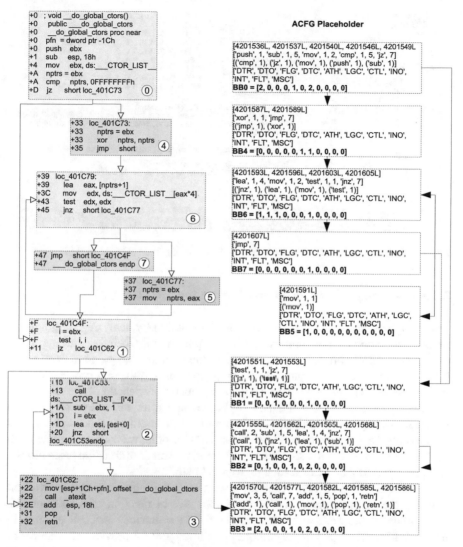

Fig. 3.6 ACFG construction of `__do_global_ctors()` compiler function

transformed and normalized based on a set of features describing the type, category, and frequency of instructions (mnemonics and operands). The raw signature (prior to fuzzy hashing) of function (fingerprint) is illustrated in Fig. 3.7. The signature of each basic block overlaid on the adjacency matrix and combined with the sequential patterns of the minimum spanning tree forms the encoded canonical values. We define various conversion/annotation patterns based on the logical combination of instruction categories, canonical values, and the symbolic feature vectors to generate an identifiable signature for each compiler function.

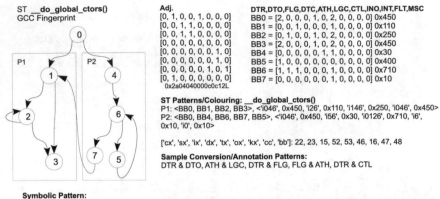

Fig. 3.7 Fingerprint of `__do_global_ctors()` compiler function based on ACFG

3.2.3.3 Compiler Constructor and Terminator (CCT)

The compiler-specific call sequences can be identified by analyzing program call graphs and control flow graphs. Each compiler family behaves differently in setting up the program startup code, initialization routines, and program termination (OS transition) code. The program initialization and termination processes entail multiple compiler functions that manage the preparation/cleanup of the call stacks, required libraries, and OS interactions before and after the execution of main function. Multiple function calls can be observed during these processes. As part of the compiler constructor and terminator (CCT) profile, we capture features such as the sequence of initialization/termination code, number of function basic blocks, and properties of caller/callee functions on the path.

In order to generate CCT signatures, we traverse the program call graph until reaching the main function. We store the sequence of function calls and function fingerprints of the pre/post main (initialization, termination) and call patterns to imported libraries as part of the compiler profile. Figure 3.8 provides an example of a constructor and terminator graph for the GCC compiler.

3.2.3.4 Detection Method

The subgraph matching technique is helpful in matching CCT profiles as it allows us to compare the initialization and termination flows with the reference patterns of compiler behavior. A common method for graph comparison is based on canonical encoding of graph structures. The resolution can be defined at basic block, single function, or multiple function levels. For the purpose of this tier, we combine subgraph encoding with neighborhood hashing techniques to reach the required granularity levels.

Fig. 3.8 Sample of GCC compiler constructor and terminator

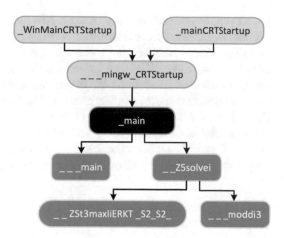

A neighborhood hash graph kernel (NHGK) is applied on the subsets of the call graph to generate fingerprints of adjacent nodes [146]. In this scheme, a bit vector of length n is created based on an input set of annotated graphs AG, using the function G.

$$G : AG \rightarrow \{0, 1\}^n. \tag{3.5}$$

The neighborhood hash value h for a target function f_t and the corresponding set of neighbor functions N_{f_t} can be obtained as follows [160]:

$$h(f_t) = shr_1(G(f_t)) \oplus (\oplus_{f_k \in N_{f_t}} G(f_k)), \tag{3.6}$$

where shr_1 indicates a single-bit shift to the right and $\oplus$ denotes the XOR function.

3.3 ECP Approach

In this section, we provide an overview of the approach proposed in [252] that will be referred to as ECP in this chapter. We reimplement the proposed system and present our obtained evaluation results, discuss the details of our findings, and highlight the limitations of ECP.

3.3.1 ECP Overview

ECP models compiler identification as a structured classification problem and labels each byte of the binaries with the information on whether it is compiled with one or two compilers (statically linked code). The authors use wildcards idiom features, which are defined as short sequences of instructions that neglect details such as literal arguments and memory offsets. After extracting the features from a large number of binaries, redundant features can be found, which are related to the user functions or the architecture. Therefore, the authors consider top-ranked features based on the results of mutual information computation between the features and compiler classes. They train the linear-chain model's parameters to assign high probabilities to correct compiler classes. The proposed technique is performed on three sets of binaries containing code from three compilers: GNU C Compiler (GCC), Intel C Compiler (ICC), and Visual Studio (VS). The dataset is collected for GCC and VS on Linux and Windows workstations, respectively. In addition, they have compiled various open-source software packages with the ICC compiler.

3.3.2   Dataset Generation

Most of the aforementioned binaries are not publicly available. Therefore, we have collected different source files from different years of the Google Code Jam [18] competition (referred to as the G dataset) (2008–2014). We have also gathered several source code samples from our university (referred to as the U dataset). Our experimental corpus comprises three sets of binaries: GNU C Compiler (GCC), Intel C Compiler (ICC), and Visual Studio compiler (VS). We disassemble each program binary using IDA PRO [45] disassembler. Furthermore, we test the ECP approach with an additional compiler, Clang (Xcode). We build our dataset after considering all possible combinations of compilers, and optimization levels on various combinations of the binaries.

3.3.3   ECP Evaluation Results

In what follows, we discuss our results based on a specific process of validation. First, we split the training data into ten sets, reserving one set as a testing set. We then train a classifier, on the remaining sets, and evaluate its accuracy on the testing set. In addition, we perform various experiments: (1) changing the number of files; (2) modifying the threshold value of the top-ranked features; and (3) mixing various percentages of binaries taken from our dataset in order to observe the effect of diverse binaries. Finally, we measure the time by showing the relationship between the number of features and the total elapsed time.

Accuracy: The ECP approach can attain relatively high accuracy, as shown in Fig. 3.9, where the accuracy for the G dataset is between 0.89 and 0.98. This is higher than the accuracy obtained using the U dataset (min = 0.82, max = 0.95). By analyzing the source code, we find out that the user contribution in the U dataset is greater than that of the G dataset. The U dataset is also more complex than the G dataset, as it consists of more advanced code structures, classes, methods, etc.

Fig. 3.9 Accuracy results

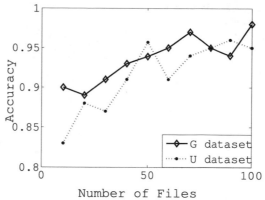

Fig. 3.10 Impact of the
threshold value

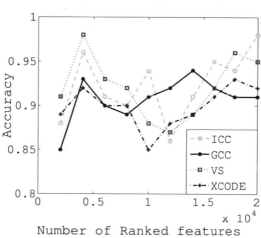

Impact of Threshold Value: In addition, we studied how changing the threshold
value for the number of top-ranked features affects accuracy. We find out that the
accuracy of the ECP method may depend on the choice of the threshold value,
as shown in Fig. 3.10. For instance, the best threshold values for GCC and Xcode
compilers are 16,000 and 18,000, respectively. In practice, finding the best threshold
for a given compiler and dataset combination may be a task that is both time-
consuming and error prone.

Impact of Dataset: Finally, we perform an experiment to study the effects of
dataset diversity on accuracy, as illustrated in Fig. 3.11. We consider different
percentages of mixed datasets (e.g., 100% *G* dataset and 20% *G*–80% *U* datasets).
As shown, the accuracy decreases when the diversity of the dataset increases,
especially when the percentage of university projects increases, since the user
contribution in the *U* dataset is higher than that of the *G* dataset.

Fig. 3.11 Diversity in
datasets

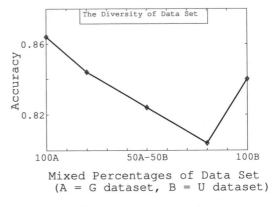

Fig. 3.12 Time efficiency

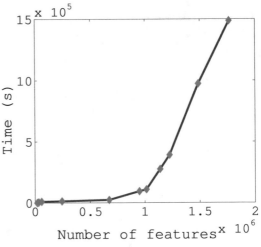

Efficiency: We measure the time efficiency of the ECP approach by calculating the
total required time for feature extraction and feature ranking. Figure 3.12 shows the
total time versus the number of features for different experiments.

3.3.4 Discussion

The ECP approach represents a pioneering effort on compiler identification and
may attain relatively high accuracy. This approach can also identify the compilers
of binaries containing a mixture of code from multiple compilers, such as statically
linked library code. However, a few limitations can be observed. First, as the number
of features increases, the running time may increase even more rapidly. Second, the
features of specific compilers may only become apparent after examining a large
number of binaries. Third, the accuracy may depend on both the dataset and the
choice of threshold.

3.4 BINCOMP Evaluation

In this section, first we introduce our dataset and then we provide the evaluation results of BINCOMP.

3.4.1 Dataset Preparation

Gathering a data corpus for the evaluation of compiler provenance attribution is challenging. For example, despite the fact that collecting code from open-source projects may be attractive, the source files usually have numerous dependencies which complicates the compilation process. Nonetheless, we choose four free open-source projects to test BINCOMP. In addition, we have gathered programs written for the Google Code Jam [18] competition as well as university projects from a programming course at our university. All of our datasets are publicly accessible.[1]

We generate the binaries to build our dataset by compiling the source code with possible combinations of compiler versions and optimization levels (O0 and O2), as shown in Table 3.5. Our dataset consists of 1177 files, 232 of which belong to the Google Code Jam dataset, 933 of which belong to the students code projects, and 12 of which belong to the open-source projects.

3.4.2 Evaluation Results

We evaluate the proposed compiler provenance approach using the aforementioned datasets (Sect. 3.4.1). We split the training data into ten sets, reserving one set as a testing set, and using nine sets as training sets to evaluate our approach; we repeat this process numerous times. Since the application domain is characterized

Table 3.5 Different compilers and compilation settings used to build the dataset

Compiler	Version	Optimization
GCC	3.4	O0
	4.4	O2
ICC	10	O0
	11	O2
VS	2010	O0
	2012	O2
XCODE	5.1	O0
	6.1	O2

---

[1]https://github.com/BinSigma/BinComp/tree/master/Dataset.

Table 3.6 F-measure results

Feature	$F_{0.5}$ (dataset = 500 files)	$F_{0.5}$ (dataset = 1000 files)
Idioms	0.789	0.812
Compiler transformation profile (CTP)	0.694	0.708
Compiler constructor and terminator (CCT)	0.807	0.877
Compiler tags (CT)	0.689	0.700
Annotated control flow graph (ACFG)	0.634	0.671

by a heightened sensitivity to false positives than false negatives, the F-measure is employed to evaluate the proposed approach as follows:

$$F_{0.5} = 1.25 \cdot \frac{PR}{0.25P + R} \qquad (3.7)$$

$$P = \frac{TP}{TP + FP} \qquad (3.8)$$

$$R = \frac{TP}{TP + FN}. \qquad (3.9)$$

The obtained results of $F_{0.5}$ measure are summarized in Table 3.6.

We also test BINCOMP against different compilers as illustrated in Fig. 3.13. As depicted in Fig. 3.13a, BINCOMP can detect the VS compiler with an average accuracy of 0.97, while ECP average accuracy is 0.93. The main explanation for this difference lies in the type of features used in the technique; BINCOMP uses different kinds of features (syntactical, structural, and semantic), whereas ECP uses only syntactical features.

In addition, we record the overall run time and compare BINCOMP and ECP approaches in terms of computation time, as shown in Fig. 3.14.

Moreover, we test BINCOMP using different variations of compiler versions and optimization levels, as shown in Tables 3.7 and 3.8. Table 3.7 indicates that identifying the version of compiler is significantly more difficult than recognizing the compiler and optimization levels. For instance, the accuracy to identify the version of Xcode compiler is below 0.80. In addition, we observe that the features of VS and Xcode compilers are slightly different when we change either the versions or the optimization levels, which makes the detection process more challenging. However, the GCC and ICC compilers produce more diverse code among compiler versions compared to the VS and Xcode compilers.

We find that up to 75% of the functions in our dataset are identical when generated by Visual Studio 2010 or 2012 with the same optimization level. In other

Fig. 3.13 The accuracy
against different compilers.
(**a**) MSVC. (**b**) ICC. (**c**) GCC.
(**d**) CLang

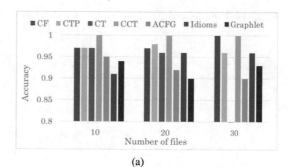

(a)

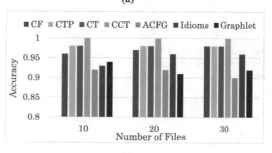

(b)

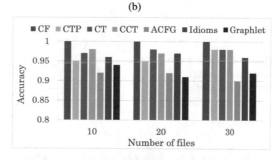

(c)

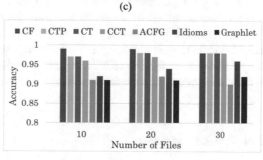

(d)

Fig. 3.14 Time efficiency

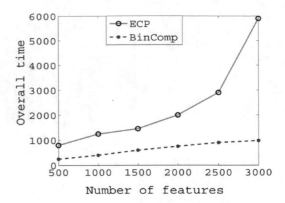

Table 3.7 Accuracy results
for variations of compiler
versions

Compiler	Version	Accuracy
GCC	3.4.x	86%
	4.4.x	89%
ICC	10.x	83%
	11.x	90%
VS	2010	70%
	2012	71%
Xcode	5.x	78%
	6.1	74%

Table 3.8 Accuracy for
variations of compiler
optimization levels

Compiler	Optimization level	Average accuracy
GCC	O0, O2	91%
ICC	O0, O2	89%
VS	O0, O2	95%

words, the code generator in Visual Studio has remained relatively stable between
these versions, which offers an explanation for the low accuracy for VS version
detection. On the other hand, we found that up to 85% of the functions of Xcode
are identical between two versions. However, we have observed changes in our
proposed features for the GCC and ICC compilers, which allow us to detect the
version and optimization level by measuring the differences in the features.

3.4.3 Comparison

We performed a comparison between BINCOMP, ECP, and IDA PRO on four
open-source projects, namely SQLite, libpng, zlib, and OpenSSL, where the
obtained results are illustrated in Fig. 3.15. We compile SQLite and zlib with
VS 2010 (O2), and the compiler is successfully identified by these three approaches;
whereas libpng and OpenSSL are compiled with GCC (O2), on which IDA PRO

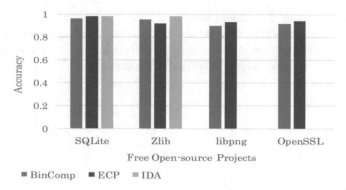

Fig. 3.15 Accuracy results comparison between BINCOMP, ECP, and IDA PRO

is not able to identify the source compiler of these binaries. BINCOMP and ECP provide more accurate results in identifying the VS compiler, while IDA cannot identify the GCC compiler.

3.5 Limitations and Concluding Remarks

In this chapter, we presented BINCOMP, which allows to recover compiler provenance of program binaries accurately and automatically. BINCOMP extracts syntactic semantic, and structural features from program binaries for building representative and meaningful signatures to capture compiler characteristics. We examined the applicability of our proposed features and the features used in the existing techniques (e.g., idioms) to identify the compiler, version, and optimization levels. For instance, the binaries that are compiled with the same compiler have the same CT feature. Furthermore, we formulated the compiler transformation profile (CTP) that maps the instructions underlying a binary according to the most likely compiler family by which it was probably generated. Furthermore, we introduced features that capture detailed provenance at function-level granularity, allowing us to recover the optimization levels used to produce the binary code. We design ACFG and compiler constructor terminator (CCT) features to explicitly capture such changes and identify the version. We evaluated compiler provenance recovery on different datasets across several compiler families, versions, and optimization levels. Our results demonstrate that compiler provenance can be extracted accurately and efficiently, and thus, the proposed approach can be considered as a practical approach for real-world binary analysis.

However, BINCOMP exhibits some limitations. For instance, similar to most existing methods, BINCOMP works under the assumption that the binary code is already de-obfuscated. BINCOMP also assumes that the binary code is not stripped, even though it supports limited statistical analysis on stripped binaries via numerical vectors. In addition, only Intel x86/x86-64 architecture is considered, and we evaluate BINCOMP only for C++ programs. The future work in this area (particularly machine learning-based approaches) could benefit from the set of high-value features introduced in BINCOMP to build more advanced detection models for binary analysis.

Chapter 4
Library Function Identification

Program binaries typically contain a significant amount of library functions taken from standard libraries or free open-source software packages. Automatically identifying such library functions not only enhances the quality and efficiency of threat analysis and reverse engineering tasks, but also improves their accuracy by avoiding false correlations between irrelevant code bases. Furthermore, such automation has a strong positive impact in other applications such as clone detection, function fingerprinting, authorship attribution, vulnerability analysis, and malware analysis.

To this end, this chapter proposes a scalable and robust prototype system called BINSHAPE, which allows to identify standard library functions in program binaries. The key idea of BINSHAPE is twofold. First, for each library function it derives a robust signature called the *shape* of the function based on heterogeneous features covering instruction-level features, statistical features as well as control flow graph, and function-call graph features. The *shape* of a library function captures a collection of most segregative characteristics along one or more dimensions of the features, which is automatically determined using selection evaluators, such as mutual information-based feature ranking and decision tree learning. Second, the shapes of library functions are extracted and stored in a repository and indexed using a novel data structure based on B^+ trees for efficient matching against a target function.

The chapter is organized as follows. First, the library function identification problem and the approach overview are discussed in Sect. 4.1. Then, the feature extraction process and the detection methodology are presented in Sects. 4.2 and 4.3, respectively. Next, the evaluation of the proposed technique is presented in Sect. 4.4. Finally, the limitations of BINSHAPE along with the conclusions and future research areas are presented in Sect. 4.5.

© Springer Nature Switzerland AG 2020
S. Alrabaee et al., *Binary Code Fingerprinting for Cybersecurity*, Advances in Information Security 78, https://doi.org/10.1007/978-3-030-34238-8_4

4.1 Introduction

With the rapid development of the information technology, modern software contains a significant amount of third-party library functions taken from standard library functions or free open-source software packages. Automatically identifying such library functions enhances the efficiency and accuracy of the binary analysis task, thus avoiding false correlations between irrelevant code bases.

Automating the process of accurately identifying library functions in binary programs poses the following challenges: (1) *Robustness:* the distortion of features in the binary file may be attributed to different sources arising from the platform, compiler, or programming language, each of which may change the structures, syntax, or sequences of features. Hence, it is challenging to extract robust features that would be less affected by different compilers, slight changes in the source code as well as obfuscation techniques. (2) *Efficiency:* another challenge is to efficiently extract, index, and match features from program binaries in order to detect a given target function within a reasonable time, considering the fact that many known matching approaches have high complexity [200]. (3) *Scalability:* due to the dramatic growth of software packages as well as malware binaries, threat analysts and reverse engineers deal with large numbers of binaries on a daily basis. Therefore, designing a system that could scale up to millions of binary functions is an absolute necessity. Accordingly, it is important to design efficient data structures to store and match against a large number of candidate functions in a repository.

To address the library identification problem, security researchers elaborated techniques to automatically identify library functions in binaries. For instance, the widely used IDA FLIRT [122, 151] applies signature matching to patterns generated according to the first invariant byte sequence of the function. This simple method is indeed very efficient but the robustness is a major issue. It suffers from the limitation of signature collisions and might require a new signature for each new version as the result of a slight modification, since various compilers and build options usually affect byte-level patterns. Similarly, most other existing methods, e.g., UNSTRIP [165], which is based on the interaction of wrapper functions with the system call interfaces, and LIBV [236], which employs data flow analysis and graph isomorphism, also rely on one type of features and thus might also be easily affected by compiler families and compilation settings. Furthermore, these methods are usually not as efficient as FLIRT due to the need for complex operations, e.g., graph isomorphism testing.

In this context, this chapter, we aim to address the aforementioned challenges and the limitations of existing works. Specifically, we focus on the following research problems. *Can we generate a "robust" signature for each library function to be resilient against compiler effects and obfuscation techniques? Can we rely on only those features, whose extraction, indexing, and matching can be performed in an efficient manner? Can we design an efficient data structure to perform large-scale function matching (e.g., against millions of functions) relatively quickly (e.g., less than a second)?*

The main advantages of BINSHAPE are as follows. First, by relying mostly on lightweight features and the proposed data structure, our technique is *efficient*, and outperforms other techniques that rely on time-consuming computations such as graph isomorphism. Second, incorporating different types of features significantly reduces the chance of signature collisions compared to most existing works which rely on a single feature type. Therefore, by extracting the aforementioned heterogeneous features and furthermore selecting the best features among them, our approach achieves a high level of *robustness*. Third, our technique is general in the sense that it is not limited to a particular type of function, e.g., the wrapper functions provided by standard system libraries [165]. Finally, the ability to conduct an experimental evaluation against a large number (over a million) of functions in a repository confirms the *efficiency* and *scalability* of our system.

4.1.1 Motivating Example

Most of the existing works rely on features of a particular type and they typically organize those features as a vector. In addition, for every version of the function, a new signature must be generated and indexed in the repository. Our first observation here is that, instead of using one feature type, as in FLIRT, the diverse nature of library functions demands a rich collection of features in order to increase the robustness of detection. In addition, as will be demonstrated shortly in Fig. 4.1, the most segregative features for different library functions will likely be different, and therefore a feature vector may not be the best way of representing a signature.

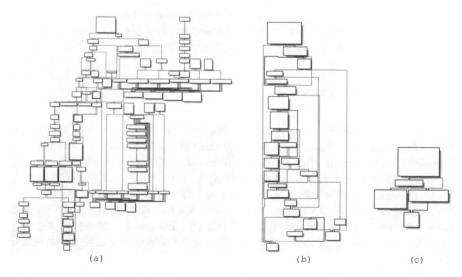

(a)   (b)   (c)

Fig. 4.1 Control flow graphs of (**a**) _memmove, (**b**) _memchr, and (**c**) _lock_file library functions

Specifically, the CFGs of _memmove, _memchr, and _lock_file functions are depicted in Fig. 4.1. We observe that two graph features of _memmove function are enough to make the function distinguishable from others in our repository. On the other hand, the CFG of _lock_file function contains smaller number of nodes (i.e., five), and the CFG of _memchr function is almost flat. Therefore, the best features to identify two different functions, one with few basic blocks and one with a large and complex CFG, would be very different; for instance, basic block level features for the former, and graph features for the latter.

4.1.2   Threat Model

In-Scope Threats: In designing the features and the methodology of our system, we take into consideration several ways by which adversaries may attempt to evade detection by our system. First, adversaries may intentionally apply obfuscation techniques to alter the syntax of binary files. Second, since the syntax of a program binary can be significantly altered by simply changing the compilers or compilation settings, adversaries may adopt such strategies to evade detection. Finally, attackers may slightly modify the source code of library functions and reuse them so as to evade detection.

Out-of-Scope Threats: However, our system is not intended to replace threat analysts or reverse engineers. Thus, it is not designed to overcome the hurdles imposed by packers, obfuscation, or encryption. Instead, our system focuses on identifying library functions in binaries that are already unpacked, de-obfuscated, and decrypted using existing tools [124, 175, 206]. Therefore, the scope of our work is limited to function identification, and our tool is designed to work together with other reverse engineering tools or related initiatives [124, 206] (e.g., those for de-obfuscation) instead of replacing such tools completely.

4.1.3   Approach Overview

Our approach is divided into two phases: offline preparation (indexing) and online search (detection). As illustrated in the upper part of Fig. 4.2, the offline preparation includes: (S) feature extraction discussed in Sect. 4.2, (1) feature selection presented in Sect. 4.2.5, which includes feature ranking to extract the elements of function shape, as well as the best feature selection and (2) signature generation to index the functions in a repository explained in Sect. 4.2.5.2. The lower part of Fig. 4.2 depicts online search, which includes: (S) feature extraction explained in Sect. 4.2; (A) filtering process discussed in Sect. 4.3.2; and (B) detection technique presented in Sect. 4.3.

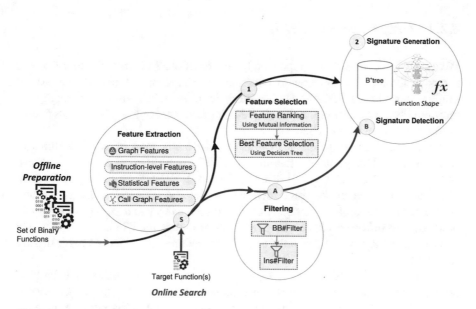

Fig. 4.2 Approach overview

First, the binaries in our training set are disassembled by IDA Pro disassembler [45]. Second, the graph features (Sect. 4.2.1) along with the instruction-level features (Sect. 4.2.2), statistical features (Sect. 4.2.3), and function-call graphs (Sect. 4.2.4) are extracted. To select the subsets of the features that are useful to build the best signature, mutual information (Sect. 4.2.5.1) is employed on the extracted features. The top-ranked features are fed into a decision tree [142], and the outcome of the decision tree is stored in the proposed data structure (Sect. 4.3.1) to form a signature for each library function. In addition to such signatures, we also store the top-ranked features that compose the signature of each function. For detection, all the features are extracted from a given target binary. Then, two filters (Sect. 4.3.2) based on the number of basic blocks ($BB\#$) and the number of instructions ($Ins\#$) are used to prune the search space. Consequently, a set of candidate functions are returned as the result of filtering, and finally the best matches are returned as the final results.

4.2 Feature Extraction

This section first describes different types of features, then presents feature selection, and finally defines the so-called function shape.

4.2.1 Graph Feature Metrics

We extract the control flow graph of a binary function. To extract the best features for each library function and to describe the shape of a function, we extract graph features based on different characteristics of the CFG. Among existing graph metrics [149], we only employ those which are inexpensive to extract. The selected graph features are listed in Table 4.1.

Below we show an example to illustrate the application of graph features to two functions. Our graph metrics are applied to two different library functions, memcpy_s and strcpy_s, as listed in Table 4.2. The corresponding CFGs have identical feature values for some metrics; for instance, *numnodes*, *numedges*, and *cc* are equal, while other metrics, such as *graph_energy* and *pearson* (shown in boldface) are different and can be used to discriminate the CFGs in this example (more generally, we will certainly need more features to uniquely characterize a function).

As discussed before (Sect. 4.1.1), the graph features of _memmove function could be part of the best features, since these features can segregate _memmove function from others. However, graph features alone are not sufficient since there are cases where all the graph features of two different functions are identical, especially for functions of relatively small size. On the other hand, the CFG (and consequently the graph metrics) of a library function may differ due to compilation settings or slight changes in the source file. Therefore, we consider additional features discussed in the following subsections.

Table 4.1 Examples of graph metrics

Graph metric	Description
n, numnodes	Number of nodes
e, numedges	Number of edges
p, num_conn_comp	Number of connected components
CC	Cyclomatic complexity: $e - n + 2p$
num_conn_triples	Number of connected triples
num_loop	Number of independent loops
leaf_nodes	Number of leaves
average_degree	$2 * e/n$
ave_path_length	Average distance between any two nodes
r, graph_radius	Minimum vertex eccentricity
link_density	$e/(n(n-1)/2)$
s_metric	Sum of products of degrees across all edges
rich_club_metric	Extent to which well-connected nodes also connect to each other
graph_energy	Sum of the absolute values of the real components of the eigenvalues
algeb_connectivity	Second smallest eigenvalue of the Laplacian
pearson	Pearson coefficient for degree sequence of all edges
weighted_clust_coeff	Maximum value of the vector of node weighted clustering coefficients

Table 4.2 Comparing graph features of _*memcpy_s* and _*strcpy_s*

Graph metric	_memcpy_s	_strcpy_s
n, numnodes	13	13
e, numedges	18	18
p, num_conn_comp	1	1
CC	7	7
num_conn_triples	6	6
num_loop	6	6
leaf_nodes	7	7
average_degree	2.7692	2.7692
ave_path_length	**2.2308**	**2.5**
r, graph_radius	**5**	**6**
link_density	0.2308	0.2308
s_metric	**150**	**159**
rich_club_metric	**0.2778**	**0.2778**
graph_energy	**18.7268**	**18.0511**
algeb_connectivity	**1**	**0.3820**
pearson	**0.4635**	**0.3415**
weighted_clust_coeff	**0.3334**	**0.5**

Table 4.3 Example of instruction-level features

Feature	Description
retType	Return type
declaration	Declaration type
argsnum	Number of arguments
argsize	Size of arguments
localvarsize	Size of local variables
instrnum	Number of instructions
numReg	Number of registers
#mnemonics	Number of mnemonics
#operand	Number of operands
#constants	Number of constants
#strings	Number of strings
#call list	Number of callees

4.2.2 Instruction-Level Features

Instruction-level features carry both syntax and semantic information of a disassembled function. Some instruction-level features are shown in Table 4.3, such as the number of constants (*#constants*) and the number of callees (*#call lis1smartba*). In addition, inspired by Kruegel et al. [184], we categorize the instructions according to their operation types, as shown in Table 4.4. We record the frequency of each instruction category as a feature. By enriching standard CFGs with information such as different colors, there is a better chance to distinguish two functions even if they

Table 4.4 Example of mnemonic groups

Mnemonic group	Description
DTR	Data transfer operations (e.g., mov)
STK	Stack operations (e.g., push, pop)
CMP	Compare operations (e.g., cmp, test)
ATH	Arithmetic operations (e.g., add, sub)
LGC	Logical operations (e.g., and, or)
CTL	Control transfer (e.g., jmp, jne)
FLG	Flag manipulation (e.g., lahf, sahf)
FLT	Float operations (e.g., f2xm1, fabs)
CaLe	System and interrupt operations (e.g., sysexit)

have the same CFG structure. This relates to the observation that categories carry some information about the functionality of a program; for instance, encryption algorithms perform more logical and arithmetic operations.

4.2.3   Statistical Features

Statistical analysis of binary code can be used to capture the semantics of a function. Several works have applied opcode analysis to binary code; for instance, opcode frequencies are used to detect metamorphic malware in [237, 278]. Therefore, each set of opcodes that belong to a specific function will likely follow a specific distribution according to the functionality they implement. For this purpose, we calculate the *skewness* and *kurtosis* measures to convert these distributions into scores as per equations 4.1 and 4.2 proposed in [24], as follows:

$$Sk = (\frac{\sqrt{N(N-1)}}{N-1})(\frac{\sum_{i=1}^{N}(Y_i - \overline{Y})^3/N}{s^3}) \tag{4.1}$$

$$Kz = \frac{\sum_{i=1}^{N}(Y_i - \overline{Y})^4/N}{s^4} - 3, \tag{4.2}$$

where Y_i is the frequency of each opcode, $\overline{Y}$ is the mean, s is the standard deviation, and N is the number of data points. Similarly, we calculate *z-score* [85, 301] for each opcode (mnemonic), where the corpus includes all the functions in our repository.

Normalization: Each assembly instruction consists of a mnemonic and a sequence of up to three operands. The operands can be classified into three categories: memory references, registers, and constant values. We may have two fragments of a code that are both structurally and syntactically identical, but differ in terms of memory references or registers [134]. Hence, it is essential that the assembly code be normalized prior to comparison. Therefore, the memory references and constant values are normalized to MEM and VAL, respectively. The registers can be generalized according to the various levels of normalization. The top-most level generalizes all registers regardless of types to REG. The next level differentiates general registers (e.g., `eax`, `ebx`), segment registers (e.g., `cs`, `ds`), and index and pointer registers (e.g., `esi`, `edi`). The third level breaks down the general registers into three groups by size—namely, 32, 16, and 8-bit registers.

4.2.4 Function-Call Graph

Function-call graph is a structural representation that abstracts away instruction-level details, and can provide an approximation of a program functionality. Moreover, function-call graph is more resilient to instruction-level obfuscation that are usually employed by malware authors to evade the detection systems [146]. In addition, it offers a robust representation to detect variants of malware programs [162]. Hence, the caller–callee relationship of the library functions is extracted.

The derived function-call graphs from those relationships are directed graphs containing a node corresponding to each function and edges representing calls from callers to callees. For labelling the nodes to exploit properties shared between functions, a neighbor hash graph kernel (NHGK) is applied to subsets of the call graph [160]. Those subsets include library functions and their neighbor functions (callees and callers). The function G maps the features of function f_i to a bit vector of length l, where l is the number of mnemonic categories (9 in total) as shown in Table 4.4. Function G checks each value of the mnemonic groups of a function; if the value is greater than 0, the corresponding bit vector is set to 1; otherwise, it will be 0.

$$G : f_i \rightarrow v_i = \{0, 1\}^l. \tag{4.3}$$

The neighborhood hash value h for a function f_i and its set of neighbor functions N_{f_i} is computed by the following formula [146]:

$$h(f_i) = shr_1(G(f_i)) \oplus (\oplus_{f_j \in N_{f_i}} G(f_j)), \tag{4.4}$$

where shr_1 denotes a one-bit shift right operation and $\oplus$ indicates a bit-wise XOR. The time complexity of this computation is constant time, $O(ld)$, where d is the summation of out-degrees and in-degrees, and l is the length of the bit vector. For instance, suppose f_i is called by two other functions f_1 and f_2, and f_i ($i \notin 1, 2, 3$) calls another function f_3. Therefore, the bit vectors based on the mnemonic group values of each function are generated (by the function G) to construct the set of neighbor function $N_{f_i} = \{v_1, v_2, v_3\}$. Finally, the hash value $h(f_i)$ would be equal to $(shr_1(v_i) \oplus (v_1 \oplus v_2 \oplus v_3))$.

4.2.5 Feature Selection

After extracting all the aforementioned features, we will end up with a number of features among which some might be the most relevant ones—those that appear more frequently and are most segregative in one function. Therefore, a feature selection process is conducted to reduce the number of features as well as to find the best ones. Our feature selection phase contains two major steps: feature ranking and best feature selection, which are described next.

4.2.5.1 Feature Ranking

We measure the relevance of the aforementioned features based on the frequency of their appearance in each library function. Mutual information (MI) [230] represents the degree to which the uncertainty of knowing the value of a random variable is reduced, given the value of another variable. To this end, we employ a mutual information measure to indicate the dependency degree between features X and library function labels Y as follows:

$$MI(X, Y) = \sum_{x \in X} \sum_{y \in Y} p(x, y) log_2 \frac{p(x, y)}{p(x)p(y)}, \qquad (4.5)$$

where x is the feature frequency, y is the class of library function (e.g., memset), $p(x, y)$ is the joint probability distribution function of x and y, and $p(x)$ and $p(y)$ are the marginal probability distribution functions of x and y. The main intention of this feature ranking is to shorten the training time. We measure mutual information-based feature ranking on all categories of aforementioned features. In addition to mutual information, we also apply feature selection evaluators, such as *ChiSquared* [243], *GainRatio* [243], and *InfoGain* [248] using WEKA [16]. Finally, the top-ranked features of our training dataset are selected based on the MI measure.

4.2.5.2 Best Feature Selection

Our aim is to build a classification system which separates library functions from non-library functions. As such, we choose to apply a decision tree classifier on the top-ranked features obtained from the feature ranking process. Each library function is passed through the decision tree and the best provided features for that specific function are recorded. This automated task is performed on all library functions to create a signature for each function. For instance, according to our dataset, the best features for _strstr function are *#DataTransConv*, *instrnum*, *algeb_connectivity*, *#id_to_constants*, and *average_degree* as shown in Listing 4.1.

Listing 4.1 `_strstr` best feature selection

```
#DataTransConv > 32.500
| instrnum > 237: other {_strstr=0,other=69}
| instrnum ? 237: _strstr {_strstr=11,other=0}
#DataTransConv ? 32.500
| algebraic_connectivity > 2.949
| | #id_to_constants > 3
| | | average_degree > 2.847: other {_strstr=0,other=591}
| | | average_degree ? 2.847
| | | | instrnum > 171: _strstr {_strstr=1,other=0}
| | | | instrnum ? 171: other {_strstr=0,other=48}
| | #id_to_constants ? 3: _strstr {_strstr=2,other=0}
| algebraic_connectivity ? 2.949:other{_strstr=0,other=4745}
```

4.3 Detection

Given a target binary function, the disassembled function is passed through two filters to obtain a set of candidate functions from the repository. The classical approach to detection would be to employ the closest Euclidean distances [128] between all top-ranked features of target function and candidate functions. However, such an approach may not be scalable enough for handling millions of functions. Therefore, we design a novel data structure, called B^{++}tree, to efficiently organize the signatures of all the functions, and to find the best matches. Our experimental results (Sect. 4.4) confirm the scalability of our method.

4.3.1 B^{++}tree Data Structure

Due to the growing number of free open-source libraries and the fact that binaries and malware are becoming bigger and more complex, indexing the signatures of millions of library functions to enable efficient detection has thus become a demanding task. One classical approach is to store $(key, value)$ pairs as well as the indices of best features; however, the time complexity of indexing/detection would be $O(n)$, where n is the number of functions in the repository.

To reduce the time complexity, we design a data structure, called B^{++}tree, that basically indexes the best feature values of all library functions in the repository in separate B^+trees, and links those B^+tree to corresponding features and functions. We also augment the B^+tree structure by adding *backward* and *forward* sibling pointers attached to each leaf node, which point to the previous and next leaf nodes, respectively. The number of neighbors is obtained by a user-defined *distance*. Consequently, slight changes in the values that might be due to the compiler effects or the slight changes in the source code are captured by the modified structure. Therefore, the indexing/detection time complexity will be reduced to $O(log(n))$,

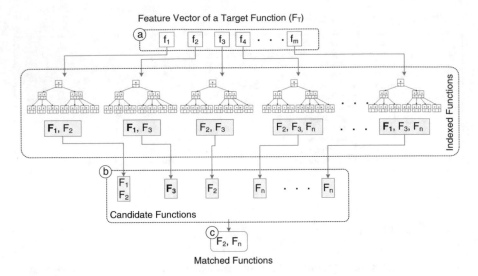

Fig. 4.3 Indexing and detection structure

which is asymptotically better. It is worth noting that the B^+ tree could be replaced with similar data structures such as red-black tree [105]. In addition, we store all top-ranked features for each library function as a signature for the function *shape* as well as for additional experiments.

We explain the B^{++} tree structure with a small example illustrated in Fig. 4.3. The best features of all library functions in our repository are indexed in B^+ trees depicted in the middle box. For instance, the best features of library function F_1 are f_1, f_2, and f_m; hence, these three feature values linked to the function F_1 are indexed in the corresponding B^+ trees (shown in boldface). For the purpose of detection, (a) all the features of a given target function are extracted. For each feature value, a lookup is performed on the corresponding B^+ tree and (b) a set of candidate functions based on the closest values and the user-defined *distance* are returned (we assume that $\{F_1, F_2, F_3, F_n\}$ are returned as the set of candidate functions). For instance, one match is found for the f_2 feature with the second feature of function F_3 (shown in boldface in part b), whereas this feature is indexed as the best feature for F_1 function as well. Finally, the candidate functions are sorted based on the distance and total number of matches: $\{F_2, F_n, F_1, F_3\}$. If we consider the first most frequent functions ($t = 1$), the final candidates would be $\{F_2, F_n\}$ functions.

The details are shown in Algorithm 1. Let f_T be the target function, and F retains the set of candidate functions and their frequency as output. First, all top-ranked features are extracted from the given target binary f_T (line 7). By performing m (total number of features) lookups in each B^+ tree (line 8), a set of candidate functions will be returned (line 9). In order to choose the top t functions, the most t frequent functions are returned as the final set of matched functions (line 11).

Algorithm 1: Function detection

Input: f_T: Target function.
Output: F: Set of candidate functions.
1 $m \leftarrow$ total number of features;
2 $n \leftarrow$ total number of functions in the repository;
3 $F_c \leftarrow \{\}$; dictionary of candidate functions ;
4 $t \leftarrow$ number of most frequent functions to be considered;
5 $distance \leftarrow$ user-defined distance;
6 $feature[m] \leftarrow$ array of size m to hold all the extracted features;
  begin
7   feature[] = featureExtraction(f_T);
8   **foreach** $feature[i] \subset F_T$ **do**
9 | $F_c = F_c + B^+TreeLookup(feature[i], distance)$;
10   **end**
11      $F = t\_most\_frequent\_functions(F_c, t)$;
12   **return** F;
13 **end**

4.3.2   Filtering

To address the scalability issue of dealing with large datasets, a filtering process is necessary. Instead of a pairwise comparison, we prune the search space by excluding functions that are unlikely to be matched. In the literature, DISCOVRE [130] applies the k-nearest neighbors algorithm (kNN) on numerical features as a filter to find similar functions. However, GENIUS [136] re-evaluates DISCOVRE, and illustrates that pre-filtering significantly reduces the accuracy of DISCOVRE. To this end, two simple filters are used in our work, which are described hereafter.

4.3.2.1   Basic Blocks Filter

It is unlikely that a function with four basic blocks can be matched to a function with 100 basic blocks. In addition, due to the compilation settings and various versions of the source code, there exist some differences in the number of basic blocks. Thus, a user-defined threshold value (γ) is employed, which should not be too small or too large to prevent discarding the correct match. Therefore, given a target function f_T, the functions in the repository which have $\gamma\%$ more or less basic blocks than the f_T are considered as candidate functions for the final matching. Based on our experiments with our dataset, we consider $\gamma = \pm 35$.

4.3.2.2   Instruction Filter

Similarly, given a target function f_T, the differences between the number of instructions of target function f_T and the functions in the repository are calculated;

if the difference in the number of instructions is less than a user-defined threshold value λ, then the function is considered as a candidate function. Based on our dataset and experiments, we consider $\lambda = 35\%$.

4.4   Evaluation

In this section, we present the evaluation results of the proposed technique. First, we present the details of the experimental setup followed by the dataset description. Then, the main accuracy results of library function identification are presented. Furthermore, we study the impact of compilers on the proposed approach and discuss the results. Additionally, we examine the effect of feature selection on our accuracy results. We then evaluate the scalability of BINSHAPE on a large dataset. Finally, we study the effectiveness of BINSHAPE on a real malware samples.

4.4.1   Experimental Setup

We developed a proof-of-concept implementation in Python to evaluate our technique. All of our experiments have been conducted on machines running Windows 7 and Ubuntu 15.04 with Core i7 3.4 GHz CPU and 16 GB RAM. The Matlab software has been used for the graph feature extraction. A subset of Python scripts in the proposed system is used in tandem with IDA Pro disassembler. The MongoDB [27] database is utilized to store our features for efficiency and scalability purposes. For the sake of usability, we implemented a graphical user interface in which binaries can be uploaded and analyzed. Any particular selection of data may not be representative of another selection. Hence, to mitigate the possibility that results may be biased by the particular choice of training and testing data, a $C4.5(J48)$ decision tree is evaluated on a 90:10 training/test split of the dataset.

4.4.2   Dataset Preparation

We evaluate our approach on a set of binaries, as detailed in Table 4.5. In order to create the ground truth, we download the source code of all C-library functions [22], as well as different versions of various open-source applications, such as 7-zip. The source code is compiled with Microsoft Visual Studio (VS 2010 and 2012), and GNU Compiler Collection (GCC 4.1.2) compilers, where the /MT and -static options, respectively, are set to statically link C/C++ libraries. In addition, the $O0-O3$ options are used to examine the effects of optimization settings. Program debug databases (PDBs) holding debugging information are also generated for the ground truth. Furthermore, we obtain binaries and corresponding PDBs from their official

Table 4.5 An excerpt of the projects included in our the dataset

Program/project	Version	Number of functions	Size (Kb)
7zip/7z	15.14	133	1074
7zip/7z	15.11	133	1068
7-Zip/7zg	15.05 beta	3041	323
7-Zip/7zfm	15.05 beta	4901	476
expat	0.0.0.0	357	140
firefox	44.0	173,095	37,887
fltk	1.3.2	7587	2833
glew	1.5.1.0	563	306
jsoncpp	0.5.0	1056	13
lcms	8.0.920.14	668	182
libcurl	10.2.0.232	1456	427
libgd	1.3.0.27	883	497
libgmp	0.0.0.0	750	669
libjpeg	0.0.0.0	352	133
libpng	1.2.51	202	60
libpng	1.2.37	419	254
libssh2	0.12	429	115
libtheora	0.0.0.0	460	226
libtiff	3.6.1.1501	728	432
libxml2	27.3000.0.6	2815	1021
Notepad++	6,8,8	7796	2015
Notepad++	6.8.7	7768	2009
nspr	4.10.2.0	881	181
nss	27.0.1.5156	5979	1745
openssl	0.9.8	1376	415
avgntopensslx	14.0.0.4576	3687	976
pcre3	3.9.0.0	52	48
python	3.5.1	1538	28,070
python	2.7.1	358	18,200
putty/putty	0.66 beta	1506	512
putty/plink	0.66 beta	1057	332
putty/pscp	0.66 beta	1157	344
putty/psftp	0.66 beta	1166	352
WireShark/Qt5Core	2.0.1	17,723	3987
SQLite	2013	2498	1006
SQLite	2010	2462	965
SQLite	11.0.0.379	1252	307
tinyXML	2.0.2	533	147
Winedt	9.1	87	8617
WinMerge	2.14.0	405	6283
WireShark	2.0.1	70,502	39,658
WireShark/libjpeg	2.0.1	383	192
WireShark/libpng	2.0.1	509	171
xampp	5.6.15	5594	111,436

websites (e.g., `WireShark`); the compiler of these binaries is detected by a packer tool called EXEINFOPE [43]. Finally, the prepared dataset is used as the ground truth for our system, since we can verify our results by referring to the source code. In order to demonstrate the effectiveness of our approach to identify library functions in malware binaries, we additionally choose `Zeus` malware version 2.0.8.9, where the source code was leaked in 2011 and is reused in our work.[1]

4.4.3 Function Identification Accuracy Results

Our ultimate goal is to discover as many relevant functions as possible with less concern about false positives. Consequently, in our experiments we use the F-measure,

$$F_1 = 2 \cdot \frac{P \cdot R}{P + R}, \tag{4.6}$$

where P is the precision, and R is the recall. Additionally, we show the ROC curve for each set of features used by BINSHAPE. To evaluate our system, we split the binaries in the ground truth into ten sets, reserving one as a testing set and using the remaining nine as training sets. We repeat this process 1000 times and report the results that are summarized in Fig. 4.4.

We obtain a slightly higher true positive rate when using graph features (including function-call graph feature) and statistical features. This small difference can be inferred due to the graph similarity between two library functions that are

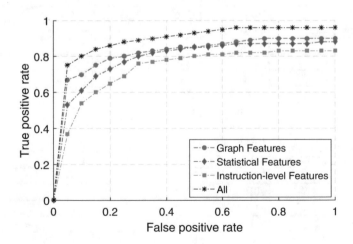

Fig. 4.4 ROC curve for BINSHAPE features

---

[1]https://github.com/Visgean/Zeus.

semantically close. Similarly, statistical features convey information related to the functionality of a function, which cause a slight higher accuracy. On the other hand, instruction-level features return lower true positive rate. However, when all the features are combined together, our system returns an average F_1 measure of 0.89.

4.4.4 Impact of Compilers

In this section, we examine the effects of compilers on a random subset of binaries as follows. (1) *The impact of compiler version*. We train our system with binaries compiled with VS 2010 at optimization level $O2$ and test it with binaries compiled with VS 2012 with the same optimization level. (2) *The impact of optimization levels*. We train our system with binaries compiled with VS 2010 at optimization level $O1$, and test it with the same compiler at optimization level $O2$. (3) *The impact of different compilers*. We collect binaries compiled with VS 2010 and optimization level $O2$ as training dataset, and test the system with binaries compiled with GCC 4.1.2 compiler at optimization level $O2$. The obtained precision and recall for the scenarios are reported in Table 4.6. We observe that our system is not affected significantly by changing either the compiler versions or the optimization levels. However, different compilers affect the accuracy. Examining the effects of more possible scenarios, such as comparing binaries compiled with the same compiler and at optimization levels $O1$ and $O3$, is one of the subjects of feature work.

4.4.5 Impact of Feature Selection

We carry out a set of experiments to measure the impact of the feature selection process, including top-ranked feature selection as well as best feature selection. First, we test our system to determine the best threshold value for top-ranked

Table 4.6 Impact of compiler versions, optimization settings, and compilers families

Project	Version (VS2010-O2 vs VS2012-O2)		Optimization (VS2010-O1 vs VS2010-O2)		Compiler (VS2010 vs GCC-4.1.2)	
	Precision	Recall	Precision	Recall	Precision	Recall
bzip2	1.00	0.98	0.90	0.85	0.82	0.80
OpenSSL	0.93	0.78	0.91	0.80	0.83	0.78
Notepad++	0.98	0.97	0.95	0.82	0.84	0.72
libpng	1.00	1.00	0.91	0.74	0.81	0.72
TestSTL	0.98	1.00	0.90	0.84	0.81	0.75
libjpeg	0.93	0.90	0.88	0.76	0.81	0.69
SQLite	0.91	0.87	0.89	0.85	0.78	0.71
tinyXML	1.00	0.99	0.90	0.82	0.84	0.79

Fig. 4.5 Impact of
top-ranked features

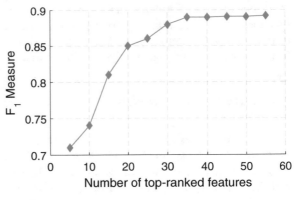

Fig. 4.6 Impact of best
features

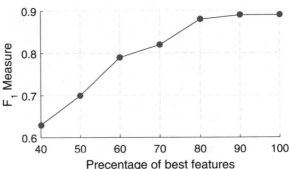

features as shown in Fig. 4.5. We start by considering five top-ranked features and
report the F_1 measure of 0.71. We increment the number of top-ranked features by
five each time. When the number of top-ranked features reaches 35 classes, the F_1
measure is increased to 0.89 and it remains almost constant afterwards. Based on
our findings, we choose 35 as the threshold value for the top-ranked feature classes.

Next, we pass the top-ranked features into the decision tree in order to select
the best features for each function. The goal is to investigate whether considering
the subset of best features would be enough to segregate the functions. In order to
examine the effect of best features, we perform a breadth first search (BFS) on the
corresponding trees to sort best features based on their importance in the function;
since the closer the feature is to the root, the more it is segregative. Our experiments
examine the F_1 measure while varying the percentage of best features. We start
by 40% of the top-ranked best features and increment them by 10% each time.
Figure 4.6 shows the relationship between the percentage of best features and the
F_1 measure. Based on our experiments, we find that 90% of the best features results
in an F_1 measure of 0.89. However, for the sake of simplicity, we consider all the
selected best features in our experiments.

4.4.6 Impact of Filtering

We study the impact of the proposed filters (e.g., *BB#* and *Ins#*) on the accuracy of BINSHAPE. For this purpose, we perform four experiments by applying: (1) no filter (2) *BB#* filter, (3) *Ins#* filter, and (4) both of the aforementioned two filters. As shown in Fig. 4.7, the drop in accuracy caused by the proposed filters is negligible. For instance, when we test our system with two filters, the highest drop in accuracy is about 0.017.

4.4.7 Scalability Study

To evaluate the scalability of our system, we prepare a large collection of binaries consisting of different ".exe" or ".dll" files (e.g., `msvcr100.dll`) containing more than 3,020,000 disassembled functions. We gradually index this collection of functions in a random order, and query the `7-zip` binary file of version 15.14 on our system at an indexing interval of every 500,000 assembly functions. We collect the average indexing time for each function to be indexed, as well as the average time it takes to respond to a function detection. The indexing time includes feature extraction and storing them in the B^+ trees. Figure 4.8 depicts the average indexing and detection time for each function.

The results suggest that our system scales well with respect to the repository size. When the number of functions increases from 500,000 to 3,020,000, the impact on response time of our system is negligible (0.14 s on average to detect a function among three million functions in the repository). We notice through our experiments that the ranking time and filtering time are very small and negligible. For instance, ranking 5000 features takes 0.0003 ms, and filtering highly likely similar functions

Fig. 4.7 Impact of filtering

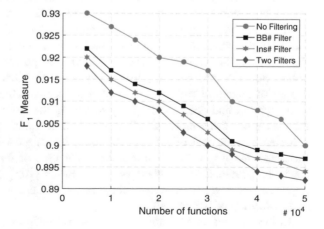

Fig. 4.8 Scalability study

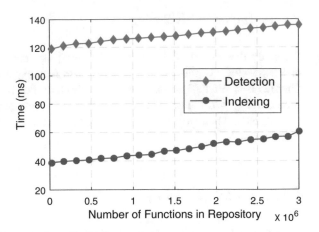

in the repository to a function having 100 basic blocks and 10,000 instructions, takes 0.009 ms. Besides, the feature extraction time varies for different types of features; e.g., the graph feature extraction takes more time than instruction-level and call-graph feature extractions.

4.5   Limitations and Concluding Remarks

In this chapter, we have presented a pioneering investigation into the possibility of representing a function based on its shape. We have proposed a robust signature for each library function based on a diverse collection of heterogeneous features, covering CFGs, instruction-level characteristics, statistical features, and function-call graphs. In addition, we have designed a novel data structure, which includes B^+ tree, in order to efficiently support accurate and scalable detection. Experimental results have demonstrated the effectiveness of BINSHAPE.

The main advantages of BINSHAPE are as follows. First, by relying mostly on lightweight features and the proposed data structure, it is *efficient*, and outperforms other techniques that rely on time-consuming computations such as graph isomorphism. Second, incorporating different types of features significantly reduces the chance of signature collisions compared to most existing works which rely on a single type of features. Therefore, by extracting the aforementioned heterogeneous features and furthermore selecting the best features among them, BINSHAPE achieves a great deal of *robustness*. Third, the proposed technique is general in the sense that it is not limited to a particular type of functions, e.g., the wrapper functions provided by standard system libraries [165]. Finally, testing against a large number (over a million) of functions in a repository confirms the *efficiency* and *scalability* of BINSHAPE.

However, the proposed approach has the following limitations: (1) We have not scrutinized the impact of inline functions. (2) Our system is able to tackle some code transformation such as instruction reordering, however, some other obfuscation techniques, such as control flow flattening, affect the accuracy of BINSHAPE. In addition, the proposed approach is not able to handle the packed, encrypted, and obfuscated binaries. (3) We have tested BINSHAPE with VS and GCC compilers, however, binaries compiled with ICC and Clang have not been examined. (4) We have not investigated the impact of hardware architectures, such as MIPS or ARM in this study. These limitations are the subjects of future work.

Chapter 5
Identifying Reused Functions in Binary Code

Discovering reused binary functions is crucial for many security applications, especially considering the fact that many modern malware typically contain a significant amount of functions borrowed from open-source software packages. This process will not only reduce the odds of common libraries leading to false correlations between unrelated code bases but also improve the efficiency of reverse engineering. We introduce a system for fingerprinting reused functions in binary code. More specifically, we introduce a new representation, namely, the semantic integrated graph (SIG), which integrates control flow graph, register flow graph, function-call graph, and other structural information, into a joint data structure. Such a comprehensive representation captures different semantic descriptors of common functionalities in a unified manner as graph traces of SIG graphs.

In this chapter, we first review existing binary representations in Sect. 5.1. The proposed approach and the evaluation results are presented in Sects. 5.2 and 5.3, respectively. Finally, the chapter concludes in Sect. 5.4.

5.1 Existing Representations of Binary Code

Different binary representations have been developed for binary code analysis, such as data flow graphs, control flow graphs (CFGs), call graphs, register flow graphs [59] (RFGs), and program dependence graphs. These representations can certainly be employed to characterize the code and also to identify reused functions in binary code. To illustrate these representations, we introduce in the following a running example using the bubble sort code presented in Listing 5.1.

© Springer Nature Switzerland AG 2020

S. Alrabaee et al., *Binary Code Fingerprinting for Cybersecurity*, Advances in Information Security 78, https://doi.org/10.1007/978-3-030-34238-8_5

5.1.1 Control Flow Graph

The control flow graph (CFG) is one of the most widely used features in the literature. In this context, a control flow graph is a standard code representation in reverse engineering to aid in understanding the structure and the semantics of a function. It describes the order of statements to be executed as well as the conditions that need to be met for a particular path of execution. To this end, basic blocks are represented by nodes connected by directed edges to indicate the transfer of control. Therefore, a label `true(t)`, `false(f)`, or ϵ is assigned to each edge. In particular, a normal node has one outgoing edge labelled ϵ, whereas a predicate node has two outgoing edges corresponding to a `true` or `false` evaluation of the predicate. As an example, the CFG for bubble sort is shown in Fig. 5.1. However, while CFGs expose the control flow of a given code, they fail to provide other useful information, such as the way registers are manipulated by the code and the interaction between different functions.

Listing 5.1 Bubble sort source code

```
void bubble_sort(int arr[], int size) {
        bool not_sorted = true;
        int j=0,tmp;

        while (not_sorted)        {
                not_sorted = false;
                j++;
                for (int i = 0; i < size - j; i++){
                        if (arr[i] > arr[i + 1]) {
                                tmp = arr[i];
                                arr[i] = arr[i + 1];
                                arr[i + 1] = tmp;
                                not_sorted = true;
                        }//end of if
                        print_array(arr,5);
                }//end of for loop
        }//end of while loop
}//end of bubble_sort
```

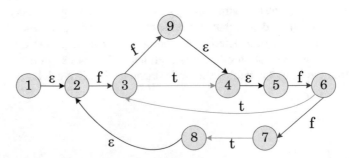

Fig. 5.1 Control flow graph for bubble sort function

Table 5.1 Original classes of register access

Class	Arithmetic	Logical	Generic	Stack
1	0	0	0	0
2	0	0	0	1
3	0	0	1	0
4	0	0	1	1
5	0	1	0	0
6	0	1	0	1
7	0	1	1	0
8	0	1	1	1
9	1	0	0	0
10	1	0	0	1
11	1	0	1	0
12	1	0	1	1
13	1	1	0	0
14	1	1	0	1
15	1	1	1	0
16	1	1	1	1

5.1.2   Register Flow Graph

A register flow graph (RFG) is used to capture the way the registers are manipulated within a function in binary code, which is originally designed for authorship identification of binary code [59]. RFGs describe the flow and dependencies between registers as an important semantic aspect of the behavior of a program, which might indicate authorship as well as functionality. Moreover, in a RFG, assembly instructions are classified into four categories of stack, arithmetic, logical operation, and generic operations as follows:

- Arithmetic class, such as add, sub, mul, div, imul, idiv, etc.
- Logical class, such as or, and, xor, test, shl, etc.
- Generic class, such as mov, lea, call, jmp, jle, etc.
- Stack class, such as push and pop.

The steps involved in constructing the RFG for the registers are as follows:

1. Counting the number of compare (e.g., cmp) instructions,
2. Identifying the registers used in each compare instruction,
3. Checking the flow of each register from the beginning until reaching the compare instruction,
4. Classifying the registers according to the 16 classes illustrated in Table 5.1 proposed by Alrabaee et al. [59].

We employ an example to show how to extract the RFG. In this pursuit, the first step is to highlight the compare instructions in the main function. For illustration purpose, we base our discussion upon a randomly selected function presented in Listings 5.2 as follows:

Listing 5.2 main function

```
            (00411670 main)
            push    ebp
            mov     ebp, esp
            sub     esp, 0D8h
            push    ebx
            push    esi
            push    edi
            lea     edi, [ebp+var_D8]
            mov     ecx, 0CCCCCh
            rep stosd
            mov     esi, esp
            push    offset ?tt@3HA ;
            push    offset Format ;
            call    ds:__imp__scanf
            add     esp, 8
            cmp     esi, esp
            call    j___RTC_CheckEsp
            mov     esi, esp
            push    offset ?s@@3A ;
            call    ds:__imp__gets
            cdd     esp, 4
            cmp     esi, esp
```

We note that the illustrated code fragment contains two compare (cmp) instructions. Therefore, two RFGs can be constructed according to each cmp instruction.
To this end, we filter the instructions and keep only the ones which are related to the
registers of compare instructions. The first graph is constructed as follows:

Step1: Keep all the instructions until the first compare (e.g., cmp esi, esp)
instruction as listed in Listing 5.3.

Listing 5.3 main function

```
(00411670 main)
push    ebp
mov     ebp, esp
sub     esp, 0D8h
push    ebx
push    esi
push    edi
lea     edi, [ebp+var_D8]
mov     ecx, 0CCCCCh
rep stosd
mov     esi, esp
push    offset ?tt@3HA ;
push    offset Format ;
call    ds:__imp__scanf
add     esp, 8
cmp     esi, esp
```

Step 2: Filter these instructions by eliminating the instructions that are not related to the registers of the compare instructions (`esi` and `esp`), so the sequences will be as in Listing 5.4.

Listing 5.4 Instructions related to `esi` and `esp` registers, selected from Listing 5.3

```
1.  mov   ebp,  esp
2.  sub   esp,  0D8h
3.  push esi
4.  mov   esi,  esp
5.  add   esp,  8
6.  cmp   esi,  esp
```

Step 3: Construct the state graph from the previous sequences as depicted in Fig. 5.2a. We start from the last instruction and for each of the involved registers, we step backward till reaching to the first select instruction as shown in Listing 5.4.

Step 4: Reshape Fig. 5.2a for the sake of simplicity to construct the RFG, as the new graph shown in Fig. 5.2b. The left-hand side nodes are referring to the instructions which use `esi` register (number 3 and 4 in Listing 5.4), which represent stack and data transfer (generic) operations, respectively. According to the category presented in Table 5.1, the bit vector of [0, 0, 1, 1] belongs to class 4. Therefore, we replace the two nodes by one node (C4). Similarly, the right-hand side nodes employ `esp` register representing data transfer and arithmetic operations. By referring to Table 5.1, the vector [1, 0, 1, 0] is of class 11.

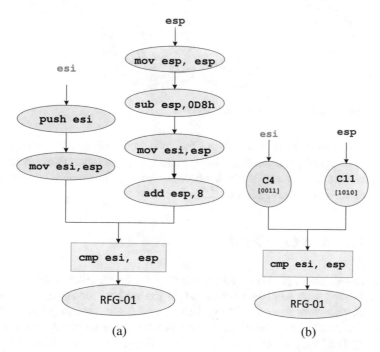

Fig. 5.2 Register flow graph construction. (**a**) The states of `esi` and `esp` registers. (**b**) The classes in RFG

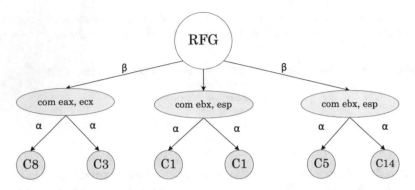

Fig. 5.3 Register flow graph for bubble sort function

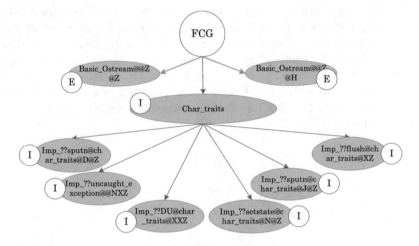

Fig. 5.4 Function-call graph for bubble sort function

Moreover, two costs of α and β are assigned to the edges of a RFG; α is the cost that is assigned based on the flow of registers values (instruction counts), and β represents the ID of the basic block where the compare instruction belongs to. An example of RFG is presented in Fig. 5.3.

5.1.3   Function-Call Graph

A function-call graph (FCG) is the representation of a function in binary code as a directed graph with labelled vertices, where the vertices correspond to functions and the edges to function calls. Two labels, I and E are assigned to the nodes; I represents internal library functions and E represents external library functions. An example of FCG for the bubble sort function is shown in Fig. 5.4. In the literature, external call graphs have been used for malware detection [127]. In such a case, model graphs and data graphs are compared in order to distinguish call graphs representing benign programs from those based on malware samples [127, 247].

5.2   Reused Function Identification

In this section, we first provide an overview of the proposed SIGMA approach in Sect. 5.2.1. We then describe the three building blocks of an *SIG* in Sect. 5.2.2. We introduce the *SIG* concept in Sect. 5.2.3. Finally, we describe methods for *SIG* graph matching in Sect. 5.2.4.

5.2.1   Overview

The overall architecture of our SIGMA approach is depicted in Fig. 5.5, which is composed of two main phases of training and testing detailed next.

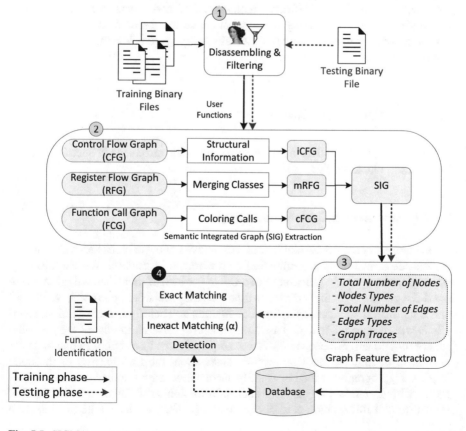

Fig. 5.5 SIGMA approach overview

The training phase consists of the following steps: (1) Disassembling the binary code and filtering out compiler-related functions; (2) Constructing the semantic integrated graph *SIG* by (2.a) generating the CFG, RFG, and FCG from user functions; (2.b) applying structural information to CFG to obtain the information control flow graph *iCFG* (Sect. 5.2.2.1); applying new merged classes to RFG to obtain a merged register flow graph *mRFG* (Sect. 5.2.2.2); (2.c) applying color classes to FCG to obtain the colored function-call graph *cFCG* (Sect. 5.2.2.3). Finally, merging the previous graphs into a single semantic integrated graph of *SIG*. (3) Decomposing the *SIG* into a set of traces aiming to identify fragments in the functions and considering various properties of the *SIG*, such as the total number of nodes, node types (such as data, or control), edge types, total number of edges, the depth of graph, etc. We record these features into our database for each function.

Given a set of unknown assembly instructions, the testing phase constructs the *SIG* of each function and further extracts the properties of the constructed graph (Steps 1–3 in Fig. 5.5) and compares them with the existing *SIG*s in the database (Step 4). We propose two graph matching methods: (1) *Exact matching*: two graphs are deemed as an exact match if they have the same properties. Similarly, a specific fragment g_i belongs to a specific function f_i, if and only if f_i has a fragment with the same properties as g_i. (2) *Inexact matching*: the edit distance between two graphs is calculated and the similarity score is compared to a predefined threshold value. Two functions are deemed similar if their similarity score is less than the predefined threshold value.

5.2.2   Building SIG Blocks

In this section, we extend the existing representations introduced in Sect. 5.1 to form the building blocks of *SIG*.

5.2.2.1   Information Control Flow Graph

As mentioned in Sect. 5.1, traditional CFGs consist of basic blocks each of which is a sequence of instructions terminating with a branch instruction. We can thus only obtain the structure of a function from a CFG. The lack of more detailed information in CFGs means two entirely different functions may yield the same CFG, which will cause confusion for identifying similar functions. Therefore, we extend standard CFGs with a colored scheme based on structural information about the probable role or functionality of each node. For example, if most instructions in one node are arithmetic or logical, this may provide clues about the functionality of the node (e.g., a cryptographic function usually involves a large number of for loops). By enriching standard CFGs with such information as different colors of nodes, which we call information control flow graph (*iCFG*), we have a better chance to

Table 5.2 Structural information categories

Category	Description
Data Transfer (DT)	Data transfer instructions, such as mov, movzx, movsx
Test	Test instructions, such as cmp, test
ArLo	Arithmetic and logical instructions, such as add, sub, mul, div, imul, idiv, and, or, xor, sar, shr
CaLe	System and API calls, and load effective instructions, such as lea
Stack	Stack-related instructions, such as push, pop

Table 5.3 Color classes for *iCFG*

Color classes	Majority	Minority$_1$	Minority$_2$	Minority$_3$
1–2–3	DT-Test	ArLo	Stack	CaLe
4–5–6	DT-ArLo	Test	CaLe	Stack
7–8–9	DT-CaLe	ArLo	Stack	Test
10–11–12	DT-Stack	Test	CaLe	ArLo
13–14–15	Test-ArLo	DT	CaLe	Stack
16–17–18	Test-CaLe	DT	ArLo	Stack
19–20–21	Test-Stack	DT	ArLo	CaLe
22–23–24	ArLo-Stack	Test	DT	CaLe
25–26–27	ArLo-CaLe	Stack	DT	Test
28–29–30	Stack-Cale	Test	DT	ArLo

distinguish two functions even if they have the same CFG structure. Table 5.2 shows some example categories of structural information that we consider in coloring the nodes.

The assignment of classes depends on two percentages: (1) the two highest percentages and (2) the lowest percentage, among the proposed categories. By considering the highest percentages, we aim to measure the majority category in the function. We choose two highest percentages because we have noticed that some classes, such as data transfer (DT), are always dominant in many cases such that considering an additional second highest percentage would provide more reliable coloring. Table 5.3 shows some example of colored classes. For instance, the first entry in Table 5.3 shows three classes of 1, 2, and 3, indicating that class 2 occurs when the majority of the mnemonics is DT and Test and the minority is Stack operations.

As an example, by applying the color classes in Table 5.3 to Fig. 5.1, we can obtain the *iCFG* shown in Fig. 5.6. This *iCFG* involves five color classes: 22, 4, 3, 10, and 1. Table 5.3 demonstrates that a majority of those classes belong to ArLo-Stack, DT-ArLo, DT-Test, DT-Stack, and DT-Test. This is reasonably expected since the main functionality of the bubble sort algorithm is

Fig. 5.6 iCFG for bubble
sort function

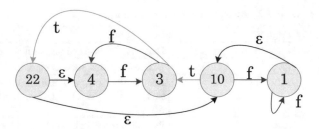

manipulating values in an array and consequently the main action is the transfer
of values from one location to another, which explains the large number of DT
instructions. As demonstrated by the example, by using this extended control flow
graph *iCFG*, we can capture more semantic information that might be helpful in
identifying functions in binary code. Nonetheless, the *iCFG* only contains control
information about basic blocks, and it lacks other useful semantics, such as the way
registers are manipulated and the way functions interact with each other. Hence, we
introduce two other building blocks in addition to *iCFG*.

5.2.2.2 Merged Register Flow Graph

As mentioned in Sect. 5.1, RFG is a binary code representation for capturing
program behaviors based on an important semantics of the code, i.e., how registers
are manipulated. The original RFG designed for authorship attribution lacks support
for handling some cases that are important for function identification: when (1) both
operands of cmp instruction are constants (C), (2) one of the operands is a constant
value and the other one is a register (reg), (3) both operands are memory locations
(ML), (4) one of the operands is a memory location and the other one is a register,
and (5) the operands are a mixture of constant values and memory locations. These
cases are especially important for identifying functions in binary code, and hence
we extend the RFG by adding several new classes as shown in Table 5.4.

Moreover, since the original RFG depends on only the cmp instructions, we also
extend RFG instructions to the test instruction. Finally, as another improvement
over the original RFG, we merge certain nodes to one node, for instance, class 1 and
class 2 together are equivalent to class 5. Consequently, we reduce the number of
nodes which improves the efficiency of analyzing the RFG.

After applying the aforementioned extensions and modifications, we obtain
a new representation called *mRFG*, as shown in Fig. 5.7. The *mRFG* has three
more nodes than its corresponding RFG; one of these is the test instruction,
and the other two are related to the immediate memory address and the constant
values. Moreover, we merge the original classes (in Fig. 5.3) as: $(C8, C3) \rightarrow C8$,
$(C1, C1) \rightarrow C1$, and $(C5, C14) \rightarrow C11$. The reference to the new classes (e.g.,
$C17$ and $C19$) may capture useful semantics about the functions, e.g., a bubble sort
function mainly deals with constant values and sorts them in memory locations.

Table 5.4 Updated register classes for Table 5.1

Class	Arithmetic	Logical	Generic	Stack	C-C	C-Reg	ML-ML	ML-Reg	ML-C
1	1	0	0	0	0	0	0	0	0
2	0	1	0	0	0	0	0	0	0
3	0	0	1	0	0	0	0	0	0
4	0	0	0	1	0	0	0	0	0
5	1	1	0	0	0	0	0	0	0
6	1	0	1	0	0	0	0	0	0
7	1	0	0	1	0	0	0	0	0
8	1	1	1	0	0	0	0	0	0
9	1	1	0	1	0	0	0	0	0
10	1	0	1	0	0	0	0	0	0
11	1	1	1	1	0	0	0	0	0
12	0	1	1	0	0	0	0	0	0
13	0	1	0	1	0	0	0	0	0
14	0	0	1	1	0	0	0	0	0
15	0	1	1	1	0	0	0	0	0
16	0	0	0	0	1	0	0	0	0
17	0	0	0	0	0	1	0	0	0
18	0	0	0	0	0	0	1	0	0
19	0	0	0	0	0	0	0	1	0
20	0	0	0	0	0	0	0	0	1

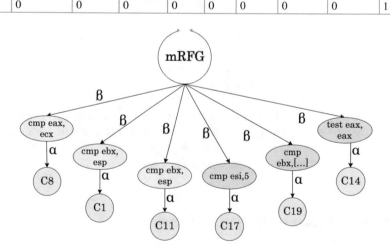

Fig. 5.7 mRFG for bubble sort function

5.2.2.3   Color Function-Call Graph

As mentioned in Sect. 5.1, traditional FCGs represent system calls in a binary code.
Among a set of system calls $C = \{C_1, C_2, \ldots, C_n\}$, each call may be either internal
(local) or external. To distinguish these calls, we extend FCGs with a color scheme

Fig. 5.8 cFCG for bubble
sort function

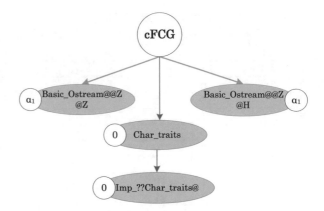

as follows. The label function for labelling edges l defines the label class α in two
cases. For an internal call, we assign one label indicating the type of the call. As
for external calls, we define the label classes using a range of values $0 < \alpha < 1$,
because we may have various external system calls potentially connecting to an API
that is very important for identifying functions. More precisely, we extend FCGs to
a new representation named cFCG, using the label function defined as follows:

$$f(l) = \begin{cases} \alpha = 0 & \text{if } l \text{ is internal system call} \\ 0 < \alpha < 1 & \text{if } l \text{ is external system call} \end{cases} \tag{5.1}$$

As an example, having applied this new representation to our running example,
we obtain the cFCG shown in Fig. 5.8. Besides serving as a building block of
our proposed approach, the cFCG representation may also be helpful in other
applications by highlighting the difference between various types of the calls. For
instance, clustering external system calls will aid for malware classification, and can
provide analysts with a list of API call graph properties derived from external calls,
which will assist for writing pattern-based signatures.

5.2.3   *SIG: Semantic Integrated Graph*

The building blocks introduced in the previous section provide complementary
views on binary code by emphasizing on different aspects of the underlying
function semantics. Inspired by the work introduced in [292], in which different
representations of source code are combined for vulnerability detection in source
code (which is a different problem from ours, as binary code lacks much of
the useful information available in source code), we combine those different but
complementary representations of binary code into a joint data structure. This

can facilitate more efficient graph matching between different binary codes for identifying reused functions. Formally, a semantic integrated graph (*SIG*) is defined as follows.

Definition 5.1

1. A semantic graph $G = (N,V,\zeta,\gamma,\vartheta,\lambda,\omega)$ is a directed attributed graph where N is a set of nodes, $V \subseteq (N \times N)$ is a set of edges and ζ is the edge labelling function which assigns a label to each edge: $\zeta \longrightarrow \gamma$, where γ is a set of labels. ϑ is a coloring function which colors each node $n \in N$ based on statistical classes function λ. Finally, ω is a function for coloring *mRFG*.

Definition 5.2

2. Let f_1, f_2 be two functions; we say f_1 is similar to f_2, if $\mathrm{SIG}(f_1)$ matches $\mathrm{SIG}(f_2)$.

Definition 5.3

3. Let f_1, f_2 be two functions, and $\mathrm{SIG}(f_1) \to s_1$ and let $\mathrm{SIG}(f_2) \to s_2$ denote extracting SIG traces s_1 and s_2 from f_1 and f_2. Let $\mathrm{sim}(a,b) \to [0,1]$ be a similarity function and δ a predefined threshold value $(0 < \delta < 1)$. We consider f_1 and f_2 are similar if $1 - sim(s_1, s_2) < \delta$.

A simple example of *SIG* with four nodes is illustrated in Fig. 5.9. Since an *SIG* is a graph, two nodes may be connected by multiple edges, e.g., edges corresponding to *mRFG* or *cFCG*. Moreover, A, B, C, D represent the outcomes of labelling function ϑ, and a, b, and c are the outcomes of function ζ. The $C1$, $C5$, $C2$, and $C11$ are outcomes of function ω. The labels in the oval nodes represent the number of outcomes of the color function for *cFCG*, where 0 represents an internal call, and α_1, α_2, and α_3 represent three different external calls.

To utilize the *SIG* for inexact matching and matching for fragments of a function, we need to consider meaningful subgraphs of *SIG*. Inspired by Yamaguchi et al. [292], we decompose an *SIG* into short paths called *traces*, where each trace is a function $\varrho : S(N) \longrightarrow S(N')$ that maps a set of nodes in an *SIG* to another set of nodes according to given criteria, where $S(N)$ denotes the power set of N. The main advantage of such a definition is that the composition of multiple traces

Fig. 5.9 Simple example of *SIG*

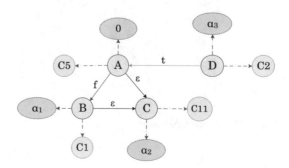

always yields other traces, i.e., ϱ_0 and ϱ_1, that can be chained together ($\varrho_0 \circ \varrho_1$). We define a number of elementary traces that serve as a basis for the construction of other traces, and some examples are shown in the following:

$$Out_{I,L,K}(Y) = \bigcup_{n \in Y} \{m : (n, m) \in V \text{ and } \vartheta(n, m) = I \text{ and } \lambda(n, m)$$

$$= L \text{ and } \omega(n, m) = K\} \tag{5.2}$$

$$IN_{I,L,K}(Y) = \bigcup_{n \in Y} \{m : (n, m) \in V \text{ and } \vartheta(n, m) = I \text{ and } \lambda(n, m)$$

$$= L \text{ and } \omega(n, m) = K\} \tag{5.3}$$

$$OR(\varrho_1, \varrho_2, \cdots, \varrho_n) = \varrho_1 \cup \varrho_2 \cup \cdots \cup \varrho_n \tag{5.4}$$

$$AND(\varrho_1, \varrho_2, \cdots, \varrho_n) = \varrho_1 \cap \varrho_2 \cap \cdots \cap \varrho_n. \tag{5.5}$$

The trace $Out_{I,L,K}$ returns all nodes reachable over edge I and connected to the node of the other graph with label L, and all nodes connected with the node of the other graph with label K. Trace $IN_{I,L,K}$ is similarly defined to move backwards in the graph, and the two traces OR and AND aggregate the outputs of the other traces.

Example: The *SIG* for the bubble sort function is shown in Fig. 5.10. We show the traces of nodes 22, 4, and 3 in Table 5.5 as well as the corresponding *AND* and *OR* traces. Moreover, the additional features from the *SIG* are listed in Table 5.6, such as total number of nodes, number of control edges (e.g., 22), number of flow edges (e.g., 0), number of flow nodes (e.g., C8), etc. These features together with the *SIG* traces are sufficient for the exact matching of *SIG*s. We discuss inexact matching in the next section (Sect. 5.2.4).

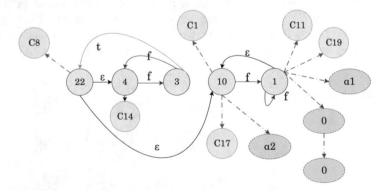

Fig. 5.10 *SIG* for bubble sort

Table 5.5 Part of traces for
SIG bubble sort function

Node	Traces	Traces type
22	$\epsilon, \epsilon, C8$	out
	t	in
4	f, C14	out
	ϵ, f	in
22 OR 4	ϵ, C8, C14, f	out
	f, t, ϵ	in
4 AND 3	f	out
	f	in

Table 5.6 Graph features for
exact matching

Features	Frequency
Total number of nodes	15
Total number of edges	18
Number of control nodes	5
Number of control edges	8
Number of call nodes	4
Number of call edges	4
Number of register nodes	6

5.2.4   Graph Edit Distance

For performing inexact matching between the *SIG*s, we need a distance metric. In
this chapter, we employ the graph edit distance for this purpose. The edit distance
between two graphs measures their similarity in terms of the number of edits needed
to transform one into the other [162]. We implement this concept as follows.

Given two *SIG*s, we define the following two elementary traces to transform
one graph into another: (1) *Edge-edit traces*, including κ_r, re-labels the edge, and
(2) *Node-edit traces*, including v_r, re-colors the node by merging nodes from
the other graph into one node. An edit edge $V_{G,H}$ between two *SIG*s G and
H is defined as a set of sequences $(\varrho_1, \varrho_2, \ldots, \varrho_n)$ of traces such that $G =
\varrho_n(\varrho_1(\varrho_{n-1}(H) \ldots \varrho_1(H) \ldots))$. To quantify this similarity, the weight of all edit
traces i.e., $V = (\varrho_n, \varrho_2, \ldots, \varrho_n)$ is measured as $w(V) = \sum_{i=1}^{n} w(\varrho_i)$. The edit
distance between two *SIG*s is thus defined as the minimum weight of all edit edges
and nodes between them, i.e., $sim(G, H) = min\ w(V_{G,H})$. The distance measure
between the nodes follows the same reasoning, with operations instead of traces.
In Algorithm 1, we calculate the graph edit distance between two *SIG*s, G and H,
by measuring the cost of transforming G to H. The algorithm starts by labelling
the edges of the two graphs as mentioned earlier, and then checks the cost of
transforming each node in G to nodes in H, and finally calculates the total cost.

Algorithm 1: Graph edit distance

---

    input : G: semantic integrated graph
               H: semantic integrated graph
               R: total set of edges
               e: last element of edges
    output: sim: Similarity result for two graphs

1 **begin**
2   // Edge labeling
3      $(G, V') \leftarrow ExtractEdges\,(G, V)$;
4      $(H, V'') \leftarrow ExtractEdges\,(H, V)$;
5
6   **for** *each v_i in V'* **do**
7   **for** *each v_j in V''* **do**
8   **if** $v_j.\varrho = v_i.\varrho$ **then**
9               $sim(G, H) \leftarrow \varrho$ in v_j;

10   **for** *each r in R* **do**
11   **for** *each $1 < e$* **do**
12          $w(V) \leftarrow w\,(\varrho_i)$;

13   **return** $sim(G, H) = minw(V_{G,H})$

We define the dissimilarity between two *SIG*s G and H as follows:

Definition 5.4

5. The dissimilarity $\rho(G, H)$ between two *SIG*s is a value in $[0, 1]$, where 0 indicates the graphs are the most similar and 1 the least similar, as formulated in the following:

$$\rho(G, H) = \frac{w(V_{G,H})}{|N_G| + |N_H| + |V_G| + |V_H| + |\varrho_G| + |\varrho_H|}, \qquad (5.6)$$

where $w(V_{G,H})$ is the weight cost of traces, $|N_G|$ the number of nodes in G, $|N_H|$ the number of nodes in H, $|V_G|$ the number of edges in G, $|V_H|$ the number of edges in H, and $|\varrho|$ the number of traces in both *SIG*s.

5.3   Evaluation

We perform three sets of experiments to examine our proposed approach. First, we test SIGMA, with variants of sorting algorithms and encryption algorithms. Then, we evaluate our system against different program binaries compiled with different compilers. Finally, we examine the effects of light obfuscation and refactoring techniques on these program binaries.

5.3.1 Dataset

We evaluate our system against 30 programs for which we have the source code. These programs are only used to extract the ground truth by compiling the source code with four different compilers (VS, GCC, ICC, and Clang) and the debugging information. Table 5.7 summarizes the 30 programs, including the program identifier, program name, binary code statistics, and the source compiler. The binary code information, such as the type of executable generated (PE or ELF) and the number of functions, is extracted using IDA PRO [45] by capturing

Table 5.7 Programs used in our system evaluation

ID	Program	Binary code		Compiler
		Type	#Functions	
1	SQlite	PE	3920	VS, GCC, ICC, Clang
2	OpenSSL	PE	2163	VS, GCC
3	info-zip	PE	1784	VS, ICC
4	jabber	PE	5910	VS, GCC
5	Hashdeep	PE	2905	VS, Clang, GCC
6	libpng	PE	9226	VS, GCC
7	ultraVNC	PE	3526	VS, GCC
8	lcms	PE	1082	Clang, ICC, GCC
9	ibavcodec	PE	739	VS, GCC, ICC
10	TrueCrypt	PE	1093	VS, GCC
11	libjsoncpp	PE	4114	VS, ICC
12	7z	PE	2179	VS, GCC, ICC
13	7zG	PE	2530	VS, GCC, ICC
14	7zFM	PE	3149	VS, GCC, ICC
15	lzip	ELF	33	VS, GCC
16	tinyXMLTest	ELF	2744	VS, GCC, ICC, Clang
17	libxml2	ELF	58	VS, GCC, ICC
18	Mersenne Twister	ELF	2740	VS, GCC
19	bzip2	ELF	285	VS, GCC
20	lshw	ELF	1429	VS, GCC
21	smartctl	ELF	457	VS, GCC
22	pdftohtml	ELF	499	VS, GCC, Clang
23	ELF statifier	ELF	2340	VS, GCC
24	FileZilla	PE	6250	VS, GCC
25	ncat	PE	1855	VS, GCC
26	Hasher	PE	436	VS, GCC, ICC, Clang
27	tfshark	ELF	439	VS, GCC
28	dumpcap	ELF	448	VS, GCC
29	tshark	ELF	1008	VS, GCC
30	pageant	ELF	2212	VS, GCC

the debugging information. Our dataset is composed of open-source projects from SourceForge [34], and the GNU software repository [32]. We include multiple programs from the same project and compile them with different compilers in order to demonstrate the capability and efficiency of our system. Three projects are compiled with four compilers, eight projects are compiled with three compilers, and 19 projects are compiled with two compilers. The dependencies of the programs restrict us to compiling all the projects with the four compilers. Our dataset includes 17 of PE binaries and 13 of ELF binaries.

5.3.2   Accuracy Results of Sorting and Encryption Algorithms

We test the proposed technique, SIGMA, with variants of sorting algorithms and encryption algorithms in order to evaluate the effectiveness and correctness of the proposed method. We employed two variants for bubble sort, quick sort, merge sort, and heap sort functions, and two variants for each of the four encryption-related algorithms (e.g., RC4, MD5, Advanced Encryption Standard (AES), and the tiny encryption algorithm (TEA)). Using the proposed method, the similarity scores of these samples based on the graph edit distance are calculated as depicted in Fig. 5.11.

As illustrated in Fig. 5.11, we achieve promising results with about 80% similarity score pairs ranging from 0.42 to 1 between the functions variants. Furthermore, the similarity score on pairs ranging from 0 to 0.2 is only about 10%. The

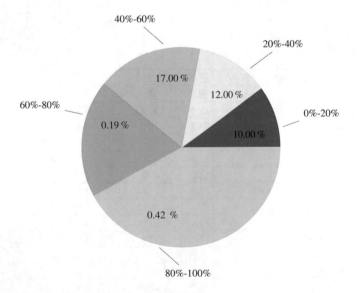

Fig. 5.11 Statistics of function variants similarities

results clearly show that our approach can capture common characteristics between functions relatively accurate. The occurrences of low-score pairs are mainly due to the significant differences in sizes of functions and variants, which result into different features, such as number of nodes, edges, and traces. For instance, the number of nodes in a bubble sort variant a is 15, whereas that of variant b is 22; the number of edges are 18 and 43, and the number of traces are 147 and 278, respectively.

The similarity scores of each pair of encryption functions are presented in Tables 5.8 and 5.9. The values (100%) in the main diagonal are the similarity scores for the variants when compared to themselves. As seen, the similarity scores among the sort functions are higher than those of encryption functions. This is due to the fact that the steps of sorting are similar among different algorithms but the steps of encryption functions vary significantly with each algorithm.

As shown in Table 5.8, the similarity score between heap and other sort algorithms is lower, because the steps of heap sort are significantly different from the other sorting algorithms steps.

Likewise, the similarity scores among encryption-related functions presented in Table 5.9 show that RC4 has a higher similarity to TEA than MD5, being similar to AES function. This is due to the fact that RC4 and TEA have common steps in the encryption process.

Table 5.8 Similarity between sort function variants

	Bubble.v1	Bubble.v2	Quick.v1	Quick.v2	Merge.v1	Merge.v2	Heap.v1	Heap.v2
Bubble.v1	100%	93%	71%	67%	62%	73%	65%	62%
Bubble.v2	96%	100%	79%	80%	70%	72%	60%	68%
Quick.v1	79%	83%	100%	94%	76%	71%	65%	60%
Quick.v2	71%	69%	95%	100%	79%	77%	74%	65%
Merge.v1	67%	76%	66%	68%	100%	97%	70%	74%
Merge.v2	73%	69%	77%	78%	94%	100%	70%	72%
Heap.v1	69%	67%	74%	73%	79%	79%	100%	96%
Heap.v2	72%	71%	64%	69%	79%	78%	95%	100%

Table 5.9 Similarity between encryption function variants

	RC4.v1	RC4.v2	TEA.v1	TEA.v2	MD5.v1	MD5.v2	AES.v1	AES.v2
RC4.v1	100%	86%	68%	57%	52%	61%	57%	62%
RC4.v2	89%	100%	74%	66%	53%	72%	50%	59%
TEA.v1	72%	79%	100%	87%	66%	61%	55%	67%
TEA.v2	68%	62%	89%	100%	72%	67%	69%	55%
MD5.v1	57%	69%	58%	51%	100%	91%	78%	74%
MD5.v2	63%	67%	67%	70%	92%	100%	78%	72%
AES.v1	69%	57%	64%	68%	79%	75%	100%	94%
AES.v2	62%	71%	69%	64%	70%	73%	89%	100%

We list the calculated dissimilarity scores between sorting algorithms and encryption algorithms in Table 5.10.

5.3.3 *Impact of Compilers and Compilation Settings*

As mentioned earlier, we compile 30 projects using different compilers. We evaluate the accuracy of our system in detecting the similarities among different binary code samples using the F_1 score. Table 5.11 summarizes the results. As seen, the average F_1 score is 0.78, while the precision ranges from 0.60 to 0.90, and the recall ranges from 0.64 to 0.92.

The accuracy results to identify C++ programs are higher than that of the C programs. This is expected since C++ programs contain classes with small-size methods, which are mostly unaffected by compilers or compilation settings; however, they may be inlined. Moreover, C programmers are not constrained by the object-oriented paradigm and often place functions with different semantics in the same source file. For instance the function `tfshark.c` in the `tfshark` project combines string processing, message processing (read/write/print), along

Table 5.10 Dissimilarity between sort and encryption functions

	Bubble.v1	Quick.v1	Merge.v1	Heap.v1
RC4.v1	86%	93%	79%	87%
TEA.v1	96%	91%	79%	89%
MD5.v1	79%	88%	90%	94%
AES.v1	89%	91%	95%	84%

Table 5.11 Our system accuracy in determining the similarity between binaries

Library	Precision	Recall	F_1	Library	Precision	Recall	F_1
SQlite	0.75	0.88	0.81	tinyXMLTest	0.72	0.79	0.75
OpenSSL	0.72	0.66	0.69	libxml2	0.78	0.82	0.80
info-zip	0.68	0.9	0.77	Mersenne Twister	0.78	0.88	0.83
jabber	0.67	0.88	0.76	bzip2	0.82	0.9	0.86
Hashdeep	0.63	0.72	0.67	lshw	0.83	0.83	0.83
libpng	0.82	0.68	0.74	smartctl	0.89	0.92	0.90
ultraVNC	0.81	0.67	0.73	pdftohtml	0.85	0.75	0.80
lcms	0.75	0.66	0.70	ELF statifier	0.83	0.74	0.78
ibavcodec	0.77	0.81	0.79	FileZilla	0.90	0.92	0.90
TrueCrypt	0.90	0.88	0.89	ncat	0.72	0.71	0.71
libjsoncpp	0.85	0.67	0.75	Hasher	0.71	0.68	0.69
7z	0.74	0.77	0.73	tfshark	0.70	0.65	0.67
7zG	0.66	0.81	0.73	dumpcap	0.62	0.64	0.63
7zFM	0.66	0.82	0.76	tshark	0.60	0.68	0.64
lzip	0.66	0.9	0.75	pageant	0.67	0.67	0.67

with common functions for program output. These functions are technically similar in semantic representation, but the presence of all three reduces the F_1 score to 0.64 when using automated ground truth based on source files. Moreover, C programs have less modularity than C++ programs so it may be harder to extract the semantics of the code. SIGMA can identify FileZilla with the highest F_1 score of 0.90, while the dumpcap has the lowest F_1 score of 0.63.

5.3.4 Impact of Obfuscation and Refactoring Techniques

In this subsection, we apply obfuscation and refactoring techniques to demonstrate the accuracy of SIGMA. First, we consider a random set of 15 binary code samples from our dataset and compile them with Visual Studio 2010. The binaries are converted into assembly files through the disassembler, and the code is then obfuscated using the DaLin generator [196]. This generator applies the following light obfuscation: (1) Register renaming (RR), which is one of the oldest and simplest techniques used in metamorphic generators; (2) Instruction reordering (IR), which transposes instructions that do not depend on the output of previous instructions; (3) Dead-code insertion (DCI), which injects a piece of code that has no effect on program execution (i.e., may not execute or may execute with no effect); and (4) Equivalent instruction replacement (EIR). We perform initial tests on the selected files and report the accuracy measurements. Light obfuscation is then applied and new accuracy measurements are obtained and analyzed.

Moreover, we use existing open-source tools for the C++ refactoring process [30, 41]. We consider the techniques of (1) renaming a variable (RV), (2) moving a method from a superclass to its subclasses (MM), and (3) extracting a few statements and placing them into a new method (NM). In-depth explanations of these techniques are detailed in [140]. The results shown in Table 5.12 demonstrate that our system performs well in identifying similarities; however, we obtain lower accuracy when we apply refactoring as opposed to when we apply light obfuscation.

Table 5.12 Results after applying light obfuscation techniques and the refactoring process

Method	Precision	Recall	F_1
Register renaming (RR)	0.89	0.88	0.88
Instruction reordering (IR)	0.91	0.92	0.91
Dead-code insertion (DCI)	0.87	0.93	0.90
Equivalent instruction replacement (EIR)	0.81	0.82	0.81
Renaming a variable (RV)	0.87	0.90	0.88
Moving a method (MM)	0.85	0.82	0.83
New method (NM)	0.67	0.72	0.70

5.4   Limitations and Concluding Remarks

In this chapter, we presented a novel approach called SIGMA for effectively identifying reused functions in binary code. Instead of relying on one source of information, our approach combines multiple representations into one joint data structure called semantic integrated graph (SIG). SIGMA also supports inexact matching and exact matching based on traces of the SIG which deal with function fragments. The experimental results have demonstrated the effectiveness of the presented method.

Nonetheless, the approach has the following limitations, which are the subject of future work. (1) Similar to most existing approaches, SIGMA assumes that binary code is already de-obfuscated. However, SIGMA can in fact address certain forms of obfuscation, such as register reassignments and instruction reordering. (2) As a learning-based approach, SIGMA also requires training data of known functionalities with multiple variants in order to collect sufficient features prior to its application to a given code. To this end, building a feature database for common functionalities is desired. (3) The capability of the proposed method for dealing with fragments of functions has not been evaluated.

Chapter 6
Function Fingerprinting

Binary code fingerprinting is a challenging problem that requires an in-depth analysis of binary components for deriving identifiable signatures. In this chapter, we present a binary function fingerprinting framework called BINSIGN. The main objective is to provide an accurate and scalable solution to binary code fingerprinting by computing and matching structural and syntactic code profiles for disassemblies. We describe the proposed methodology and evaluate its performance in several use cases, including function reuse, malware analysis, and indexing scalability.

This chapter is organized as follows. In Sect. 6.1, we present an overview of the proposed approach and then introduce the threat model. In Sect. 6.2, we provide the details of the fingerprinting and detection approaches. Section 6.3 presents the evaluation results. Finally, Sect. 6.4 concludes this chapter.

6.1 Introduction

Reverse engineering is a common approach to recover design-level abstractions from an unknown (target) code or system in order to understand, as much as possible, its functionality, architecture, and the inner workings of its internal components [279]. Most of the time, the target system is represented by a binary program, consisting of a set of modules, instructions, basic blocks, data and code sequences. The reverse engineering process entails a series of interleaving steps for static and dynamic analyses [266]. During the initial phases of this process, efforts are made for obtaining essential information about the potential capabilities and objectives of the binary sample. One benefit of this information is in pinpointing the target of suspicious code and directing the detection and mitigation processes of infected systems [241].

One of the critical topics in computer security is malware analysis [76, 124, 220, 273, 297]. It has gained unprecedented attention due to an ever increasing

© Springer Nature Switzerland AG 2020
S. Alrabaee et al., *Binary Code Fingerprinting for Cybersecurity*, Advances in Information Security 78, https://doi.org/10.1007/978-3-030-34238-8_6

array of cyber threats. Over the past few years, the number and complexity of malware attacks witnessed a significant growth. Almost 431 million new malware variants were uncovered in 2015 [7]. In order to address and remediate the emerging threats, advanced techniques and tools are required to support automated reverse engineering and malware analysis. One example of such techniques is binary fingerprinting.

Although clone detection is one application of function fingerprinting, it can be used for several other purposes. Another advantage of binary fingerprinting is the ability to share information about a binary function by sharing the fingerprint without the need to share the binary piece of code itself since a binary function fingerprint conveys valuable information that describes different aspects of the function.

The main objective of this chapter consists in defining an approach for binary function fingerprinting and matching. This is achieved by designing an approach that integrates important features of binary functions to produce a meaningful function fingerprint. Additionally, the approach should allow for matching a target fingerprint against a large repository of fingerprints and calculating a similarity score between two fingerprints.

6.1.1   Overview

An effective fingerprinting approach should construct a unique, compact representation of the binary function functionality. Similar fingerprints should be assigned to binary functions with similar functionalities. In addition, the generated fingerprint must be robust to byte-level discrepancies and tolerant of variations in the structure of basic blocks, call graphs, and control flow graphs. Moreover, the probability of generating the same fingerprint for two different functions with different functionalities must be negligible. Thus, in this chapter, we present BINSIGN, a framework for binary function fingerprinting. The framework consists of two main components: (1) Fingerprint generation and indexing in a scalable manner. (2) Fingerprint matching against an existing database of fingerprints.

The fingerprint is generated based on a collection of features that are extracted from an assembly function as a whole (global features). These features are combined with features that convey structural information from the CFG of a function by dividing the CFG into tracelets that carry semantic information while allowing the approach to be more scalable than an approach that considers all CFG paths. As such, BINSIGN fingerprints capture not only the syntactic information of a function, but also its semantics and underlying structure. Figure 6.1 depicts a high-level overview of the BINSIGN system.

In order to achieve effective scalability in fingerprint matching, we design and implement an efficient fingerprint matching framework to match a target fingerprint against a large repository of fingerprints. In order to avoid pairwise comparison of a large volume of fingerprints, we use three mechanisms to assist in attaining

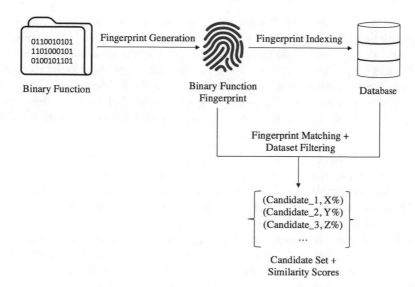

Fig. 6.1 BINSIGN system

a matching process that is scalable. The first mechanism is leveraging locality sensitive hashing (LSH) [192] combined with min-hashing [65] to select fingerprint candidates. The second mechanism is applying a filter to further prune the search space based on the number of basic blocks of the CFG of the binary function. It is highly unlikely for a pair of functions to match if the difference in the number of their basic blocks is significant. The third mechanism is distributing the computation on several machines using RabbitMQ [11] in order to boost the performance and scalability even more. BINSIGN framework computes the similarity scores between the target function and each selected candidate using Jaccard similarity [192]. To improve the accuracy of the matching process, the features of the fingerprint are ranked and weighted according to their significance. These weights are used while calculating the similarity score of two fingerprints.

6.1.2   Threat Model

In-Scope Threats: We design BINSIGN for the purpose of facilitating the reverse engineering process and helping the reverse engineer throughout the process. By matching binary function fingerprints, BINSIGN can assist in multiple processes associated with reverse engineering including compiler identification, clone detection, library function identification, code similarity, malware detection and classification, provenance analysis, vulnerability detection, and authorship attribution among other uses. BINSIGN is designed to be resilient to changes in the binary code such as those introduced into the code by the use of different compilers and selecting different optimization levels when compiling the code. Moreover, the fingerprinting and matching techniques are also designed to be resilient to any light obfuscation methods that do not alter in a major way the structure of the function CFG and/or the binary instructions in its code. These light obfuscation techniques include register replacement, register reassignment, dead-code insertion, and code substitution among others. Name stripping and removal of symbolic information (stripped binaries), for instance, are other factors that do not affect the proposed fingerprinting and matching processes.

Out-of-Scope Threats: The use of BINSIGN as a tool is not intended for replacing the reverse engineering process entirely, but just to assist and support it. Some binary code, such as malware, is often packed or encrypted to avoid inspection by anti-virus software. In order to analyze and examine such pieces of code, various unpacking techniques can be used [71, 104]. Obfuscation methods also pose a challenge against reverse engineers who attempt to analyze an obfuscated piece of code. Automated tools have been developed that implement several de-obfuscation techniques [257, 281]. However, unpacking and de-obfuscating a piece of code lie outside the scope of our considered threat model. We assume the binary code is already unpacked and de-obfuscated before going through the proposed fingerprint generation or matching processes. Moreover, our fingerprinting methodology is not designed to be resilient to any heavy obfuscation techniques, which result in significant modifications in the structure of a function CFG or heavily changed instructions of a binary function. Therefore, a function would not be successfully matched after going through heavy obfuscation (such as control flow flattening or extensive instruction substitution).

6.2 Function Fingerprinting

6.2.1 Feature Extraction

A fingerprint provides valuable insights regarding a binary piece of code. These insights should not only cover the syntactic elements of a code fragment but should also capture its semantics and underlying structure. Thus, it is important to select the suitable set of assembly features that characterizes the essential semantics and functionality of programs. Also, certain factors, such as name stripping and removal of symbolic information can eliminate access to some features thus complicating the matching process.

Indeed, some features such as strings and function names are unavailable in stripped binary files. In order to overcome these complications, the semantics of code operations are captured by analyzing mnemonic groups and operand types even if the symbols are stripped. Feature-driven fingerprint generation entails several steps of feature extraction and normalization. Each function fingerprint includes a feature vector $\mathbf{v}_{f_i} \in \mathbf{V}$ that captures all the available features of a function f_i in the form of key/value pairs (k_i, v_i). Choosing the right combination of features that carry enough code semantics has a direct impact on the fingerprinting results and fingerprint matching accuracy. In what follows, we present the features considered by the BINSIGN fingerprint.

The features are extracted at two different levels from a binary function, namely global features and tracelet features. Features that describe each individual basic block such as the instructions and constants are extracted from each block and then are combined together to form the tracelet features. Therefore, the structural information of the function CFG is captured through these tracelet features. Table 6.1 depicts the list of extracted tracelet features.

However, features that occur once per function and describe the function as a whole (such as the return type, number of arguments, and function size, for example) constitute the global features. The extracted global features are listed in Table 6.2. Some features are considered to be common to both tracelet features and global features as well. For instance, the number of instructions in each basic block is extracted as a tracelet feature and the total number of instructions of the function is extracted as a global feature.

During the feature extraction process, functions are examined in different layers. Each group of features encapsulates lower level features into higher levels of abstractions. We take into consideration the following groups of information, each of which describes a different aspect of an assembly function during the feature extraction and fingerprint generation processes. In the following, we describe the groups of features in more detail.

Table 6.1 Tracelet features

Feature	Example
Data constants	Constants
	Strings
	Number of constants
	Number of strings
Tracelet information	Number of instructions
	Number of operands
	Code Refs.
	Number of code Refs.
	Function calls
	Number of function calls
	Imported functions
	Number of imported functions
Functionality tags	Number of API tags
	Number of library tags
	Number of mnemonic groups

Table 6.2 Global features

Feature	Example
Data constants	Number of constants
	Number of strings
Prototypes	Return type
	Arguments
	Number of arguments
	Size of arguments
Function information	Number of instructions
	Size of local variables
	Function flags
	Number of code Refs.
	Number of function calls
	Number of imported functions
	Size of function
	Number of basic blocks
	Tracelets
	Number of tracelets
Functionality tags	Number of API tags
	Number of library tags
	Number of mnemonic groups

6.2.1.1   Characterization of Function Prototype

A function prototype provides meaningful information about the function, such as the return type, and the number, size, and types of arguments. Therefore, we consider this information provided by the prototype in the feature extraction and fingerprint generation processes.

6.2.1.2   Composition of CFG Instructions

This group of features captures information describing the CFG structure and instructions in its basic blocks such as the number of basic blocks, number of tracelets, as well as the number and types of instructions that appear in each basic block. The mnemonic and operand features of each instruction are extracted and normalized.

The normalized mnemonics act as generalized representations of assembly instructions. In these generalized instructions, the operands are numbered according to their types. For instance, general register operands ($reg : eax...edx$) are coded as 1, memory references (mem) are coded as 2, immediate values (imm) are coded as 5, and so on. The mnemonics list is then reduced to a compact form following a frequency analysis: the number of occurrences of each assembly instruction and the total number of calls to registers and memory addresses are calculated.

Table 6.3 Mnemonic groups

Mnemonic group	Mnemonics
Data transfer	`mov, xchg, cmpxchg, movz, movzx, movs, movsx, movsb, movsw`
Data comparison	`cmp, cpx, cpy, test, cmn, teq, tst`
Logical operations	`xor, or, and, not`
Stack operations	`push, pop, pushf, popf, pusha, popa, pushad, popad`
Flag manipulation	`sti, cli , std, cld, stc, clc, cmc, sahf, lahf, popfw, popf, popflq, popfl, pushfw, pushf, pushflq, pushfl`
Binary arithmetic	`sub, add, inc, dec, mul, div, shl, sal, sar, shr, ror, rcl, rcr, rol`
Control transfer	`jz, jnz, je, jne, jg, jge, ja, jae, jl, jle, jb, jbe, jo, jno, jc, jnc, js, jns, jecxz`
Floating operations	`fbld, fbstp, fcmovb, fcmovbe, fcmove, fcmovnb, fcmovnbe, fcmovne, fcmovnu, fcmovu, fild, fist, fistp, fld, fst, fstp, fxch, fabs, fadd, faddp, fchs, fdiv, fdivr, fdivrp, fiadd, fidiv, fidivr, fimul, fisub, fisubr, fmul, fmulp, fprem, fprem1, frndint, fscale, fsqrt, fsub, fsubp, fsubr, fsubrp, fxtract, fcom, fcomi, fcomip, fcomp, fcompp, ficom, ficomp, ftst, fucom, fucomi, fucomip, fucomp, fucompp, fxam, f2xm1, fcos, fpatan, fptan, fsin, fsincos, fyl2x, fyl2xp1, fld1, fldl2e, fldl2t, fldlg2, fldln2, fldpi, fldz, fclex, fdecstp, ffree, fincstp, finit, fldcw, fldenv, fnclex, fninit, fnop, fnsave, fnstcw, fnstenv, fnstsw, frstor, fsave, fstcw, fstenv, fstsw, fwait`
String manipulation	`cmps, cmpsq, cmpsb, cmpsd, cmpsl, cmpsw, lods, lodsq, lodsb, lodsl, lodsd, lodsw, movs, movsq, movsb, movsl, movsd, smovl, movsw, smovw, scas, scasq, scasb, scasl, scasd, scasw, stos, stosq, stosb, stosl, stosd, stosw`
Repeat operations	`rep, repe, repz, repne, repnz`
Call operation	`call`
Jump operation	`jmp`
Halt operation	`hlt`
Load operations	`lea, les`
Interrupt system	`Mnemonics with sys_ prefix`

Following this step, the instruction mnemonics are classified into 15 groups according to their operation group. Table 6.3 lists these mnemonic groups and the mnemonics that belong to each of them. After that, the total number of instructions and the distinct number of instructions of each mnemonic group are computed. Any data constants and strings that occur in these instructions as operands are also captured in the fingerprint as well as the local variables.

6.2.1.3 Types of Function Calls

The number and types of function calls that take place in the code of a binary function represent the other features that are considered. System and API calls are important features that need to be taken into account for inexact pattern matching since they are good indicators of the code functionality. Examples of API categories are shown in Table 6.4.

Each function can be classified based on its execution outcome on a target system. System calls are considered as interaction points with the operating system. Therefore, they provide valuable information on the potential runtime behavior and functionality of the function. These system and API calls are used to allocate functionality tags to the function.

Functionality tags are code annotations that are allocated to code fragments in a function and convey a high-level description of the code context and side effects. Functionality tags are useful for fast identification and localization of particular groups of operations in disassemblies. Assigning context-based tags to assembly-level functions provides many benefits when statically analyzing the binary function. Functionality tags provide hints to the reverse engineer about the potential computations that may take place in a certain function. As described in [241], a function is given multiple tags if it contains multiple system calls. When combined with cross referencing of code and data, the tags can be used for semantic code search and for tracking code functionality.

For instance, finding crypto-related keys is an important step in malware reverse engineering. Hence, automatic assignment of crypto-related functionality tags (e.g., CRY, HSH, CER) to disassembly functions could limit the search space, reduce the amount of manual work, and highlight the most likely code fragments to look for keys. Combinations of different functionality tags provide a description of the overall functionality of the code regions and highlight the sequence of actions carried out to perform the functionality (e.g., CRY+FIL+NET is translated into crypto-operations on a file, followed by network communication).

Table 6.4 Examples of API categories

Category	API functions
File	CreateFileMapping, GetFileAttributes, ReplaceFile
Network	gethostbyname, getaddrinfo, recv, WSAAccept
Registry	RegCreateKey, RegQueryValue, SHRegSetPath
Crypto	CryptGenKey, CryptSetKey, CryptDecodeObject
Service	QueryServiceLockStatus, SetServiceObjectSecurity
Memory	VirtualAlloc, VirtualUnlock, ReadProcessMemory

6.2.2 Fingerprint Generation

This subsection is dedicated to describing the details of the steps involved in the fingerprint generation process. Our approach for generating binary function fingerprints is depicted in Fig. 6.2. The approach consists of four steps: (1) Disassembling the binary file and extracting the function CFG, (2) tracelet generation from function CFG, (3) global feature and tracelet feature extraction, and (4) feature min-hashing. In the following, we describe each of these steps in more detail.

6.2.2.1 Disassembling and CFG Extraction

A significant aspect of our proposed methodology is related to generating fingerprints for functions in the binary format. To this end, we introduce a function fingerprinting approach for the generation and matching of abstracted representations from assembly functions. This approach enables us to fingerprint structural and syntactic function properties. The first step is to disassemble the binary file using the disassembler IDA Pro [45]. Each disassembled binary executable file contains a set of assembly functions. We consider the function CFG to capture the structural information of a function. Each node in a CFG of a function represents a basic block and each edge denotes a branching instruction that results in a jump from one basic block in the CFG to another. CFGs are important because they capture syntactic elements (assembly instructions in basic blocks) and relationships (jumps/calls) between basic blocks.

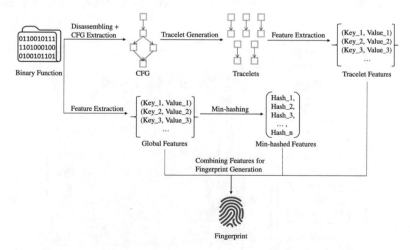

Fig. 6.2 Fingerprint generation process

6.2.2.2   Tracelet Generation

As mentioned previously, one of the main intentions of BINSIGN is to capture the core CFG structure of the functions in addition to the syntactic information. To this end, we decompose the CFG into traces of execution and extract features from the CFG traces. The aim is to include information about all possible execution traces of a function. It is computationally expensive to obtain information about all possible paths of a CFG, especially for extremely large functions. Furthermore, it would be redundant and space consuming to consider the information captured from repeated nodes that are common between different paths multiple times. In order to counter these issues, we adopt the idea presented in [112], by decomposing each CFG into partial traces of execution, namely tracelets. In [112], tracelets are used after the instructions are put through a simple rewriting engine for the purpose of code search in order to find similar functions in a code base.

For our purposes however, we use the tracelets as part of the fingerprint that represents a binary function. Each tracelet is only considered once in the fingerprint and is not repeated. In BINSIGN, tracelets include two basic blocks. Therefore, every edge in the CFG of a function results in one tracelet. An alternative would be to consider a larger number of basic blocks in a tracelet. However, that would result in repetitive information without offering any further benefits. Including only two basic blocks allows us to generate tracelets more efficiently, without losing any functionality information since all CFG nodes and edges are visited at least once and the information they provide is captured in the fingerprint.

For example, consider the CFG presented in Fig. 6.3. The CFG consists of five basic blocks that are connected by means of six edges. Therefore, information describing six distinct tracelets would be included in the fingerprint of the binary

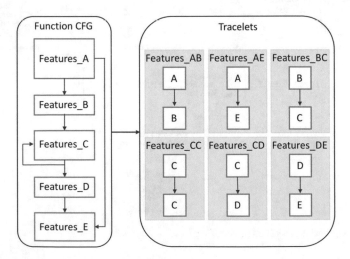

Fig. 6.3 Example of tracelet generation

function represented by this CFG. Following the labelling of the basic blocks as in Fig. 6.3, the generated tracelets can be summarized by a set of pairs of basic blocks as follows: $\{(A, B), (A, E), (B, C), (C, C), (C, D), (D, E)\}$. It is worth noting that the CFG contains a loop at the basic block labelled as C. The loop is traversed only once when decomposing the CFG into a set of tracelets.

6.2.2.3 Feature Extraction

After function disassembly, CFG extraction, and decomposition into tracelets, the features previously mentioned in Sect. 6.2.1 are extracted. These features are then combined to form the global features and tracelet features. The global features are extracted once from the function as a whole, and the tracelet features are extracted from the basic blocks of each tracelet. The collection of these features aggregates a descriptive fingerprint that contains a significant amount of valuable information about the binary function.

6.2.2.4 Signature Hashing

We take advantage of the *min-hashing* technique [65] to represent the signature in a compact way. Min-hashing is a technique that is used to reduce the dimensionality of a set of values using a number of hash functions. The algorithm for generating the signature hash takes, as input, an assembly function and produces, as output, the hash of the function's signature.

It is important to mention that the min-hashing process is not applicable to all the features being extracted, i.e., it is restricted to the numerical features. Therefore, we do not apply min-hashing to all the extracted features. Instead, min-hashing is applied to the normalized instructions of the assembly function. The normalized instructions construct an appropriate representation of the binary function's functionality and can be used effectively later on to filter the functions in the dataset during the fingerprint matching process to acquire a candidate set of fingerprints that are most similar to the target function's fingerprint.

Each instruction in the function's binary code is normalized by encoding the operands using numbers that represent the type of the operand. After normalizing the instructions of a binary function, each hash function is used to hash all normalized instructions and we select the minimum resulting hash value. Several random seeds are used in combination with the MD5 hash function in order to produce many different hash functions for the min-hashing process. The seeds are random numbers that are generated in advance. The same seeds are used every time a new fingerprint is generated. This is necessary for the signature hashes of different fingerprints to be comparable to each other.

After conducting several experiments, we select 210 hash functions to be used in the min-hashing process to generate the signature. Our experiments show that this is a suitable number of hash functions to generate an effective signature. The collection

Table 6.5 Example of signature hash generation

Instructions	HashFunction$_1$	HashFunction$_2$	...	HashFunction$_m$
Inst$_1$	123	2	...	705
Inst$_2$	294	946	...	60
Inst$_3$	874	212	...	381
Inst$_4$	42	100	...	529
Inst$_5$	509	87	...	91
Inst$_6$	15	446	...	173
...	...	...	...	...
Inst$_n$	39	568	...	446

of the minimum hash values resulting from hashing the normalized instructions using all the hash functions represents the signature hash. In other words, the signature hash consists of a vector of m min-hash values, where m is the number of hash functions. In Sect. 6.2.3, we describe how this min-hash signature is used in the fingerprint matching process in order to filter the functions in the dataset and acquire a candidate set.

Table 6.5 shows an example of the process of deriving the hash signature of a function from its normalized instructions. Each row in the table represents one normalized instruction and each column represents one hash function derived from the hash function MD5 using different seeds. Each cell in the table holds a hash value resulting from hashing the normalized instruction in the left most cell of the row using the hash function at the top of the column. The number of instructions in this example is denoted by n and the number of hash functions is denoted by m. In order to generate the signature hash for this example, the minimum hash value from each column is selected. Therefore, the signature hash can be represented through the following list of hash values: $[15, 2, \ldots, 60]$. This list is of length m.

6.2.2.5   Fingerprint Components

The fingerprint generated through BINSIGN methodology is composed of three different parts. As depicted in Fig. 6.2, the parts that make up a fingerprint in BINSIGN are: (1) the function global features, (2) the tracelet features, and (3) the signature hash of the normalized instructions. Having different types of features as part of the fingerprint allows the resulting fingerprint to carry various information about the syntax, semantics, structure, and functionality of a binary function.

The signature hash component of the fingerprint is mainly used in the fingerprint matching process in order to filter all the fingerprints in the dataset and acquire a candidate set. The similarity score is then calculated between each candidate fingerprint in the candidate set and the target fingerprint based on how similar the function global features and tracelet features are. Moreover, BINSIGN fingerprints can additionally be used to share information about a binary function without sharing the actual binary code of the function, by just sharing the fingerprint. The normalized instructions are only used to generate the signature hash values without being stored as part of the fingerprint. Therefore, the instructions are not leaked when sharing a function fingerprint. After generating the fingerprints, the functions are indexed in parallel into a *Cassandra* [2] database.

The CFG of a sample function is depicted in Fig. 6.4. The details of the function fingerprint are shown in Table 6.6. In this example, features with the value 0 and empty lists are not included in Table 6.6 for simplicity purposes. In the tracelet features, the features of each basic block are enclosed between the symbols "{" and "}". Each tracelet includes two basic blocks, which are separated by the symbol "-".

6.2.3 Fingerprint Matching

The fingerprint matching process aims at recognizing target functions and identifying functions of a target disassembly that share similar features with fingerprints of other functions in the dataset. Figure 6.5 depicts an overview of BINSIGN matching process. Through the fingerprint matching process, a candidate set is selected from the entire dataset as being similar to the target fingerprint. Then, the similarity between each candidate fingerprint and the target fingerprint is computed. The fingerprints whose similarity lies above a certain threshold are then selected.

6.2.3.1 Fingerprint Candidate Selection

In order to select a candidate set when matching a function fingerprint and reduce false positives, two filtering methods are put in place: filtering based on the number of basic blocks and LSH [192]. First, the functions in the dataset are filtered by the number of basic blocks in the function CFG. We choose this filter because it is improbable for a function with a very small number of basic blocks to be a suitable match of a function with a significantly larger number of basic blocks. Accordingly, we set a threshold that is proportional to the number of basic blocks. More precisely, if the difference in the number of basic blocks between the target fingerprint and a fingerprint in the dataset is larger than 30% of the number of basic blocks of the target fingerprint, then the candidate function is filtered out and it is not considered as a candidate match.

Second, LSH is used in order to reduce the number of functions being considered. The min-hash signatures are divided into bands, where each band contains several hash values. A fingerprint from the dataset is selected as a candidate match to a target function if all its hash values equal the hash values of the target signature in at least one of the bands. Each band is used to create a query to obtain candidates. The final candidate set comprises the results of all the queries from all bands. For instance, in the illustrating example depicted in Fig. 6.6, $Signature_1$ and $Signature_n$ are selected as candidates since all the hash values of at least one of their bands

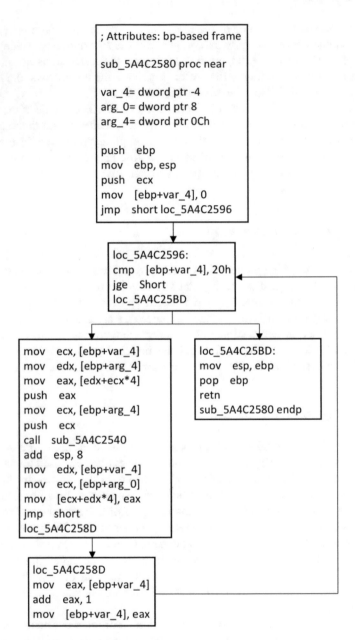

Fig. 6.4 Sample of a function CFG

Table 6.6 Example of a function fingerprint illustrated in Fig. 6.4

Feature	Function fingerprint
Global features	`[(function_name, sub_5A4C2580), (basic_blocks_number,` `5), (function_size, 65), (argument_size,8),` `(argument_number,2), (local_variables_size, 4), (flags,` `17424), (arguments, [dword, dword]), (return_type, None),` `(instructions_number, 29)]`
Tracelet features	`{instructions_number: 6, constants: [0L],` `mnemonic_groups: ['Stack', 'DataTransfer', 'Stack',` `'DataTransfer', 'Jump', 'DataTransfer'],` `constants_number: 1}, {instructions_number: 3, constants:` `[32L] , mnemonic_groups: ['Compare', 'Branch',` `'DataTransfer'], constants_number: 1} -` `{instructions_number: 4, constants: [1L, 32L],` `mnemonic_groups: ['DataTransfer', 'Arithmetic',` `'DataTransfer', 'Compare'], constants_number: 2},` `{instructions_number: 3, constants: [32L],` `mnemonic_groups: ['Compare', 'Branch', 'DataTransfer'],` `constants_number: 1} - {instructions_number: 3,` `constants: [32L], mnemonic_groups: ['Compare', 'Branch',` `'DataTransfer'], constants_number: 1},` `{instructions_number: 13, constants: [8L], calls:` `['sub_5A4C2540'], mnemonic_groups: ['DataTransfer',` `'DataTransfer', 'DataTransfer', 'Stack', 'DataTransfer',` `'Stack', 'Call', 'Arithmetic', 'DataTransfer',` `'DataTransfer', 'DataTransfer', 'Jump', 'DataTransfer'],` `constants_number: 1, calls_number: 1} -` `{instructions_number: 3, constants: [32L],` `mnemonic_groups: ['Compare', 'Branch', 'DataTransfer'],` `constants_number: 1}, {instructions_number: 3,` `mnemonic_groups: ['DataTransfer', 'Stack']} -` `{instructions_number: 13, constants: [8L], calls:` `['sub_5A4C2540'], mnemonic_groups: ['DataTransfer',` `'DataTransfer', 'DataTransfer', 'Stack', 'DataTransfer',` `'Stack', 'Call', 'Arithmetic', 'DataTransfer',` `'DataTransfer', 'DataTransfer', 'Jump', 'DataTransfer'],` `constants_number: 1, calls_number: 1},` `{instructions_number: 4, constants: [1L, 32L],` `mnemonic_groups: ['DataTransfer', 'Arithmetic',` `'DataTransfer', 'Compare'], constants_number: 2}`
Signature hash	`[6685L, 643L, 7535L, 462L, 6978L, 14480L, 2965L, 3813L,` `10682L, 1184L, 4993L, 21866L, 4582L, 19074L, 9137L, 694L,` `4819L, 4939L, 7646L, 10449L, 2242L, 9081L, 5877L, 2914L,` `3766L, 1061L, 3674L, 87L, 7301L, 13164L, 16519L, 7426L,` `11339L, 5366L, 1024L, 6416L, 8080L, 5980L, 3931L, 41L,` `5920L, 12543L, 10032L, 19143L, 4521L, 667L, 17382L, 630L,` `3476L, 6095L, 4708L, 4666L, 394L, 2075L, 6405L, 15590L,` `12420L, 4866L, 15238L, 9420L, 18267L, 500L, 6134L,` `11105L, 2414L, 10262L, 14855L, 6275L, 9454L, 702L, 5986L,`

(continued)

Table 6.6 (continued)

Feature	Function fingerprint
	7724L, 1326L, 3316L, 3595L, 5039L, 4919L, 13202L, 6449L, 581L, 10544L, 12750L, 558L, 9293L, 7255L, 3047L, 6526L, 2666L, 15273L, 3382L, 7677L, 9423L, 6666L, 8875L, 2222L, 19026L, 558L, 1534L, 5743L, 2865L, 14064L, 3086L, 6723L, 3701L, 6408L, 3412L, 23757L, 1205L, 2170L, 322L, 17558L, 6017L, 2229L, 3528L, 12931L, 1912L, 11654L, 4350L, 7752L, 4061L, 154L, 1108L, 1755L, 5416L, 16351L, 3334L, 7483L, 614L, 2818L, 1800L, 2185L, 12577L, 3171L, 4091L, 5375L, 6826L, 18492L, 11674L, 1332L, 521L, 9078L, 4934L, 3832L, 7271L, 18534L, 14107L, 468L, 731L, 9682L, 352L, 8749L, 14527L, 4195L, 13255L, 7341L, 2252L, 1526L, 4323L, 8914L, 4140L, 990L, 510L, 1427L, 18539L, 313L, 10923L, 2368L, 16289L, 2908L, 3866L, 3312L, 1799L, 4379L, 18681L, 6426L, 15823L, 3940L, 4604L, 565L, 100L, 863L, 4734L, 2423L, 1057L, 7348L, 11822L, 8594L, 838L, 7281L, 4429L, 184L, 5673L, 409L, 21617L, 18332L, 18251L, 11619L, 5693L, 2711L, 7436L, 880L, 14349L, 18036L, 8601L, 3447L, 6277L, 1848L, 7638L, 8870L, 12025L]

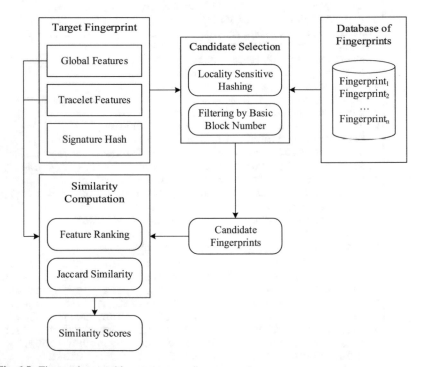

Fig. 6.5 Fingerprint matching process

		Target Signature	Signature₁	Signature₂	...	Signatureₙ
Band₁	Hash₁	1465	4486	145		**1465**
	Hash₂	614	614	56		**614**
	Hash₃	60	1715	478		**60**
Band₂	Hash₄	945	**945**	8675		45
	Hash₅	9247	**9247**	601		8965
	Hash₆	4559	**4559**	23775		2237
	...					
Bandₓ	Hashₘ₋₂	605	1908	12560		9458
	Hashₘ₋₁	190	25	7206		16759
	Hashₘ	3127	999	189		15

Fig. 6.6 Example of candidate selection. The boldfaced values represent the hashes that match with the corresponding band in the target signature

(*Band₂* of *Signature₁* and *Band₁* of *Signatureₙ*) match the hash values of the corresponding band in the target signature.

In order to reduce the number of false positives, we conduct extensive experiments to identify the best number and size of bands. The smaller the band size, the more inclusive the candidate set, which leads to more false positives. However, if the band size is too large, true matches with some modifications will not be included in the candidate set. We find via thorough experimentation that a band size of *seven* hash values and a total of *thirty* bands compose a fitting signature. This means that 210 different hash functions are used in the min-hashing process to generate the signature. LSH approximates the Jaccard similarity. This particular choice of band size and number of bands results in a similarity threshold of around 60%. As mentioned in [192] the threshold can be calculated as b represents the number of bands and r represents the size of each band. Therefore, fingerprints with a similarity score between the normalized instructions of less than 60% are not included in the candidate set of similar functions.

6.2.3.2 Fingerprint Similarity Computation

When matching a function fingerprint, we need to calculate the similarity between a pair of functions. Hence, a similarity score between the target fingerprint and each candidate fingerprint is calculated. The Jaccard similarity coefficient is used in order to calculate the similarity score between the target fingerprint and each candidate fingerprint. The Jaccard similarity between the global features of the target fingerprint and the candidate fingerprint is calculated and then combined with the Jaccard similarity between the tracelet features of both fingerprints. The combined Jaccard similarity coefficient of the global features and tracelet features is then considered to be the similarity score of the two fingerprints.

Table 6.7 Feature weights

Feature	Weight	Feature	Weight
Return type	1.0000	Out calls	0.9678
Arguments	1.0000	Number of out calls	0.9678
Tracelets	0.9815	Number of instructions	0.9644
Mnemonic group	0.9815	Number of operands	0.9644
Strings	0.9815	Number of basic blocks	0.9621
Constants	0.9815	Size of arguments	0.9528
Imports	0.9815	Number of arguments	0.9528
Number of imports	0.9815	Number of constants	0.9392
Number of tracelets	0.9787	Size of local variables	0.9230
Number of strings	0.9787	API tags	0.9230
Calls	0.9785	Function flags	0.1000
Number of calls	0.9785	Number of library tags	0.1000
Size of function	0.9691	Number of API tags	0.1000

Each feature affects the resulting similarity score differently since some features are more meaningful than others. Consequently, each feature is assigned a different weight as displayed in Table 6.7. The weights of the features are given after using WEKA [16] for ranking the features. WEKA provides implementations of a number of machine learning algorithms. The gain ratio attribute evaluation algorithm [176] is used through WEKA in order to rank the different features and assign weights to the features accordingly. The names of the functions used for feature ranking were known. Therefore, this is executed using supervised machine learning. All the considered features are extracted from each function in the dataset before ranking the features using the gain ratio attribute evaluation algorithm.

6.3   Evaluation

We perform several experiments in order to evaluate multiple aspects of BIN-SIGN methodologies including its accuracy, performance, and scalability. These experiments include function matching, function reuse detection, library function detection, malware similarity analysis, and function indexing scalability. We provide some insight into the effects of different compiler optimization levels and the use of some obfuscation techniques on the proposed fingerprint matching methodology. We also compare BINSIGN results with the results of other tools in terms of function matching. In the following, we discuss the experiments and results in detail.

6.3.1 Dataset Preparation

We apply our experiments on a dataset that consists of widely used, well-known libraries and malware samples. Table 6.8 summarizes the details of the functions included in our dataset.

The dataset includes different versions of the libraries: libpng, sqlite, and zlib, such as, libpng v.1.5.22, libpng v.1.6.17, sqlite 3.8.1, sqlite 3.8.9, zlib v.1.2.5, and zlib v.1.2.8. The dataset includes 16 different library files. These files are compiled using Visual Studio (MSVC) compilers 2010 and 2013. Zeus and Citadel botnet malware samples are also included in the dataset. The dataset includes 642 binary functions from Zeus and 896 binary functions from Citadel. We also include functions from the applications AdobeARM.exe, Cassandra.dll, and SFTP.exe as noise functions to increase the number of functions in the dataset. The total number of binary functions in the dataset is 23,569 functions. In order to evaluate the scalability of our system, we add dynamic library system functions files obtained from Microsoft Windows operating system to generate fingerprints for 6 million functions.

Table 6.8 Dataset details

Binary type	File name	Number of functions	Size
Library functions	libpng1.5.22-MSVC2010	525	250 KB
	libpng1.5.22-MSVC2013	539	257 KB
	libpng1.6.17-MSVC2010	604	277 KB
	libpng1.6.17-MSVC2013	620	285 KB
	sqlite3.8.1-MSVC2010	2290	965 KB
	sqlite3.8.1-MSVC2013	2308	1.006 MB
	sqlite3.8.9-MSVC2010	1460	525 KB
	sqlite3.8.9-MSVC2013	1471	565 KB
	zlib1.2.5-MSVC2010	164	92 KB
	zlib1.2.5-MSVC2013	169	93 KB
	zlib1.2.6-MSVC2010	179	92 KB
	zlib1.2.6-MSVC2013	183	93 KB
	zlib1.2.7-MSVC2010	174	92 KB
	zlib1.2.7-MSVC2013	178	93 KB
	zlib1.2.8-MSVC2010	174	92 KB
	zlib1.2.8-MSVC2013	178	93 KB
Malware samples	Citadel	896	4.505 MB
	Zeus	642	2.705 MB
Noise functions	Cassandra	5493	1.39 MB
	SFTP	620	207 KB
	AdobeARM	4702	1.01 MB
Total:	–	23,569	14.687 MB

6.3.2   Comparison with Existing Tools

We perform this experiment in order to compare the accuracy of BINSIGN against
DIAPHORA [5] and PATCHDIFF2 [10] when used to match similar functions. Both
tools DIAPHORA and PATCHDIFF2 are IDA Pro plugins for comparing binary files.
After comparing two binary files, the tools produce a mapping between the similar
functions of the two files. In this experiment, we compare two versions of the
same binary file. For each function in the target binary file, we use BINSIGN to
match that target function with the corresponding function in the other binary file
such that the matching function is the one with the highest similarity score on top
of the candidate set. DIAPHORA offers different options. We deactivate unreliable
methods. We assume that function names are not available during the matching
process. Therefore, we activate the option of ignoring the function names. We only
use the function names as the ground truth for verification purposes.

To perform this experiment, we use the binary files resulting from compiling
the libraries `libpng`, `sqlite`, and `zlib` using two compilers: MSVC 2010
and MSVC 2013 compilers. In this manner, some differences are introduced by the
compilers between the binary functions. After that, we match the functions in the
binary file compiled by MSVC 2010 as the target set. We match each function by
selecting the candidate function with the highest similarity score to that specific
function. The function names in both binary files are stripped away during this
experiment and are not used as part of the matching process. However, we verify
the correct matches using the function names in the program debug database as the
ground truth. If the candidate with the highest similarity score does not have the
same name as the target function, we examine both functions manually in order to
determine whether the function is the correct match or not.

We display the results of the comparison in Table 6.9. The percentage of the
correctly matched functions to the total number of functions being matched in the
binary file represents the accuracy. The accuracy of DIAPHORA when matching
these library files ranges between 44.12% and 65.81%. The resulting accuracy

Table 6.9 Function matching comparison

Tool Name	Library	# Target functions	# Correct matches	Accuracy
DIAPHORA	`libpng`	620	408	65.81%
	`sqlite`	1489	657	44.12%
	`zlib`	156	79	50.64%
PATCHDIFF2	`libpng`	620	510	82.26%
	`sqlite`	1489	937	62.92%
	`zlib`	156	122	78.21%
BINSIGN	`libpng`	620	553	**89.19%**
	`sqlite`	1489	1391	**93.42%**
	`zlib`	156	134	**85.90%**

The bold values demonstrate BINSIGN achieves the highest accuracy in this experiment.

of PATCHDIFF2 when matching these files ranges between 68.92% and 82.26%. BINSIGN achieves an accuracy that ranges between 85.90% and 93.42% when matching these binary files. Table 6.9 shows that BINSIGN consistently achieves the highest accuracy in this experiment. This is because BINSIGN is using a fuzzy technique for matching fingerprints. Therefore, BINSIGN is more lenient when comparing functions with modifications introduced by different compilers.

6.3.3 Function Reuse Detection

Through this experiment, we attempt to detect reused functions. The function reuse detection is performed between different versions of the same library and between different libraries. Different versions of the well-known zlib library are used for this experiment. The experiment is performed using versions 1.2.5, 1.2.6, 1.2.7, and 1.2.8 of this library. In order to detect reused functions between different libraries, we also use version 1.6.17 of the libpng library. Each fingerprint in the dataset must pass through two filters in order to be considered in the candidate set. Therefore, only functions with the number of basic blocks similar enough to the candidate function and with a similar min-hash signature to the one of the target function are included in the candidate set. We perform this experiment using different similarity thresholds for the hash signature to analyze how this change affects the accuracy of the matching process. As mentioned previously in Sect. 6.2.3.1, an approximation of the threshold is calculated as b represents the number of bands and r represents the size of each band. Therefore, we set the threshold one time at 60% (30 bands with 7 hash values in each band) and another time at 65% (30 bands with 8 hash values in each band). This experiment was performed on a PC with an Intel Core i7 CPU 920 @2.67 GHz and 12 GB of RAM running Microsoft Windows 7 64-bit.

6.3.3.1 Function Reuse Between Zlib Versions

In this experiment, we attempt to match the functions with the same symbolic name since we assume they perform similar functionality throughout the different versions of the library. Each version is used to attempt to match the corresponding functions in its consecutive version of the library. The function is correctly matched if the candidate function with the highest similarity score is the corresponding function in the other version of the library. If the candidate with the highest similarity score does not have the same name as the target function, we examine both functions manually in order to determine if the function is reused or not.

The results of this experiment are shown in Table 6.10. The accuracy is calculated by finding the percentage of the correctly matched functions to the total number of functions in the binary file. It is worth mentioning that although the accuracy is computed using the total number of functions in each binary file, not all functions

Table 6.10 Results of function reuse detection

Library versions	#Target functions	LSH-Threshold	Accuracy	#Candidates	Average time
zlib1.2.5-zlib1.2.6	169	60%	89.47%	24,970	3.9 s
		65%	78.11%	11372	2.8 s
zlib1.2.6-zlib1.2.7	183	60%	94.67%	30,881	3.7 s
		65%	90.71%	14,947	2.5 s
zlib1.2.7-zlib1.2.8	178	60%	98.79%	26,965	4.5 s
		65%	88.76%	12,003	3.7 s
zlib1.2.8-libpng1.6.17	52	60%	100%	4474	4.7 s
		65%	100%	2147	4.4 s

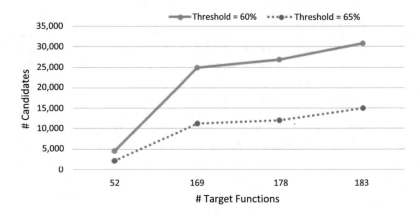

Fig. 6.7 Number of target functions vs. number of candidate functions

are necessarily being reused in the consecutive version of the library. The number of candidates displayed in Table 6.10 shows the sum of the sizes of all the candidate sets acquired when matching all target fingerprints. In other words, the number of candidates represents the number of functions with fingerprints that passed through the two filters: number of basic block filtering and LSH. The average time denotes the average time it takes for matching each function and acquiring a candidate set. As we can see from the results, changing the LSH threshold from 60% to 65% decreases the accuracy score. This is expected since increasing the threshold can result in a true match being filtered out by the LSH filter.

A plot of the number of target functions against the total number of candidates is presented in Fig. 6.7 when the LSH threshold is set to 60% and 65%. We can see that as the number of functions being matched increases, the total number of candidates also increases as expected. However, there are other factors that affect the total number of candidates. The size of the target functions is one of these factors. This is because smaller functions usually contain less distinctive features. As a result, a smaller target function tends to have a larger candidate set, which increases the total number of candidates. The total number of candidates depends on the characteristics and size of the target functions as well as on the number of

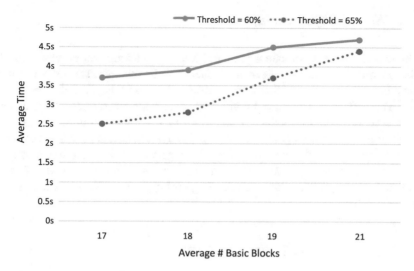

Fig. 6.8 Impact of number of basic blocks on the matching time

target functions. It is clear that the slope decreases in Fig. 6.7. Therefore, we can deduce that a further increase in the number of target functions results in a smaller increase in the total number of candidates.

The effect of the number of basic blocks of the target functions on the matching time is shown in Fig. 6.8. Computing the similarity scores between the target function and each candidate function is where most of the time is spent. A smaller portion of that time is spent on obtaining the candidate set. Consequently, the matching time is affected by the number of candidates and the size of the functions. The larger the functions being compared, the more time it requires for the matching process to be completed. It is also clear that the slope decreases in Fig. 6.8. Therefore, we can deduce that a further increase in the number of basic blocks of the target functions results in a smaller increase in the matching time.

6.3.3.2   Function Reuse Between Libraries

We also attempt to match reused functions from the zlib library in the libpng library as shown in the last row of Table 6.10. IDA Pro identifies 178 binary functions in version 1.2.8 of the zlib library and 620 binary functions in version 1.6.17 of the libpng library. We inspect the functions in both libraries manually and identify 52 reused functions. We use BINSIGN to attempt to match these functions from zlib as our target functions. BINSIGN is able to identify all 52 functions successfully with similarity scores ranging from 60% to 100%. In this case, changing the threshold does not affect the accuracy of the matching process since the correct matches still pass the filter even after modifying the size of the bands in the LSH filter.

6.3.4   Scalability Evaluation

In this experiment, we evaluate the scalability of the indexing process of fingerprints of binary functions into the *Cassandra* database. To this end, we index 6 million binary functions using BINSIGN and measure the time that the indexing process takes. These functions include library functions, malware samples, and dynamic library system functions obtained from *Microsoft Windows* operating system.

Before each function is indexed into the database, various features are extracted from the function and the function fingerprint is generated. The resulting fingerprint is then stored in the database. The indexing process takes around 0.0072 s per function on average. This time includes fingerprint generation and communication with the database.

6.3.4.1   Fingerprint Methodology Scalability

Our fingerprinting methodology takes into consideration scalability when generating the fingerprint. This is accomplished through the min-hashing process. The scalability is improved by selecting a candidate set through the banding technique as described in Sect. 6.2.3.1. Only candidates that are selected through the proposed min-hashing and LSH filter and the number of basic blocks filter are considered (instead of performing brute force matching) in order to speed up the matching process. Therefore, the similarity score is calculated only between the candidate fingerprints that pass through these filters and the target fingerprint being matched.

6.3.4.2   Implementation Scalability

In order to improve the scalability of BINSIGN, we implement a distribution mechanism using a message queuing software, namely *RabbitMQ* [11]. The latter is an open-source software that is implemented based on the international standard advanced message queuing protocol (AMQP) [1]. We find that a messaging mechanism is suitable because of its simplicity. Other, more complex distribution frameworks require a lot of processing/tools for data analysis and synchronization with the server. This leads to a lot of overhead that results in slowing the overall process.

Figure 6.9 depicts an overview of the distribution process using *RabbitMQ*. When indexing several binary files, the files are distributed across multiple workers. The distribution is done through a queue (RabbitMQ) using Round-Robin scheduling. The queue sends binaries to each worker based on the processing power of the worker machine. *RabbitMQ* uses a publish/subscribe mechanism, such that each worker subscribes to receive messages from the publisher. Each worker machine runs several instances of IDA Pro concurrently in order to process the binary files, generate the functions fingerprints, and store the fingerprints in the *Cassandra* [2]

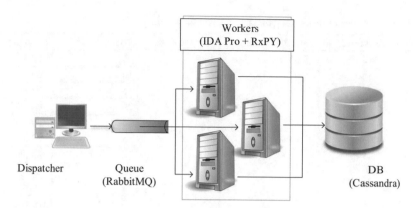

Fig. 6.9 Architecture of the distribution process

database. In order to run the code asynchronously, RxPY [12] (reactive extension) is used. RxPY is a python library for composing asynchronous and event-based programs. In our experiments, the distribution is performed on a server machine with an Intel Xeon CPU E5-2630 v3 @2.40 GHz (2 processors) and 128 GB of RAM running `Microsoft Windows` Server 2008 64-bit, along with a PC with an Intel Core i7 CPU 920 @2.67 GHz and 12 GB of RAM running `Microsoft Windows` 7 64-bit. Additional worker machines can be used in order to further improve the scalability and performance of the system. In addition to *RabbitMQ*, the built-in pooling mechanism of `Cassandra` [109] is also used to perform concurrent reads and writes to the database to improve performance and scalability.

6.3.5 Resilience to Different Compiler Optimization Levels

Through this experiment, we study the effects of using different compiler optimization levels on the accuracy of our fingerprint matching approach. We compile version 1.2.8 of the `zlib` library using `MSVC` 2013 with four different optimization levels. `MSVC` 2013 provides the following optimization levels: disabled optimization, minimize size, maximize speed, or full optimization. These optimization levels are represented by the abbreviations: Od, $O1$, $O2$, and Ox, respectively. We use as target functions the result of the compilation of the `zlib` library with full optimization (Ox). We attempt to match the target functions with `zlib` functions compiled with the other optimization levels (Od, $O1$, and $O2$).

The results of this experiment are presented in Table 6.11. As expected, the lowest accuracy score of 65.05% is the result of matching the fully optimized (Ox) functions with the functions that were compiled with disabled optimization (Od). Functions with optimization level $O1$ have a higher similarity to the fully optimized functions. Therefore, the resulting accuracy score of 87.85% is higher. In this case,

Table 6.11 Impact of different optimization levels on accuracy

Optimization levels	Overall accuracy	Average time	#Basic blocks	Accuracy
Ox vs. Od	65.05%	4.2 s	5	62.5%
			10	66.7%
			15	53.8%
			20	60.0%
			25	100.0%
Ox vs. O1	87.85%	4.3 s	5	83.3%
			10	83.3%
			15	84.6%
			20	100.0%
			25	100.0%
Ox vs. O2	100.00%	0.26 s	5	100.0%
			10	100.0%
			15	100.0%
			20	100.0%
			25	100.0%

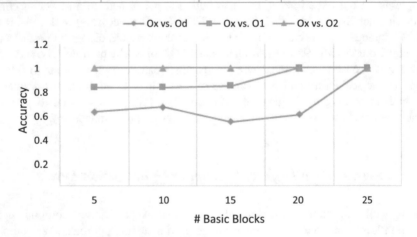

Fig. 6.10 Matching different optimization levels

the optimization levels Ox and $O2$ appear to generate identical assembly code. Therefore, the accuracy of the matching process is 100%.

After matching different optimization levels, we discover that the size of the target functions being matched affects the accuracy of the matching process. Figure 6.10 shows the change in accuracy when matching target functions with different number of basic blocks. It is consistent among the different optimization levels being compared, such that larger functions with higher number of basic blocks are matched with higher accuracy. The reason is that larger functions usually include more distinctive features than smaller functions. Small functions tend to have common features and structures. Thus, the probability of mismatching a small function is higher than the probability of mismatching a larger one.

It is notable that the accuracy of matching between the optimization levels Ox and Od is consistently lower than matching between the optimization levels Ox and $O1$. This is due to the fact that when compiling with optimization level Od, none of the optimization techniques are applied to the code. This results in code with very different characteristics than code that has undergone some optimization (such as minimizing size or maximizing speed). However, optimization level $O1$ applies some optimization techniques that minimize the size, which results in code with higher similarity to the fully optimized functions. Compiling the code with the optimization level $O2$ seems to produce identical functions to the fully optimized code regardless of the size of the function.

6.3.6 Library Function Detection

Identifying library functions in binaries is useful in the reverse engineering process. The recognition of library functions assists the analysts in understanding the context of the binary piece of code in a more rapid and more accurate manner. Another benefit of identifying library functions is to decrease the number of binary functions that call for manual inspection by the reverse engineer. IDA F.L.I.R.T. is a technology provided by the industry-standard disassembler IDA Pro. It provides a built-in capability for recognizing standard library functions by assigning labels to the identified standard library functions through exact matching of byte-level sequences. As a result, F.L.I.R.T. fails to detect the library function in the case of any slight byte-level discrepancies. In this experiment, we identify a few cases where IDA F.L.I.R.T. does not detect the library functions in the binary files and then attempt to match these library functions using BINSIGN. We identify such library functions in two files: Putty.exe and Heap.exe. Tables 6.12 and 6.13 show respectively the results of our experiments on these executables.

Table 6.12 Library function identification in Putty.exe

Function name	FLIRT detection	BINSIGN score
_memchr	Yes	1.0
_memcpy	Yes	1.0
_memset	Yes	1.0
_memcpy_s	Yes	1.0
_memcmp	No	–

Table 6.13 Library function identification in Heap.exe

Function name	FLIRT detection	BINSIGN score
_memchr	No	0.890
_memcpy	No	0.644
_memset	No	0.637
_memcpy_s	No	–
_memcmp	No	–

Table 6.12 shows that F.L.I.R.T. is able to detect the library functions except the last function, _memcmp. BINSIGN also exhibits similar results. It is worth noting that the similarity scores of the library functions matched by BINSIGN is 1.0. This is why F.L.I.R.T. is able to detect these functions through its exact matching technique. However, the version of the _memcmp function used in this binary is significantly different from the one used in F.L.I.R.T. to generate the target signature. The differences in the functions CFGs can be seen in Fig. 6.11. The differences in the basic blocks are significant enough such that BINSIGN is not able to match the function.

Table 6.13 shows the results of this experiment on the file Heap.exe. In this case, F.L.I.R.T. is not able to detect any of the library functions in this binary. However, BINSIGN is able to detect the first three library functions in the table with relatively high similarity scores. As for the functions _memcpy_s and _memcmp, neither F.L.I.R.T. nor BINSIGN were able to identify them. The differences in the basic blocks of the CFGs of these functions are significant as in the previous case. The variation in the CFG of the function _memcmp is even more drastic than _memcpy_s and the number of basic blocks increased radically as displayed in Figs. 6.11 and 6.12, respectively.

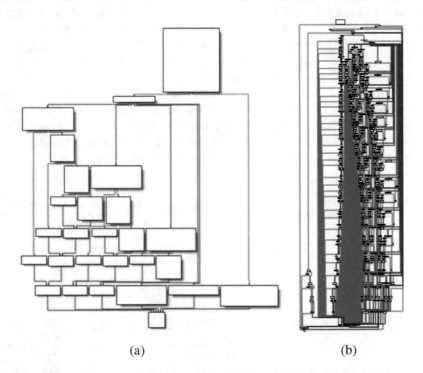

(a)   (b)

Fig. 6.11 CFG of different versions of _memcmp. (**a**) Original CFG. (**b**) Modified CFG

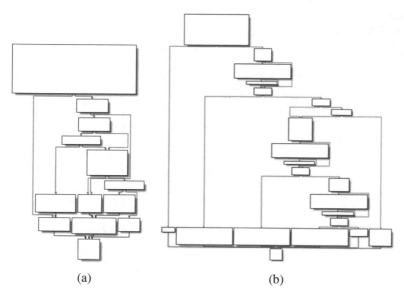

(a)   (b)

Fig. 6.12 CFG of different versions of _memcpy_s function. (**a**) Original CFG. (**b**) Modified CFG

Table 6.14 Candidates of RC4 Function from Citadel

Function	Similarity score
sub_42E92D	0.68787
sub_10034D0A	0.40042
png_set_sCAL	0.35377

6.3.7 Malware Similarity Analysis

This experiment is performed using Citadel and Zeus malware samples. The functions in Citadel are modified versions of functions from Zeus [215, 241]. Since Citadel reuses the RC4 stream cipher function from Zeus with slight modifications [241], we identify the RC4 function in both malware samples and attempt to match the two versions of this function. We attempt to identify the fingerprint of the RC4 function in Zeus using the fingerprint of the reused RC4 function from Citadel. We use IDA Pro to disassemble both Zeus and Citadel. We identify 642 functions in Zeus and 896 functions in Citadel using IDA Pro. We generate fingerprints of these functions and match the RC4 function. Functions from the previously mentioned library files are also included in the dataset. It takes 0.463 s to match the RC4 function.

After manual inspection, we find that the top matched function (as listed in Table 6.14) with a similarity score of 0.68787 is truly the modified RC4 function. The matches with lower similarity scores are different functions from the library files in the dataset. Figure 6.13a, b show the CFG of both RC4 functions in Zeus and Citadel, respectively. There are some clear modifications in the structure

Fig. 6.13 CFG of RC4
function in (**a**) Zeus and (**b**)
Citadel

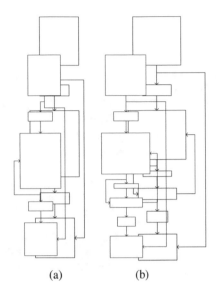

(a)   (b)

of the CFG of the function. While the number of basic blocks in the two CFGs is
different, the match is correctly identified since the difference in the number of basic
blocks does not exceed 30% of the number of basic blocks in the target function.
Therefore, the matching RC4 function passes through the filters of BINSIGN and is
selected as the function with the highest similarity score.

Moreover, we attempt to match all the functions in Zeus because numerous
functions in Citadel are modified versions of functions in Zeus. BINSIGN is
able to match 591 out of 642 functions in Zeus to functions in Citadel. Out of
these functions, 546 functions are matched with a similarity score above 70%, 532
functions are matched with a similarity score above 80%, and 517 functions are
matched with a very high similarity score above 90%.

6.3.8 Resilience to Obfuscation

Different types of obfuscation techniques can be used to make the code more
difficult to understand [77, 234]. These techniques are used in order to prevent the
reverse engineering of a software program. An obfuscator is a tool that automatically
applies obfuscation techniques to alter a piece of code in such a way that it obscures
the code, making it more difficult to understand or reverse engineer while preserving
its functionality [13].

Heavy obfuscation is not included in the scope of our threat model. However, we
provide some insight into how some obfuscation techniques affect our fingerprint
matching methodology. To that end, we use the Obfuscator-LLVM [9, 173], which
provides three different obfuscation techniques: control flow flattening, instruction
substitution, and bogus control flow [173]. The purpose of the first technique is to

fully flatten the CFG of a binary function. The control flow flattening technique offered by Obfuscator-LLVM is based on the technique described in more detail in [190]. The second obfuscation technique entails randomly selecting equivalent instruction sequences to replace standard binary operators in a manner that renders the code to be more complicated while maintaining the same functionality. The bogus control flow technique [190] adjusts the call graph of a function by adding a new basic block before the current basic block and then makes a conditional jump to the original basic block. Moreover, the original basic block is cloned and populated with random, junk instructions.

We include obfuscated functions using the three previously described obfuscation techniques to the dataset. We use the original function as the target function. The original CFG can be seen in Fig. 6.14a. Consequently, the function that went through instruction substitution is identified as a match with a similarity score of 0.84399. The function is still identified with a high similarity score which shows resilience to instruction substitution. We illustrate in Fig. 6.14c the CFG structure after applying the instruction substitution obfuscation technique. While this type of obfuscation does not modify the structure of the CFG, it does change the number and type of instructions inside each basic block.

Figure 6.15 shows the instructions contained in two basic blocks as examples of the changes that occur after applying the instruction substitution obfuscation

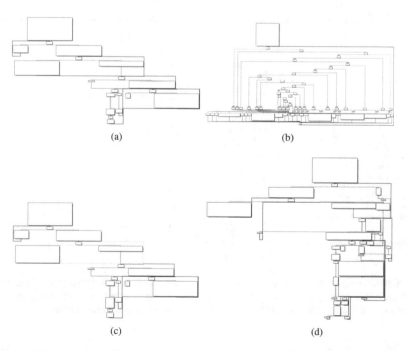

(a)

(b)

(c)

(d)

Fig. 6.14 Effects of obfuscation techniques on a CFG. (**a**) Original function CFG. (**b**) CFG after control flow flattening. (**c**) CFG after instruction substitution. (**d**) CFG after bogus control flow

```
Lea   eax,ZSt4cout@@GLIBCXX_3_4
lea   ecx, aValueAt
mov   [esp+68h+var_68], eax
mov   [esp+68h+var_64], ecx
call  __ZStlsISt11char_traitsIcEERSt13basic_ostreamIcT_ES5_PKc
mov   ecx, [ebp-24h]
mov   [esp+68h+var_68], eax
mov   [esp+68h+var_64], ecx
call  __ZNSoIsEi
lea   ecx, aIndex
mov   [esp+68h+var_68],eax
mov   [esp+68h+var_64], ecx
call __ZStlsISt11char_traitsIcEERSt13basic_ostreamIcT_ES5_PKc
mov   ecx, [ebp-24h]
mov   ecx, [ebp+ecx*4-1Ch]
mov   [esp+68h+var_68],eax
mov   [esp+68h+var_64],ecx
call  __ZNSoIsEi
lea   ecx, __ZSt4endlIcSt11char_traitsIcEERSt13basic_ostreamIT_T0_ES6_
mov   [esp+68h+var_68], eax
mov   [esp+68h+var_64], ecx
call __ZNSoIsEPFRSoS_E
mov   [ebp-48h], eax
xor   eax, eax
mov   ecx, [ebp-24h]
mov   edx,eax
sub   edx, ecx
mov   ecx,eax
sub   ecx, 1
add   edx, ecx
sub   eax, edx
mov   [ebp-24h],eax
jmp loc_8048882
```

```
lea   eax, _ZSt3cin@@GLIBCXX_3_4
lea   ecx, [ebp-18h]
mov   edx, [ebp-1Ch]
shl   edx, 2
add   ecx, edx
mov   [esp+58h+var_58], eax
mov   [esp+58h+var_54], ecx
call  __ZNSirsERi
mov   [ebp-38h], eax
mov   eax, [ebp-1Ch]
add   eax, 1
mov   [ebp-1Ch], eax
jmp   loc_80487F1
```

              (a)   (b)

```
mov   eax, [ebp-2Ch]
mov   eax, [ebp+eax*4-18h]
mov   [ebp-24h], eax
mov   eax, [ebp-2Ch]
mov   eax, [ebp+eax*4-14h]
mov   ecx, [ebp-2Ch]
mov   [ebp+ecx*4-18h], eax
mov   eax, [ebp-24h]
mov   ecx, [ebp-2Ch]
mov   [ebp+ecx*4-14h], eax
```

```
xor   eax, eax
mov   ecx, [ebp-30h]
mov   ecx, [ebp+ecx*4-1Ch]
mov   [ebp-28h], ecx
mov   ecx, [ebp-30h]
mov   edx, eax
sub   edx, 1
sub   ecx, edx
mov   ecx, [ebp+ecx*4-1Ch]
mov   edx, [ebp-30h]
mov   [ebp+edx*4-1Ch], ecx
mov   ecx, [ebp-28h]
mov   edx, [ebp-30h]
mov   esi, eax
sub   esi, edx
mov   edx, eax
sub   edx, 1
add   esi, edx
sub   eax, esi
mov   [ebp+eax*4-1Ch], ecx
```

              (c)   (d)

Fig. 6.15 Examples of instruction substitution in basic blocks. (**a**) First basic block before instruction substitution. (**b**) First basic block after instruction substitution. (**c**) Second basic block before instruction substitution. (**d**) Second basic block after instruction substitution

technique. There are visible changes in the number and types of instructions between the basic blocks before and after going through this type of obfuscation. The number of instructions significantly increased as shown in Fig. 6.15c, d. The obfuscated functions resulting from control flow flattening and bogus control flow are not matched since the instructions and control flow structure are too different from the original function as displayed in Fig. 6.14c, d. The resulting CFGs are significantly different from the original CFG. The number of basic blocks increased by more than 30%. Hence, the fingerprints of these functions are filtered out by the filtering mechanism, which relies on the number of basic blocks of the CFG.

6.4 Limitations and Concluding Remarks

In this chapter, we defined the main components of function fingerprinting and described the algorithms and the processes of fingerprint generation and matching. The methodology was evaluated in terms of function matching, malware analysis, obfuscation resilience, and scalability. We showed that the methodology is effective and can improve the accuracy of exact and inexact fingerprint matching. BINSIGN outperformed existing tools and achieved a higher accuracy score. We also described different measures undertaken to ensure BINSIGN scalability.

However, BINSIGN suffers from the following limitations, which could be considered as future work: (1) Function inlining has not been investigated. (2) Advanced obfuscation techniques, such as transforming the CFG structure (e.g., control flow flattening), could obstruct the matching process. Future research work may take into account situations involving merging basic blocks by removing unneeded jumps, such as unconditional branching instructions, or identifying unreachable and dead code, which can result in a more effective matching process.

Chapter 7
Free Open-Source Software Fingerprinting

This chapter presents an approach to fingerprint free open-source software (FOSS) packages. FOSS package identification is crucial for several important security applications, e.g., digital forensics, software license infringement, and malware detection. However, existing function identification approaches are insufficient for this purpose due to various challenges in applying practical methods of data mining and database searching, especially when the source code is inaccessible. Moreover, the task of automated detection of FOSS packages becomes more complicated with the introduction of obfuscation techniques, the use of different compilers and compilation settings, and software refactoring techniques.

In this chapter, we present a novel resilient and efficient system, namely FOSSIL, to identify FOSS functions in program binaries and malware samples. First, we provide in Sect. 7.1 an overview of the proposed approach and the considered threat model. Afterwards, we detail our approach to identify FOSS functions in Sect. 7.2. Then, the experimental results are presented in Sect. 7.3. Finally, we provide in Sect. 7.4 the limitations of the proposed approach along with the chapter conclusions.

7.1 Introduction

In the absence of source code, the identification of free open-source software (FOSS) packages in a target binary becomes essential for various security applications, such as malware detection, software license infringement, and digital forensics. The special attention placed on the reused free open-source software packages in reverse engineering is mainly due to the following reasons. First, according to a recent survey [186], the similarity identification among malware samples attributable to reused FOSS packages can help in developing profiles for malware families. For instance, Flame [81] and other malware in its family

© Springer Nature Switzerland AG 2020
S. Alrabaee et al., *Binary Code Fingerprinting for Cybersecurity*, Advances in
Information Security 78, https://doi.org/10.1007/978-3-030-34238-8_7

[80] contain code packages that are publicly available, including SQLite and LUA [186]. Second, FOSS packages are heavily used in most modern malware; as a result, the identification of those packages plays a vital role in the process of extracting information about the functionality of a malware binary. Third, it becomes more important to map between the parts of a malware binary and FOSS packages in the cases where obfuscation techniques may have been applied, as the reused FOSS packages may differ from their original source files. Fourth, to identify new malware from a known family or to decompose a malware binary based on the origin of its functions, clustering FOSS functions based on their common origin may contribute to reverse engineering.

As per our knowledge, there is no similar approach that is specifically designed for identifying FOSS packages in malware binaries and discovering their origin. There exist certain techniques that may be used for this purpose. To that end, identifying clone functions [112, 179, 202, 222, 256], determining reused functions [61], discovering shared components [255], and labelling standard compiler libraries [165, 240] in binaries are worth mentioning. However, these techniques are limited by several issues that impact their features, including compilation settings, handling indirect branches, high computational overhead, and obfuscation; these issues greatly affect the precision/recall [261] of the identification methods. Even though some of the existing techniques may detect binary similarities, their results remain difficult to be interpreted. For instance, some similarities might be identified only from the structural perspective, but not from the semantic perspective. More importantly, none of those techniques identifies free open-source software functions. On the other hand, their identification is very important as many malware usually contain a significant amount of library code borrowed from open-source software packages. For example, Flame malware [81] contains code packages that are publicly available, including SQLite and LUA [186].

There exist several challenges in the automation of FOSS function identification process as follows:

- *Usability:* The information about FOSS packages may give immediate insights about a binary file and hence, provide reverse engineers a direction to conduct their investigations. To that end, existing approaches of binary search engine, clone detection, or function identification might be useful only if the repository contains a function that exhibits a high degree of similarity to the target function. Furthermore, the effect of different compilers, compiler optimization, and obfuscation techniques may greatly impact the identification outcome. For instance, a given unknown function is less likely to be very similar to the right function in the repository, and there is little advantage in returning a list of matches with low degrees of similarity. Ideally, a resilient system should find the similar pairs with a controller process that can synthesize the available knowledge.
- *Efficiency:* An efficient system with a practical response time can greatly help reverse engineers to detect similarities at near-real time. To identify a given target function efficiently, devising efficient algorithms for extracting, indexing, and matching features from program binaries is challenging.

- *Robustness:* The robustness of a FOSS identification system may be impacted by the platform, the compiler, or the programming language, which potentially affect the structures, syntax, or sequences of features and hence, distorts the features. Therefore, it is challenging to extract robust features that would be less affected by different compilers, slight changes in the source code as well as obfuscation techniques.
- *Scalability:* It is essential to design a system that can scale up to millions of binary functions as reverse engineers usually handle very large numbers of binaries on a daily basis. Therefore, it is important to include the factors that may affect the performance of FOSS package identification with the increased repository size.
- *Stability:* Another important concern in the design of a system is to sync the repository with a new version of a FOSS package release. The update process should be supported by a system without any re-indexing of the whole package.

7.1.1 Approach Overview

An overview of the proposed approach is depicted in Fig. 7.1. First, the disassembled version of free open-source software packages is extracted and then is fed into the pre-processing module, where the assembly instructions are normalized and further ranked (discussed in Sect. 7.2.1). Then, different types of the features (opcodes, CFG Walks, and opcode frequencies) are extracted (discussed in Sect. 7.2.3). Afterwards, different detection methods are applied to the extracted features, and the FOSS function repository is updated for the purpose of identification (discussed in Sect. 7.2.5). Finally, these detection methods are integrated using a Bayesian network model in order to identify FOSS functions (discussed in Sect. 7.2.5.4).

The proposed Bayesian network controls the application of different employed detection methods, including hidden Markov model (HMM), hash subgraph pairwise (HSP) kernel-based method, and *z-score* calculation, on the extracted features. More specifically, normalized opcodes are fed into the hidden Markov model in order to detect the behavior of opcodes in a function. The HMM is chosen as the first component, since it is shown that applying the HMM to opcodes makes it possible to detect malware-morphed viruses [57] in addition to resisting different types of

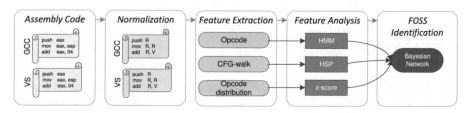

Fig. 7.1 Approach overview

light obfuscation [57, 278]. The second component, is the hash subgraph pairwise method, which provides an extremely efficient process for a high-dimensional graph, and accepts control flow graph walks to label the walks by applying the kernel function for each node together with its neighbors. Depending on the output of this component, either the function is identified, or the third component of the model is checked. To achieve this, the opcode frequencies are converted into a probability distribution whose characteristics are analyzed with the use of a *z-score* [85, 301] in order to capture the relationship between the instructions and their behaviors in a function.

7.1.2 Threat Model

In-scope Threats: We assume that target binaries might be passed through light obfuscation techniques to modify the syntax of binary files. We also assume that an adversary may change compilers or compilation settings to evade detection. Furthermore, to intentionally avoid detection by our system, adversaries may reuse FOSS packages through modifying and adapting them. Moreover, adversaries will very likely come up with more elaborated evasion techniques specifically designed for systems such as the proposed one and therefore, hardening the system against evolving countermeasures is expected to be an ongoing process.

Out-of-Scope Threats: The main goal of the proposed solution is to assist (and not to completely replace) reverse engineers and hence, we do not cover general reverse engineering tasks, such as unpacking and de-obfuscating binaries (although later in this chapter we discuss how our system can deal with some obfuscation techniques). Additionally, our system relies on existing techniques for de-obfuscating binaries. Also, encrypted code to reduce code size or to prevent reverse engineering is also beyond the scope of the present approach.

7.2 Identifying FOSS Functions

In this section, we first introduce the employed normalization, feature extraction, and selection. Afterwards, we present the proposed detection methods in detail.

7.2.1 Normalization

Due to the effect of compilers and compilation settings, it is essential to normalize the assembly instructions before analysis. Each disassembled function contains a sequence of assembly instructions, each of which is composed of a mnemonic and the operands. The operands can be classified into three categories of memory reference, registers, and constant values. The objective of the normalization step is to generalize the memory references, registers, and constant values. Constant values and registers are normalized to *VAL* and *REG*, respectively, which simply ignore the exact constant value or the register names and types. Moreover, we differentiate general registers (e.g., eax, ebx), segment registers (e.g., cs, ds), and index and pointer registers (e.g., esi, edi). Finally, we break down the general registers into three groups by size; namely, 32−, 16−, and 8−bit registers [134].

7.2.2   Feature Extraction

Recognizing free open-source functions is more challenging than identifying other types of functions (i.e., compiler functions), since the malware writer may modify the FOSS package more frequently and significantly. Therefore, we aim at selecting the features, which maximally preserve the semantics of a function. Consequently, instead of relying on syntax-based features obtained from feature templates [251], we propose using different features at various levels and the ones which are easily stored in a repository while considering the efficiency of their extraction. We also take into consideration the earlier-mentioned threat models.

7.2.3   Feature Analysis

For our system, we mainly select three kinds of features: opcodes, CFG-walks, and opcode frequencies distribution. In the following, we elaborate on each of them:

1. **Opcodes:** Opcodes are the operations that need to be executed, and are usually used to efficiently identify obfuscated or metamorphic malware [82]. However, prevalent opcodes (e.g., mov, push, and call) are not much useful indicators of malware samples [82], and based on such opcode frequencies, the resultant degree of similarity between two files could potentially be marred [114]. As a result, we devise an algorithm to evade this phenomenon and to label each opcode more relevantly by applying feature ranking based on mutual information [230] to include only the top-ranked opcodes.
2. **Control Flow Graph Walks:** Control flow graphs (CFGs) are built with a set of basic blocks, where each block indicates a sequence of instructions without an intervening control transfer instruction. CFG has been used to find variants of malware [93]. However, as CFGs may change due to both compiler and optimization settings, exact matching of CFGs might not be sufficient for our purpose. Therefore, we represent CFGs into a set of walks, where we consider the interactions between these walks. Thus, we capture a set of semantic relations (walk interactions) such that when a malware includes part of a FOSS function to implement a specific functionality, it would be captured based on these semantic

relations. Among the most prominent graph kernels, the random walk kernel [145] and the shortest path kernel [284] have been used in the literature, where a graph is decomposed into sequences of nodes generated by walks and it counts the number of identical walks that can be found in two graphs. In this chapter, we build an instance of the substructure fingerprint kernel in a suitable manner for the analysis of CFG walk relations.

Example: As an example, we consider a CFG containing ten basic blocks $(BB_0, \cdots, BB_9)$ as shown in Fig. 7.2a. For selecting the random walks, we consider two nodes BB_0 and BB_7, where the path between them (BB_0, BB_4, BB_6, BB_7) with a distance of 3 is highlighted in Fig. 7.2b. To increase the time efficiency, we follow a radius for our random walk, which is the shortest path with neighboring nodes. In Sect. 7.3, we choose the radius values: $\{0, 1, 2\}$, as illustrated in Fig. 7.2b–d, respectively. Specifically, the *radius* value 0 only includes the information about node BB_0 and node BB_7 as shown in Fig. 7.2b. For $radius = 1$, the (BB_0, BB_4) and (BB_6, BB_7) pairs represent the structural information depicted in Fig. 7.2c. The walks when *radius* is equal to 2 are (BB_0, BB_4, BB_6), and (BB_4, BB_6, BB_7). Our experimental results indicate that a *radius* of 2 is the best choice for efficiency.

3. **Opcode Frequencies Distribution:** We first consider the simple hypothesis that FOSS functions performing the same task belong to the same distribution. Second, we calculate the area of opcode frequencies distribution. Third, the distribution of the various opcodes conforms to a consistent distribution shape when it is related to a specific FOSS function, even if it is modified. Finally, if a malware writer modifies the FOSS package, the semantics will be preserved and will be discovered by the distribution curve. It is for these aforementioned reasons that we choose the opcode frequencies distribution feature.

7.2.4   Feature Selection

We choose features to represent the functionality and semantics of binary functions. Even though we extract various representations of code properties, only part of them may indicate the semantics of a function. Therefore, our aim is to choose features where the semantics of a function is best preserved. For the same reason, in addition to syntax-based features obtained from feature templates [133], we include different function features at various abstraction levels of the binary code. Our system also pays attention on efficiently extracting features from binaries and efficiently storing them in a repository. In the following, we elaborate on each selected feature.

Opcode Ranking: We apply mutual information-based ranking [92] on the opcodes and corresponding functions of each FOSS family, and hence, keep the feature set size smaller. Thus, our representation of the properties of coding

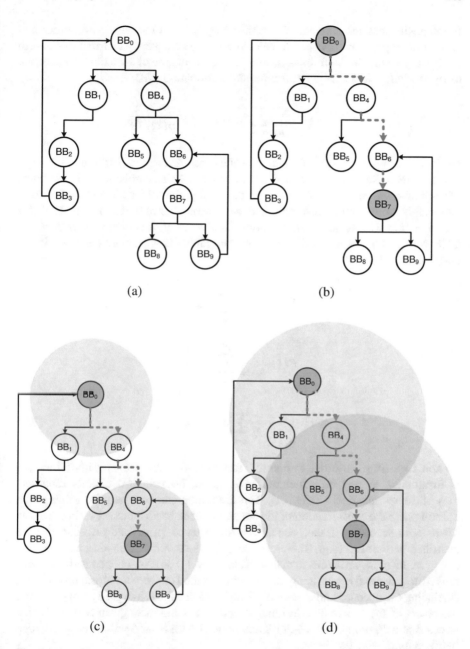

Fig. 7.2 Random walks between BB_0 and BB_7 nodes and different radius (r). (**a**) Function CFG.
(**b**) $r = 0$. (**c**) $r = 1$. (**d**) $r = 2$

functionality remains efficient. We rank the opcodes in the descending order and choose the top-ranked opcodes to calculate opcode frequency distributions and to color CFG-walks. In the following, to measure the degree of statistical dependence of two variables X and Y, we utilize mutual information (MI):

$$MI(X, Y) = \sum_{x \in X} \sum_{y \in Y} p(x, y) log_2 (\frac{p(x, y)}{p(x)p(y)}), \tag{7.1}$$

where x indicates the opcode frequency, y indicates the class of FOSS function (e.g., sqlite3MemMalloc), $p(x)$ and $p(y)$ are the marginal probability distributions of each random variable, and $p(x, y)$ is the joint probability of X and Y. The joint and marginal distributions are computed over the number of function variants N (for each function we have different versions, such as when it is compiled with VS or GCC compilers). These distributions are computed between class (function label) and feature as follows:

$$P(x) = \frac{1}{N} \sum_{i=1}^{N} \ell_{[x_i = x]}$$

$$P(y) = \frac{1}{N} \sum_{i=1}^{N} \ell_{[y_i = y]}$$

$$P(x, y) = \frac{1}{N} \sum_{i=1}^{N} \ell_{[x_i = x \wedge y_i = y]}. \tag{7.2}$$

Graph Coloring: In order to identify functions that are semantically similar, it is insufficient to rely on structural information, because two distinct functions may still have identical CFGs [61]. This limitation can be addressed using graph coloring with the consideration of the content of each basic block, as it classifies the instructions according to their semantics; for instance, push and pop opcodes are classified in one class (e.g., Stack operation). Moreover, instruction-level coloring can generate more variations than that of class-level [184]. We only consider the top-ranked opcodes and hence, apply the coloring method on the normalized instructions (including the opcodes and operands). Finally, each edge is assigned by aggregating the colors of the source and destination nodes. For instance, given two connected nodes A and B, node A with color 2 and node B with color 8 will result in an edge between them with 10.

Opcode Importance: For the measurement of opcode importance, we adopt the model from [82]. Then, converting the frequencies into a histogram and measuring the area of intersection based on the probability distribution are performed to further process top-ranked opcodes. Thus, we represent the opcode importance in terms of function behavior. The most important opcodes will be used by the third component.

Table 7.1 Top-ranked opcode distributions for different sorting algorithms

	The z-score for top-ranked opcodes					
	add	push	lea	mov	and	or
Bubble.v1	1.051211	0.412661	−0.830144	1.510222	2.100523	1.995820
Bubble.v2	1.071291	0.406912	−0.830144	1.493213	2.215012	1.969582
Quick.v1	1.059154	0.569042	−0.908245	1.618144	2.121009	1.865189
Quick.v2	1.056159	0.520013	−0.900166	1.618306	2.116910	1.860028
Heap.v1	1.097158	0.450061	−0.731512	1.590128	2.000211	1.890244
Heap.v2	1.097054	0.410901	−0.699958	1.589422	2.009144	1.894061
Merge.v1	1.029032	0.542113	−0.700193	1.500000	1.961411	1.900019
Merge.v2	1.018054	0.520393	−0.700082	1.500000	1.959009	1.901200

We show an example of opcode distribution values for the most important opcode that was found in the tested sorting algorithms (e.g., we consider two variants for each sorting algorithm) in Table 7.1.

7.2.5 Detection Method

This section introduces different components of our detection system: the hidden Markov model [278], the neighborhood hash graph kernel [299], and the *z-score*. These components are integrated through Bayesian network model.

7.2.5.1 Hidden Markov Model

The first component is based on the opcode features. An opcode-relevance file based on the top-ranked features obtained from the mutual information is created for each FOSS function. These top-ranked opcodes are used for the hidden Markov model (HMM) with chi-squared [138] testing. The HMM is chosen to be the initial component since it is computationally efficient [278]. In the case of a hidden Markov model, as its name implies, the states are not directly observed, and we can only estimate these states while observing sequences of data [271]. Therefore, we train a HMM to fit opcode sequences that are extracted from a FOSS function. Subsequently, we score functions based on the extracted opcode sequences and classify each function into a specific FOSS package. We then use chi-squared distance with a HMM in order to compute a confidence interval for this component.

In the proposed HMM model, the states represent the sequence of instructions. However, these sequences are not fully observed. Yet, the hidden states can be estimated by observing the sequences of data [271]. Therefore, we apply data flow analysis in order to discover the hidden states (e.g., instructions related to inline functions) as follows. The data flow dependency between two instructions i_1 and i_2 is defined according to the following rules:

- instruction i_1 reads from a register or a memory address, and instruction i_2 writes to the same register or memory address.
- instruction i_1 and i_2 both write to the same register or memory address.
- instruction i_1 writes to a register or memory address, and instruction i_2 reads from the same register or memory.

Consequently, if an instruction (or a set of commands) shows no evidence of a data flow dependency, it is tagged as a hidden state. It should be noted that "instructions side effects" (that represent which flags are manipulated) are treated as observations. Therefore, such observations will be annotated to the states.

In what follows, we describe the chi-squared distance, which is combined with the HMM. Suppose Z is a statistical opcode variable from a distribution under observation. Our goal is to estimate the main characteristics of the probability distribution P for statistical opcode variable Z. Statistical testing is used to decide which hypothesis best fits an observed sequence of samples $(z_1, z_2, \ldots, z_n)$. We employ Pearson's chi-squared statistical test χ^2 [138], which is commonly used to determine whether the difference between expected and observed data is significant. We denote this test as T^2, as defined in Eq. 7.3 [138]:

$$T^2 = \sum_{i=1}^{n} \frac{(\hat{m}_i - m_i)^2}{m_i} \leq \chi^2_{(\alpha, n-1)}, \qquad (7.3)$$

where $\hat{m}_i$ is the normalized frequency of opcodes in the training phase, and m_i is the normalized frequency of opcodes in the testing phase. The $\chi^2_{(\alpha, n-1)}$ represents a chi-squared distribution with $n - 1$ degrees of freedom and a type I error rate of α. The decision threshold is obtained by comparing the estimator value given by T^2 to the $\chi^2_{(\alpha, n-1)}$ distribution. For more details, we refer the reader to [271, 278]. In this component, the number of passed hypotheses along with their error rates are represented as Ψ_3, which is later used by the Bayesian network model.

Example: We consider a simplified problem involving maximum five opcodes. Suppose that function x is composed of five instructions with different opcode frequencies as shown in Table 7.2. The possible observations are test, push, mov, add, and lea.

Table 7.2 Instruction frequencies in function x

Opcode	Opcode frequency	Normalized value
test	5	0.111
push	15	0.333
mov	12	0.266
add	8	0.177
lea	5	0.111

Table 7.3 Instruction
frequencies in function y

Opcode	Frequency	Normalized value
test	9	0.204
push	22	0.500
mov	9	0.204
add	4	0.090

Moreover, consider target function y with four instructions and opcode frequencies listed in Table 7.3.

In order to classify the function as a match, we perform χ^2 test. The null hypothesis H_0 is that the function is matched, provided that the estimator function T^2 yields a score less than or equal to the corresponding χ^2 value. In order to compute the T^2, the opcode frequencies for each instruction are used.

Example: Since χ^2 is a probability distribution, the frequencies are normalized before performing this test as shown in Table 7.3. For instance, the normalized value for instruction test is 0.111. Finally, according to Eq. 7.3, T^2 is calculated as $T^2 = \frac{(0.111-0.204)^2}{0.111} + \frac{(0.333-0.5)^2}{0.0.333} + \frac{(0.266-0.204)^2}{0.0.266} + \frac{(0.177-0.090)^2}{0.0.177} + \frac{(0.111-0)^2}{0.0.111} \approx 0.3298$. We compare T^2 with $\chi^2_{(0.05,4)} = 9.488$; since $T^2 \le \chi^2_{(0.05,4)}$, we accept the null hypothesis, that is, we classify function y as a match for function x. Also, we apply the previous calculation for the categories in the function.

7.2.5.2   Neighborhood Hash Graph Kernel

The distance between CFG-walks (node–node interaction relations) has a crucial impact on obtaining the semantics of the graphs [145]. For this purpose, we use a hash subgraph pairwise (HSP) kernel-based method [300] and employ hierarchical hash labels to represent the structural information of node relations in a linear time. We use the kernel function of Gartner et al. [299] in our detection system since their function can efficiently make full use of graph structural information. The manner by which the neighborhood hash graph kernel function is generated is described in the following. The label pair feature space of graph H for each label pair (l_i, l_j) is defined as follows [299]:

$$\varphi_{l_i,l_j}(H) = \sum_{d=0}^{\infty} \tau_d |\{w \in W_d(H) : f_1(w) = l_i \wedge f_{d+1}(w) = l_j\}|, \qquad (7.4)$$

where $W_d(H)$ is the set of all possible walks with d edges in graph H, $f_1(w)$ and $f_{d+1}(w)$ are the first and last nodes of walk w, and $(\tau_0, \tau_1, \cdots, \tau_d)$ are weights of the edges. The weight of each edge is calculated by the summation of source and destination node colors (e.g., $f_C(i) + f_C(i + 1)$), where function $f_C(i)$ calculates the node color, as discussed in Sect. 7.2.4.

Corresponding to the feature map provided above, the graph kernel function based on label pairs is calculated as follows [299]:

$$K(H, H') = \langle \varphi(H), \varphi(H') \rangle = \langle L(\sum_{i=0}^{\infty} \tau_i E^i)L^T, L'(\sum_{j=0}^{\infty} \tau_j E^j)L'^T \rangle$$

$$= \sum_{m=0}^{|k|} \sum_{n=0}^{|k|} \left[L\left(\sum_{i=0}^{\infty} \tau_i E^i \right) L^T \right]_{mn} \left[L'\left(\sum_{j=0}^{\infty} \tau_j E^j \right) L'^T \right]_{mn}, \quad (7.5)$$

where E^i is the adjacency matrix of H, and L is the labelled matrix of H.

In what follows we explain the details of the label process generation. We denote a label as a binary vector $e = \{u_1, u_2, \ldots, u_r\}$ consisting of r-bits (0 or 1), representing the presence (1) of the group of instructions (discussed in Sect. 7.2.4) in a node. Let $XOR(e_i, e_j) = e_i \oplus e_j$ symbolize the XOR operation between two bit vectors of e_i and e_j. Let $ROT_o(e) = \{u_{o+1}, u_{o+2}, \ldots, u_r, u_1, \ldots, u_o\}$ denote the rotation (ROT_o) operation for $e = \{u_1, u_2, \ldots, u_r\}$, which shifts the last $r - o$ bits to the left by o bits and moves the first o bits to the right.

In order to compute the neighborhood hash of a graph, we first obtain the set of adjacent nodes $N^{adj}(n) = \{N_1^{adj}, \ldots, N_d^{adj}\}$ for each node n, and then calculate a neighborhood subgraph hash label for every node, using the Eq. 7.6 [300], where $l_i(n)$ indicates the bit label of node n as follows:

$$l_{i+1}(n) = NH(n) = ROT_1(l_i(n)) \oplus (ROT_o)(l_i(N_1^{adj})) \oplus \cdots \oplus ROT_o(l_i(N_d^{adj})). \quad (7.6)$$

In order to differentiate between the outgoing (out-degree) and incoming edges (in-degree), we set two ROT_o operations:

- If the edge $n_1 n$ is an incoming edge to node n, let $ROT_o = ROT_2$;
- If the edge $n n_1$ is an outgoing edge of node n, let $ROT_o = ROT_3$.

It is worth noting that $l_0(n)$ describes the information of node n, while $l_1(n)$ represents the label distribution of node n and its adjacent nodes. Finally, the structural information of subgraph of radius i is presented by $l_i(n)$. According to our experiments, we find a radius of $r = 2$ as the best choice for our system.

According to the hierarchical hash labels, the graph kernel is defined as [299]:

$$K(H, H') = \sum_{r=0}^{r^*} \beta r \langle Lr \sum_{i=0}^{\infty} \left(\tau_i E^i \right) (Lr)^T, Lr' \sum_{j=0}^{\infty} \left(\tau_j E^j \right) (Lr)'^T \rangle$$

$$= \sum_{r=0}^{r^*} \sum_{m=0}^{|k|} \sum_{n=0}^{|k|} \beta r \left[Lr\left(\sum_{i=0}^{\infty} \tau_i E^i \right) Lr^T \right]_{mn} \left[Lr'\left(\sum_{j=0}^{\infty} \tau_j E^j \right) Lr'^T \right]_{mn},$$

$$(7.7)$$

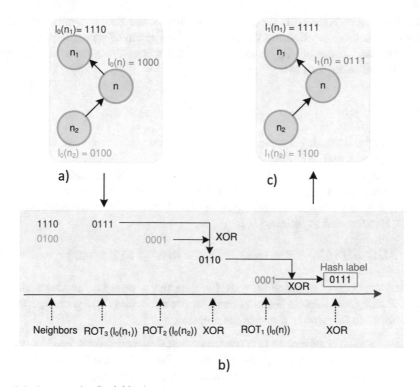

Fig. 7.3 An example of neighborhood subgraph hash labels computation

where E is the adjacency matrix of H and $L_0, L_1, \ldots, L_r$ are the hierarchical hash labels of H.

From a practical perspective, the whole process involved in calculating hierarchical hash labels is linear with respect to the size of the graph [299, 300]. For more details, we refer the reader to [299, 300]. Thus, computing the similarity between two control flow graphs will be equivalent to comparing the set of hash values.

Example: To demonstrate the manner by which the neighborhood hash graph kernel works, a small example is illustrated in Fig. 7.3. Figure 7.3a depicts a simple directed graph including three nodes labelled with a 4-bit value for simplicity. The computation of neighborhood subgraph hash label, $l_1(n)$ for node n is illustrated in Fig. 7.3b. Similarly, for each node the neighborhood subgraph hash label, $l_1(n_i)$ is calculated based on the basic bit label, $l_0(n_i)$ as shown in Fig. 7.3c.

7.2.5.3 Z-score Calculation

Each set of opcodes that belong to a specific function will likely follow a specific distribution due to the functionality they implement. Therefore, we consider the distribution of opcode frequencies in the last component, and further employ the *z-score* in order to convert these distributions into scores. The *z-score* is a statistical measure of a score relationship with the mean in a group of scores indicating how many standard deviations an element is from the mean. The *z-score* is calculated using the following formula:

$$Z = \frac{x - \mu}{SD}, \tag{7.8}$$

where x is the normalized value of opcode frequency, μ is the mean value of that specific opcode, and SD is the standard deviation.

We calculate the *z-score* for each opcode distribution to facilitate comparisons. Based on the possible values for the *z-score*, we calculate the area under the curve and create a curve representing the opcode distributions. The area under the curve (AUC) is calculated as follows [36]:

$$AUC = P(\min < Z < \max) = P(Z < \max) - P(Z > \min). \tag{7.9}$$

Thus, we obtain one value for each function that represents the area under the curve. Finally, we obtain a feature (area) for each function. The generated feature vector for each function is stored in the repository.

Example: Suppose a function (f_1) consists of six top-ranked opcodes. The opcode frequencies x_i, and the corresponding *z-score* values $Z(x_i)$ are listed in Table 7.4. The minimum and maximum *z-score* values of f_i are -1.16 and 1.01, respectively. Therefore, the area under the curve (AUC) is calculated as follows:
$$AUC = P(Z = 1.01) - P(Z = -1.16) = 0.843752 - 0.125072 = 0.71868.$$

7.2.5.4 Bayesian Network Model

A Bayesian network (BN) model is utilized to measure the knowledge obtained from the aforementioned components and to further automate the relation and interaction among them. The BN models have certain characteristics. First, the BN can encode probabilistic relationships among the outputs of each component. Second, it can handle situations where sufficient data for each component is not available for identification purpose. Third, the BN could be used to learn causal relationships; therefore, it can be used to not only gain knowledge for FOSS function identification problem, but also to predict the consequences of intervention. This feature is very

Table 7.4 Top-ranked opcode frequencies and the corresponding *z-score* values of f_1 function

	push	lea	and	or	shl	mov
x_i	21	11	8	10	9	22
$Z(x_i)$	0.84	-0.83	-1.33	-0.99	-1.16	1.01

important in the case of modifications performed by malware authors. Hence, the BN can capture both causal and probabilistic relationships, and provides an ideal representation for combining prior knowledge and data.

An described earlier, FOSSIL encompasses three main components: HMM (H), CFG-walks (W), and *z-score* (Z), which can be used to identify a FOSS function. Each component provides particular knowledge about the FOSS function, and this knowledge is measured by a factor ψ_s. If the factor ψ_s is smaller than a predefined probability threshold value of Ω set by the BN ($\psi_s \leq \Omega$), then FOSSIL invokes another component, which indicates that the knowledge obtained from the current component is not sufficient.

In addition, each component has a direct effect on the use of other component (e.g., H on W). The situation can thus be modeled with a Bayesian network model. Therefore, the joint probability function can be defined as follows:

$$P(f, H, W, Z) = P(f|H, W, Z).P(f|H, W).P(f|H).P(H) \qquad (7.10)$$

and the probability can be formulated with Bayes' law by Eq. 7.11:

$$p(y|\mathbf{x}) = \frac{p(y).p(\mathbf{x}|y)}{p(\mathbf{x})}, \qquad (7.11)$$

where $p(\mathbf{x}|y)$ is the probability of a possible input $x = (x_1, \ldots, x_n) \in \Upsilon^n$ given the output $y = (y_1, \ldots, y_n) \in \Gamma^n$.

We define a set of conditional probabilities (factors) Ψ_1, Ψ_2, and Ψ_3 for our three components. Through extensive experimentation involving logistic regression [108], we found the best values of 0.45, 0.35, and 0.2 for these factors, respectively. These factors are based on all possible features in the components, and thus represent more explicitly the underlying probability distribution of the features in each component. Each part of the joint probability is obtained using Eq. 7.12:

$$p(y|\mathbf{x}) = \frac{p(x, y)}{p(x)} = \frac{p(x, y)}{\sum_y p(x, y)} = \frac{\frac{1}{Z}\prod_{s \in S} \Psi_s(x, y)}{\frac{1}{Z}\sum_{y'}\prod_{s \in S} \Psi_s(x_s, y_s)} = \frac{1}{Z(x)}\prod_{s \in S} \Psi_s(x, y),$$

$$(7.12)$$

where Ψ_s represents the probabilities from each component, where $s = \{1, 2, 3\}$; Z is the probability distribution [209]; x is the set of features in each component; and y is the set of functions. We therefore obtain Eq. 7.13 as follows:

$$p(y, \mathbf{x}) = p(y)\frac{1}{Z(\mathbf{x})}\prod_{s \in S} \Psi_s(\mathbf{x}, y). \qquad (7.13)$$

7.3 Evaluation

In order to evaluate the effectiveness of our system, we test it on 160 real projects as well as a number of modern malware samples that are commonly known to reuse FOSS packages. We then examine the effect of light obfuscation and the robustness of the system for binaries compiled with different compilers and optimization levels.

7.3.1 Experiment Setup

We develop a proof-of-concept implementation in python to evaluate the effectiveness of our proposed approach. All our experiments are conducted on machines running Windows 7 and Ubuntu 15.04, with Core i7 3.4 GHz CPU and 16 GB RAM. The programs are disassembled using IDA Pro Disassembler [45], and the features are extracted by our IDAPython script. Function filtering is performed by employing IDA FLIRT technology [150] in order to drop the standard library functions. We use PostgreSQL database to store the features of FOSS packages. Our dataset is composed of 160 projects in addition to the five malware samples of Zeus, Citadel, Flame, Stuxnet, and Duqu to demonstrate the identification of reused FOSS functions in benign and malicious binaries. The current version of our system works with 32-bit binaries of both MS Windows (PE) and Linux (ELF).

7.3.2 Dataset Preparation

Collecting FOSS packages is a crucial step in evaluating our system. First, an initial study of the literature on malware behavior [103, 144, 294, 295] and technical reports [81, 186, 219] is conducted to determine the most important packages that must be considered and collected. Then, the FOSS packages are collected in two ways. (1) We collect the binary files and their PDBs from their official websites (e.g., WireShark); (2) We collect their source code from three different sources: GitHub [19], SourceForge [34], and Code-project [35] and then compile them with Visual Studio (VS) 2010, VS 2012, and GNU Compiler Collection (GCC) 5.1 compilers according to their dependencies. The FOSS packages were created to perform various functionalities as partially listed in Table 7.5. We tailor our system to C-family compilers because of their popularity and widespread use, especially in the development of malicious programs [198]. Therefore, we build a repository of FOSS functions from different sources and store them along with their features in our repository. Finally, we evaluate our approach on a set of binaries, a subset of which is detailed in Table 4.5.

Table 7.5 Example of the functionality of collected FOSS packages

Some examples of functionalities	
Encryption (e.g., `TrueCrypt`)	Random number generation (e.g., `Mersenne Twister`)
Compression (e.g., `info-zip`)	Multimedia protocols (e.g., `Libavutil`)
Secure connection (e.g., `libssh2`)	File manipulation (e.g., `libjsoncpp`)
MSDN libraries (e.g., `NSPR`)	Network operations (e.g., `webhp`)
Hashing (e.g., `Hashdeep`)	Terminal emulation (e.g., `xterm`)
Secure protocol (e.g., `openssl`)	Image compression (e.g., `openjpeg`)
XML parser (e.g., `TinyXML`)	Database management (e.g., `SQLite`)

7.3.3   Evaluation Metrics

Our ultimate goal is to discover as many relevant functions as possible with less concern about false positives, which means that recall has higher priority than precision. Since the F_2 measure weighs recall twice as heavily as it weighs precision, we chose to use this measure. The precision, recall, false positive rate (FPR), total accuracy (TA), and F_2 measure metrics are defined as follows [113]:

$$Precision = \frac{TP}{TP + FP} \tag{7.14}$$

$$Recall = \frac{TP}{TP + FN} \tag{7.15}$$

$$FPR = \frac{FP}{FP + TN} \tag{7.16}$$

$$TA = \frac{TP + TN}{TP + TN + FP + FN} \tag{7.17}$$

$$F_2 = 5 \times \frac{Precision \times Recall}{4 \times Precision + Recall}, \tag{7.18}$$

where TP indicates number of relevant functions that are correctly retrieved; FN represents the number of relevant functions that are not detected; FP indicates the number of irrelevant functions that are incorrectly detected; and TN provides the number of irrelevant functions that are not detected.

In our experimental setup, we split the collected binaries into ten sets, reserving one as a testing set and using the remaining nine sets as the training set. We repeat this process numerous times and report the average output of the system in terms of the aforementioned evaluation metrics. These metrics are calculated at function level (Sect. 4.3.1) and at project level (Sects. 4.3.2 and 4.4).

7.3.4   FOSSIL Accuracy

In this subsection, we first examine the effect of the Bayesian network model and then measure the accuracy across different versions of FOSS packages. We evaluate the accuracy of our system by examining its outputs on randomly collected binaries from our repository, compiled with VS 2010, VS 2012, and GCC compilers. The obtained F_2 results without and with the use of Bayesian network model are summarized in Tables 7.6 and 7.7, respectively.

We further evaluate FOSSIL with different versions of FOSS packages. For this purpose, we collect three different versions of all 160 projects in our repository, and compile them with VS 2010. The average precision, recall, and F_2 measure metrics are reported in Table 7.8. The highest obtained F_2 measure is 0.86, which is related to openssl, and the lowest one is 0.73 for lcms. The low F_2 measure for lcms can be attributed to the presence of many small functions that have been inlined.

7.3.5   Comparison

We compare our system with existing state-of-the-art systems, namely, REN-DEZVOUS [179], TRACELET [112], SARVAM [223], and LIBV [165]. We reimplement RENDEZVOUS and SARVAM as their source codes are not available. We pay special attention to the definition of their features as well as their stated assumptions. We use the available source code for TRACELET [37] and LIBV [165].

7.3.5.1   Accuracy

First we apply different systems to the same data (160 projects) and compare the true positives, false positives, and F_2 measure results, as shown in Table 7.9. As seen, FOSSIL can effectively identify FOSS functions in 160 projects. Our system returns

Table 7.6 Accuracy results without BN model

Feature	Precision	Recall	F_2
Opcodes	0.76	0.80	0.79
CFG-walks	0.72	0.76	0.75
Opcode distribution	0.70	0.72	0.71
Average	0.73	0.76	0.75

Table 7.7 Accuracy results with BN model

Feature	Precision	Recall	F_2
Opcodes	0.82	0.86	0.85
CFG-walks	0.84	0.83	0.83
Opcode Distribution	0.81	0.86	0.85
All together	0.93	0.84	0.86

Table 7.8 Accuracy results of different versions of FOSS packages

Project	Precision	Recall	F_2	Project	Precision	Recall	F_2
SQLite	0.78	0.81	0.80	libxml2	0.76	0.78	0.78
Webph	0.80	0.74	0.75	libjsoncpp	0.84	0.83	0.83
Xterm	0.79	0.81	0.81	Mersenne Twister	0.81	0.79	0.79
Hashdeep	0.81	0.85	0.84	libssh2	0.80	0.79	0.79
TinyXML	0.79	0.74	0.75	openssl	0.83	0.88	**0.86**
libpng	0.77	0.79	0.79	bzip2	0.79	0.80	0.80
ultraVNC	0.73	0.80	0.79	UCL	0.73	**0.9**	0.86
lcms	0.81	0.71	0.73	TrueCrypt	0.77	0.79	0.79
libavcodec	0.80	0.82	0.86	liblivemedia	0.80	0.81	0.81
info-zip	0.76	0.79	0.78	Libavutil	**0.84**	0.86	0.86
Firefox	0.77	0.81	0.80	Expat XML parser	0.80	0.8	0.8

The highest obtained Precision, Recall and F_1 score values are marked in bold

Table 7.9 Comparison results on 160 projects

Proposal	True positives	True negatives	F_2
RENDEZVOUS	0.68	0.28	0.69
TRACELET	0.77	0.20	0.79
SARVAM	0.56	0.34	0.59
LIBV	0.74	0.15	0.75
FOSSIL	0.85	0.10	0.86

an average of 0.85 true positives and 0.10 false positives, as shown in Table 7.9. This is superior to the TRACELET system, which returns the second highest rate of true positives of 0.77 with a 0.20 false positive rate, as well as SARVAM, which achieves the lowest rate of true positives.

One of the main reasons for the increase in the rate of true positives is that in our system, further semantic information (such as node colors) is extracted from the features, which enables the matching of functions semantically rather than just syntactically. In addition, ranking the opcodes measures the relation between opcodes and the function and extracts the opcodes which are strongly connected to that specific function. The TRACELET system is more accurate than other systems, since they apply data flow constraints on tracelets (decomposing CFGs into fixed length sub-traces, excluding jump instructions). However, the tracelet system assumes that the candidate function should contain at least 100 basic blocks; otherwise, the TRACELET system has a high rate of false positives. Additionally, the features used in RENDEZVOUS, such as n-grams and k-graph, are sensitive to code changes, whereas the features used in SARVAM are gray-scale image features. Although image features constitute a rich source, they have many irrelevant features that increase the rate of false positives. Other systems, such as LIBV, extract the data flow graphs by applying data and control flow constraints. However, this system applies two filters to reduce the time complexity of data flow graph comparison, which leads to increased false positives.

7.3.5.2 Performance

We further compare the performance of each system by computing the overall execution time, which involves the feature extraction, and searching through the repository to find matches. The purpose of measuring the performance is to evaluate the usability of each system at large scale. In particular, the execution time for FOSS function identification in FOSSIL was measured by adding the time required for each step (normalization, opcode ranking, and feature extraction in each component) to the time spent to discover the FOSS functions. Feature extraction in the first component takes 5 s for the small packages in our dataset (e.g., 100 functions) and 15 s for the large package (e.g., 50,000 functions). The proposed hash subgraph kernel takes an average of 5 s for all packages in a similar environment. The time required to extract features in the third component is negligible (less than 1 ms). Our system spends the majority of time on searching the repository; further optimizing the search using advanced indexing techniques represents a future work direction. Each search iteration takes a minimum of 7 s and a maximum of 50 s.

The average time for FOSSIL ranges from 17 to 80 s, while the average times for RENDEZVOUS, TRACY, SARVAM, and LIBV are 72.5, 115, 55, and 111.5 s, respectively. We observe that the performance of SARVAM is closer to that of FOSSIL, since the extraction of image features is relatively efficient. The performance of RENDEZVOUS is also close since it uses a Bloom filter, which speeds up the retrieval process.

7.3.6 Scalability Study

We evaluate the scalability of FOSSIL when it is used to index and retrieve matched functions on a large number of projects. To this end, we add more projects, *.dll* files, operating system applications, and other programs to our repository and bring the number of applications to 500 with approximately 1.5 million functions. Then, we measure the function detection accuracy of each component separately and all together. Figure 7.4 demonstrates that our system is scalable when the number of functions reaches to 1.5 million. As seen in Fig. 7.4a, the F_2 measure of using all components decreases slightly, from 0.9 to 0.86, which provides some insight into the scalability as well as the accuracy of the system when it deals with a large number of FOSS functions. Based on these results, we argue that our system will be efficient and practical for most real-world applications.

7.3.7 The Confidence Estimation of a Bayesian Network

A Bayesian network model provides a confidence estimator based on probability scores, where higher probability scores correspond to higher confidence. Applying different factor values to the Bayesian network model makes it possible to achieve

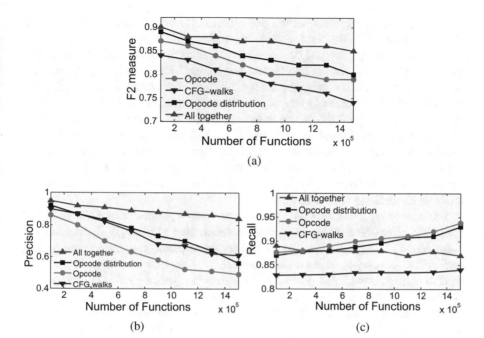

(a)

(b)   (c)

Fig. 7.4 The performance of FOSSIL against a large set of functions. (**a**) F_2 measure. (**b**) Precision. (**c**) Recall

Fig. 7.5 Confidence estimation: precision vs. recall

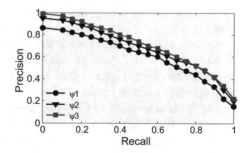

various trade-offs between precision and recall. Figure 7.5 shows the results of confidence estimation for three factors (ψ_1, ψ_2, and ψ_3), varying the trade-off between precision and recall. A precision measure of 50% is achieved with a recall measure of just under 80%; conversely, 50% recall gives over 80% precision.

7.3.8   The Impact of Evading Techniques

We consider a set of projects from our dataset in order to test FOSSIL against both source and binary code obfuscation. In what follows, we describe the details.

For source code obfuscation, we use different C++ refactoring tools [30, 41]. These refactoring tools consider various techniques, such as (1) *renaming a variable*, (2) *moving a method from a superclass to its subclasses*, and (3) *extracting a few statements and placing them into a new method*. For an in-depth explanations of these techniques, we refer the reader to [140]. For instance, we employ the Nynaeve [39] tool for the purpose of *frame pointer omission* and *function inlining*. Additionally, we apply the source code obfuscator tool known as Trigress [52]. This tool applies the following methods [52]: (1) *Virtualization*, which transforms a function into an interpreter whose bytecode language is specialized for this function; (2) *Jitting*, which transforms a function into one that generates its machine code at runtime; and (3) *JitDynamic*, which transforms a function into one that continuously modifies its machine code at runtime.

For binary-level obfuscation, we compile the projects with GCC and VS compilers, after which the binaries are obfuscated using a DaLin [196] generator and obfuscator-LLVM [173]. The DaLin obfuscator performs *instruction substitution*, *instruction reordering*, *dead-code insertion*, and *register renaming* techniques. And the obfuscator-LLVM performs (1) *instruction substitution*, (2) *control flow flattening*, and (3) *bogus control flow* obfuscations.

The obtained obfuscated binaries are passed to our system, and we then measure the accuracy of function identification, as shown in Table 7.10. The first and second columns show the tools and methods used for obfuscation, respectively. The third and fourth columns present the input and output of the obfuscation tools, respectively, which demonstrates that the employed obfuscation tools work at three levels: source, binary, and assembly. The fifth column provides the accuracy after applying the obfuscation tool, and the last column indicates which specific component of FOSSIL has been affected by the obfuscation tool.

As can be seen in Table 7.10, our system obtains an average accuracy of 83.1% in correctly identifying similar FOSS functions, which represents only a slight drop in comparison to the 86% accuracy observed without obfuscation. We also observe that the obfuscation methods of CFG flattening, and function inlining may decrease the accuracy of FOSSIL by approximately 6–12%. However, the effect of these methods on the accuracy is not significant, since FOSSIL employs a Bayesian network model to synthesize the knowledge obtained from each component by defining a confidence estimator function. Moreover, as mentioned, FOSSIL cannot deal with encrypted binaries. The current version of FOSSIL employs features belonging to static analysis. A possibility for future work is to extend FOSSIL by including dynamic features that can deal with encrypted binaries.

There are three main reasons behind this slight drop in accuracy. First, the HMM component deals with opcode frequencies at the function level; thus, in the case of *instruction reordering*, all of the reordered instructions, regardless of order, will be captured. In addition, since the operands are not considered in this component, and we also normalize the instructions, *register renaming* does not affect the accuracy. However, this component is affected slightly by *instruction substitution*, as this technique affects frequencies. Nonetheless, as previously mentioned, the chi-squared test is used to test the frequencies, and this test uses a confidence interval that varies according to user requirements.

Table 7.10 The evading techniques and their effect on the FOSSIL component

Tool	Method	Input	Output	A*	Component		
					Opcode	CFG-Walk	Opcode Distribution
OBFUSCATOR-LLVM [173]	CFG flattening	Binary	Binary	74%	○	●	○
	Instruction substitution			84%	●	○	○
	CFG bogus			81%	○	●	○
DALIN [196]	Instruction reordering	Assembly	Assembly	86%	○	○	○
	Dead-code insertion			86%	○	○	○
	Register renaming			86%	○	○	○
	Instruction substitution			84%	●	○	○
TRIGRESS [52]	Virtualization	Source	Source	82%	●	●	●
	Jitting			83%	●	○	○
	Dynamic			83%	●	○	○
PELOCK [33]	Hide procedure call	Assembly	Assembly	86%	○	○	○
	Insert fake instruction			86%	○	○	○
	Prefix junk opcode			86%	○	○	○
	Insert junk handlers			86%	○	○	○
NYNAEVE [39]	Frame pointer omission	Source	Binary	81%	●	●	○
	Function inlining			80%	○	●	○
GAS OBFUSCATOR [31]	Junk byte	Assembly	Assembly	86%	○	○	○

Accuracy results before applying the obfuscation techniques: 86%. (A*): The accuracy results after applying the obfuscation techniques (○) means there is no effect while (●) means there is an effect

Second, the CFG-walk component tolerates instruction-level obfuscation to a greater extent, since this component deals with the semantics of a function, not the syntax. To avoid *bogus control flow* as well as *function inlining* techniques, we color CFG-walks according to the most important opcodes. We also label the node with its neighbors in a novel way in order to handle any obfuscation that can affect the CFG. However, this component is affected by *CFG flattening*.

Third, the *z-score* calculates the area of opcode distribution and therefore both *instruction replacement* and *dead-code insertion* may slightly affect this component. In general, using opcode ranking, normalization, and coloring techniques reduces the impact of many obfuscation methods. However, the Bayesian network model synthesizes the knowledge obtained from the three components; therefore, if the knowledge is not sufficient, the Bayesian network model will automatically assign more weights to the other components.

7.3.9   The Impact of Compilers

To create an experimental dataset, we consider 100 projects compiled with Visual Studio (VS), GCC, ICC, and Clang compilers with Od optimization setting. Next, to measure the effect of different compilation settings, such as optimization levels, we additionally compile the source code with Od, $O2$, and OX optimization levels, and extract features for each compilation setting. The results of our system, illustrated in Table 7.11, show that the features extracted by our system are highly effective for most optimization speed levels.

The normalization process can significantly reduce the effect of GCC and VS compilers. Moreover, the top-ranked opcodes and the colored CFG-walks capture more of the semantics of a function, which help to avoid compiler effects. However, the accuracy drops significantly when ICC or Clang compilers are used, since these compilers produce more variable code compared to VS and GCC compilers. Such limitations can be handled by first identifying the compiler using existing tools, such as EXEINFO [43], and then employing the suitable features accordingly.

Table 7.11 FOSS identification with different compilers and compilation settings

Compiler	Optimization level	Precision	Recall
VS	$O0, O2, Ox$	0.95, 0.95, 0.95	0.94, 0.92, 0.92
GCC	$O0, O2, Ox$	0.92, 0.92, 0.92	0.93, 0.90, 0.89
ICC	$O0, O2, Ox$	0.78, 0.74, 0.69	0.81, 0.80, 0.78
Clang	$O0, O2, Ox$	0.65, 0.59, 0.60	0.64, 0.60, 0.58

7.3.10 Applying FOSSIL to Real Malware Binaries

We further examine FOSSIL in the context of identifying the FOSS functions in Malware binaries. Due to the lack of ground truth for evaluation, we test FOSSIL on two specific sets of malware binaries. The first set of malware is composed of the samples which are analyzed by reverse engineers and security analysts. Consequently, we can match FOSSIL findings with technical reports. The second set of malware contains 12 malware families with 5000 samples. The goal is to study the scalability of FOSSIL and to derive insights from the large-scale binaries by providing statistical analysis for certain malware families, indicating the type and percentage of FOSS packages usage.

7.3.10.1 Malware Dataset Analyzed by Technical Reports

We apply FOSSIL to Zeus, Citadel, Stuxnet, Flame, and Duqu malware binaries, which are unpacked and de-obfuscated. Statistics regarding the number of FOSS functions found in malware binaries are shown in Table 7.12. As can be seen, our system is able to determine a significant number of FOSS functions, including SQLite, webhp, xterm, hashdeep, tinysml, ultravnc, lcms, libavcodec, and info-zip, in the examined malware samples. Our system identified 87 matches between Zeus and webph, while no matches have been found between Zeus and SQLite, hashdeep, libpng, and libavcodec packages.

In addition, the results indicate similarities between pairs of malware binaries in terms of FOSS functions use. For instance, we found 55% degree of similarity in the use of FOSS functions between Zeus and Citadel malware samples, where common functions are: 80 from webph, 35 from Xterm, 81 from ultraVNC, 20 from lcms, and 60 from info-zip functions. Moreover, FOSSIL found a degree of 38% similarity among Stuxnet, Flame, and Duqu. Additionally, we compare

Table 7.12 The number of specific FOSS functions found in malware binaries

	Zeus	Citadel	Stuxnet	Flame	Duqu
SQLite	–	15	175	285	373
webph	87	134	–	5	17
Xterm	42	86	–	15	20
Hashdeep	–	5	–	25	90
TinyXML	–	10	35	70	60
libpng	–	–	30	20	60
ultraVNC	86	125	–	–	–
lcms	20	25	–	–	–
libavcodec	–	–	25	40	10
info-zip	63	100	10	33	15
Total	298	500	275	493	645

Table 7.13 Matching our findings with that of existing technical reports

Malware	FOSS package	Technical report			
		[23]	[79]	[178]	[215]
Zeus/Citadel	SQLite, webph, xterm			✗,✗,✓	✗,✓,✗
	Hashdeep, TinyXML, ultraVNC	NA	NA	✗,✗,✓	✓,✗,✓
	lcms, info-zip			✓,✓	✓,✓
Stuxnet/	SQLite, webph, xterm	✓,✗,✗	✓,✗,✗		
Flame/Duqu	Hashdeep, TinyXML, libpng	✗,✓,✓	✓,✗,✓	NA	NA
	libavcodec, info-zip	✗,✓	✗,✓		

(NA): The technical report does not provide any information. (✓): Our finding matches the finding obtained in the technical report. (✗): Our finding is not obtained in the technical report

our results with the findings in existing technical reports, as presented in Table 7.13. For instance, FOSSIL was able to detect functions in Stuxnet malware family that are related to the webph, xterm, and libavcodec FOSS packages.

7.3.10.2 General Malware Dataset

In this section, we apply FOSSIL to a large set of different malware variants, which are obtained from various resources as follows. (1) We have very large in-house data set, built since the year 2010. (2) We have also downloaded large datasets from various websites including, *VirusTotal*, *VirusShare*, *Kaggle Microsoft Malware Classification Challenge*, as well as various malware farms such as *KernelMode.info* and *contagion.org* for several years. (3) We obtained a portion of the dataset used by Jang et al. [169], which is collected by the DARPA Cyber Genome program [42]. These samples are unpacked and de-obfuscated.

There are several goals of performing the experiments as follows:

- Providing clues about the malware functionalities that can help reverse engineers and security analysts gain a better understanding of the malware.
- Determining the relation between FOSS packages and malware binaries that belong to the same family. We also provide details about the FOSS usage statistics found on malware binaries.
- Studying the relation between FOSS and malware evolution.

To this end, we perform two sets of experiments, for which the obtained results are detailed in the following.

Reused FOSS Packages in Malware Families: In order to achieve the first and second goals, we choose a set of FOSS packages and show their percentage of usage by certain malware families as illustrated in Fig. 7.6. As seen, FOSSIL is able to find the following FOSS packages in the Ramnit, Lollipop, Kelihos, Vundo, Simda, Tracur, Gatak, Locky, Kovter, Samas, Drixed, and

Fig. 7.6 Obtained FOSS
packages in malware families.
Numbers on *x*-axis represent
(1) Ramnit, (2) Lollipop,
(3) Kelihos, (4) Vundo,
(5) Simda, (6) Tracur, (7)
Gatak, (8) Locky, (9)
Kovter, (10) Samas, (11)
Drixed, (12) Ursnif
malware families.
(**a**) Compression Libraries.
(**b**) Encryption Libraries.
(**c**) Hashing Libraries.
(**d**) Parser Libraries.
(**e**) Multimedia Libraries.
(**f**) Networking Libraries.
(**g**) Database Libraries.
(**h**) JSON Libraries.
(**i**) Graphics Libraries.
(**j**) Web Libraries

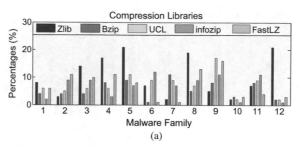

(a)

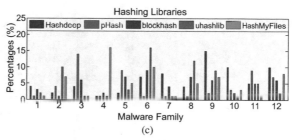

(b)

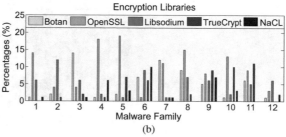

(c)

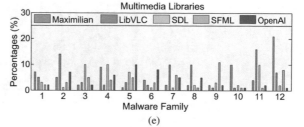

(d)

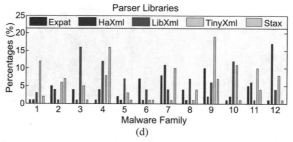

(e)

Fig. 7.6 (continued)

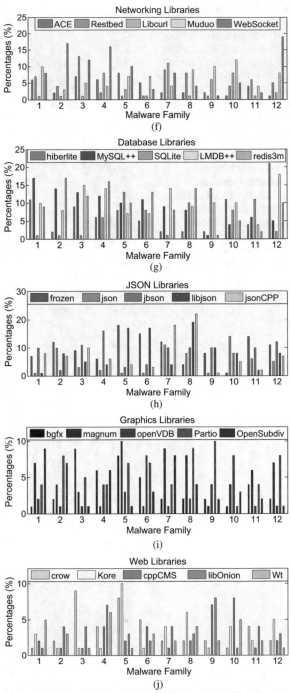

Numbers on x-axis represent (1) Ramnit (2) Lollipop (3) Kelihos
(4) Vundo (5) Simda (6) Tracur (7) Gatak (8) Locky (9) Kovter
(10) Samas (11) Drixed (12) Ursnif malware families.

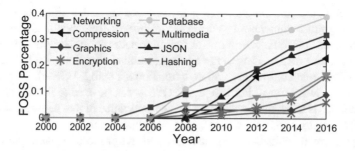

Fig. 7.7 The relationship between FOSS packages and malware evolution over 16 years

Ursnif malware families. The *compression* libraries have an average similarity of 17%, where Zlib is one of the most commonly used packages in malware binaries. The *encryption* libraries have an average similarity of 6%. The reason for this low percentage is that most malware authors use their own customized encryption algorithm. The *hashing* libraries, *parser* libraries, *multimedia* libraries, *networking* libraries, *database* libraries, *JSON* libraries, *graphics* libraries, and *web* libraries have an average similarity of 11%, 8%, 5%, 17%, 20%, 10%, 7%, and 9%, respectively.

Reused FOSS Packages and Malware Evolution: We are further interested in determining the relation between FOSS and malware lineage. We would like to verify whether a FOSS package is used over many years in the same series of the malware family. For this purpose, we use 114 samples with known evolution collected by the *Cyber Genome program* [42]. These samples include *bots*, *worms*, and *Trojans*, including KBot, BlasterWorm, MiniPanzer.A, CleanRoom.A, CleanRoom.B, MiniPanzer.B, CleanRoom.C, NBOT, Bunny, Casper, Kelihos_ver1, Kelihos_ver2, and Kelihos_ver3. We illustrate the relation between FOSS packages and the year of malware evolution in Fig. 7.7.

As seen in Fig. 7.7, the usage of FOSS packages from 2000 to 2006 is almost 0%, it increases to 10% in 2008, and starting from 2010, there is a significant rise in the FOSS packages usage. This observation supports the fact that modern malware reuse FOSS libraries. In addition, we notice that certain malware families use the same percentage of FOSS packages, which indicates that the functionality of that family has not changed over short time, whereas other malware families begin to change the FOSS packages due to their goals and functionalities.

7.4 Limitations and Concluding Remarks

In this chapter, we demonstrated how FOSSIL can be used to discover FOSS functions in binaries and malware samples. There are also other applications for our system as follows. First, the features used by FOSSIL may be used to provide clues about vulnerable functions in a given piece of code. This can be done by profiling a specific vulnerability with a set of FOSSIL features; then, once a target binary is given, FOSSIL can search for similar patterns. In addition, FOSSIL can be used as a tool for labelling certain types of binary functions, such as compiler-related, FOSS-related, and user-related functions. Finally, FOSSIL could also be applied for malware triage. For instance, FOSSIL can be used to first identify which FOSS package is used; then, according to the importance of that package, the reverse engineer or security analyst can determine the binary triage.

The performed evaluation demonstrates that the proposed system yields highly accurate results, however, it still has the following limitations: (1) We assume that the binary code under analysis is de-obfuscated. While this assumption may be reasonable for many general-purpose software, it implies the need for a pre-processing step involving de-obfuscation before applying the method to malware. (2) Function inlining has not been investigated. This problem can be circumvented by leveraging data flow analysis to the multidimensional fingerprint. (3) The proposed system deals only with x86 architecture. Dealing with multiple architectures (e.g., ARM and MIPS) could be considered as part of future work. (4) Type inference has not been considered in the proposed features. We believe that leveraging the concrete data types that are evaluated by the code will aid in verifying the matched functions and consequently reduce the number of false positives. (5) We assume the availability of a set of previously analyzed program binaries with known functionalities. Although our employed repository already has a decent size, it would need to be further enriched with a massive number of packages. However, the process of gathering FOSS packages, compiling with different compilers and optimization settings, and indexing in our repository is challenging. Each FOSS may have its unique dependencies, which makes automating the process difficult.

In addition to addressing the aforementioned issues, the future work can include extending this system as a binary search engine, and evaluating it on a larger number of FOSS packages. Thus, a small fragment of assembly code or a binary could be queried to obtain useful information related to their functionality.

Chapter 8
Clone Detection

Different clone detection techniques can be used to identify the known parts of a code and to avoid analyzing the same code portions again. Existing methods are found to be neither robust enough to accommodate the mutations brought by compilers nor scalable enough when querying against modern code base of high volume. To address these limitations, in this chapter we present BINSEQUENCE, a two-step clone detection engine. The proposed fine-grained fuzzy matching detection engine can perform code comparison accurately and as a result, the false correlation to irrelevant code can be avoided. The fingerprint-based detection engine can efficiently prune the search space without notably compromising the accuracy.

In this chapter, first we motivate the problem and provide an overview of our approach in Sect. 8.1. In Sect. 8.2, the clone detection approach is detailed. In Sect. 8.3, the evaluation results are presented. Finally, the chapter concludes in Sect. 8.4.

8.1 Introduction

Software developments do not always start from scratch. Instead, there is plenty of source code reuse in this process [217, 268]. Consequently, there exist a large number of clones in both binary code and the underlying assembly code. Due to the sheer volume of code size of modern software, the process of analyzing and manual reverse engineering often seems overwhelming. An effective clone detection tool can significantly reduce the burden of this process. It allows reverse engineers to take advantage of the massive base of already analyzed code and focus only on the newly introduced code and analyze the functionality of a relatively smaller portion of a code.

Code clone does not exist exclusively in legitimate software projects. Malware authors also tend to reuse their existing source code, or to incorporate some open-source projects. For instance, `Citadel` and `Zeus` malware share a significant

© Springer Nature Switzerland AG 2020
S. Alrabaee et al., *Binary Code Fingerprinting for Cybersecurity*, Advances in
Information Security 78, https://doi.org/10.1007/978-3-030-34238-8_8

amount of code base [83, 215], and SQLite is used by Flame as a lightweight database engine [81]. Performing clone detection on malware code cannot only help in tracking its origin but also helps analysts understand its inner behavior.

Developers and maintainers of benign software could also leverage clone detection techniques. In modern software development, it is common practice to copy and paste existing source code, or reuse third-party libraries from either standard libraries or open-source projects. If the original code portions or libraries contain a bug and the developers incorporate them without fixing the bug, the corresponding bug may be inadvertently brought into the new project. Conducting clone detection can help identify such bugs and mitigate their spread. Other important use cases of clone detection include: binary diffing, software plagiarism or GNU license infringements detection, or even vulnerability detection in firmware images of the intelligent electronic devices (IEDs) [263].

Clone detection is a challenging domain and there are already many state-of-the-art approaches. However, the existing approaches are not resilient enough against the "noises" that modern compilers might introduce. Moreover, the sheer size of large code base also makes this problem even more difficult by posing scalability issues. Function-level clone detection can be conducted by calculating the similarity of function pairs. If the obtained similarity is above certain predefined threshold, we regard these functions as clones. In the proposed approach control flow graphs (CFGs) are used to compare functions. In the rest of this chapter, we will detail the design of our tool and the means to address the aforementioned challenges.

8.1.1 Motivating Example

At source code level (take C++, for instance), we can notice that the execution across the CFG does not flow always sequentially between statements. For selection ("if," "switch," or ternary operator) and repetition ("for" or "while" loop) statements, additional edges and branches might be brought into the control flow graphs. That is to say, the execution flow will take decisions on which branch to take on the fly. Figure 8.1 shows some typical examples of these structures. Like in the source code, these structures could also be nested. Figure 8.2 depicts two nested examples. Note that we consider to implement certain functionality, compilers have virtually an unlimited number of choices. However, the compilers are bound by their mission, which is to generate reasonably efficient code. For instance, for an "if-else" statement, there are normally only two branches leading to two succeeding nodes. Although the compiler could use multiple branches and successor nodes to implement this functionality, it is highly unlikely to do that for code size and efficiency consideration.

Although different compilation environments would bring mutations into the CFGs, for instance, the compiler may use one condition move instruction such as *cmov* to replace the normal "if-else" structure which needs two branches.

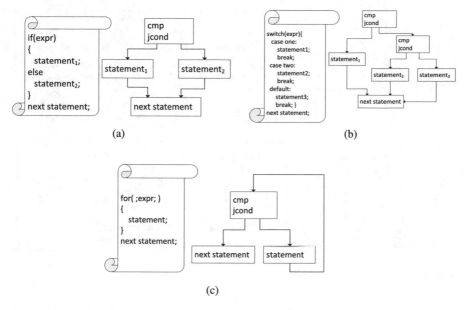

Fig. 8.1 Examples of control structures and corresponding CFGs. (**a**) The "if-else" structure. (**b**) The "switch" structure. (**c**) The "for" loop structure

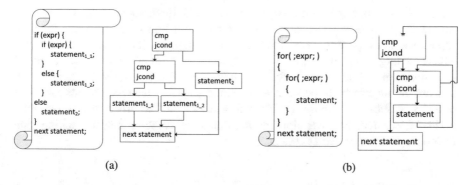

Fig. 8.2 Examples of nested control structures and corresponding CFGs. (**a**) The nested "if-else" structure. (**b**) The nested "for" loop structure

However, for functions with reasonable size, the failure to match a small substructure or several nodes will not prevent the functions to be matched, as the unmatched parts can be well compensated by the rest of structures, which are overall stable.

Based on these observations, we choose to use a CFG-centric approach to compare two functions. To accommodate the possible mutations and noises in CFGs, we adopt a fuzzy matching mechanism.

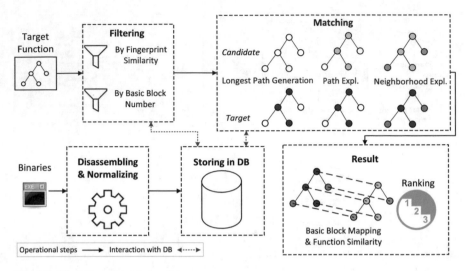

Fig. 8.3 Workflow of BINSEQUENCE

8.1.2   Overview

An overview of our approach is depicted in Fig. 8.3. First, both target and reference functions are disassembled. Then the reference function is fed into our function repository. The repository is essentially a huge database with millions of functions. Then both target function and the whole repository are fed into our fingerprint-based detection engine. More specifically, we use the target function to obtain a fingerprint, and use the fingerprint to perform a quick query against the whole repository. The output is a subset of repository. Then this subset will be processed by our fine-grained fuzzy matching detection engine, which outputs the similarity rankings and the corresponding similarity scores.

8.2   Function Clone Detection

8.2.1   Normalization

Before the actual detection phase begins, we first have to disassemble the executable into assembly functions. In this process, IDA PRO [45] is used. Instead of exporting assembly functions directly into our function repository, we choose to export their normalized representations. Figure 8.4a depicts our normalization hierarchy. We know that each assembly instruction consists of one mnemonic and a sequence of operands. When normalizing, we keep the mnemonic untouched, and classify the operands into three categories, namely registers, memory references, and immediate values. Figure 8.4b shows an example of basic block and its normalized form. The

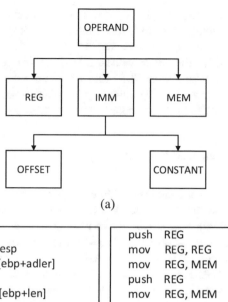

push ebp	push REG
mov ebp, esp	mov REG, REG
mov ecx, [ebp+adler]	mov REG, MEM
push ebx	push REG
mov ebx, [ebp+len]	mov REG, MEM
push esi	push REG
mov esi, ecx	mov REG, REG
and ecx, 0FFFFh	and REG, 0FFFFh
shr esi, 10h	shr REG, 10h
push 0FFFFFFFFh	push 0FFFFFFFFh
push edi	push REG
mov edi, [ebp+8]	mov REG, MEM
call sub_1001BDC0	call OFFSET
cmp dword ptr [edi+1Ch], 0	cmp MEM, 0
jnz loc_1001C030	jnz OFFSET

(b)

Fig. 8.4 Basic block normalization. (**a**) Normalization hierarchy. (**b**) An exemplary basic block and its normalized version

purpose of performing normalization is to better accommodate the instruction-level noises introduced by compilers.

The comparison of normalized instructions provides the building block when comparing two functions. To this end, a special scoring strategy [112] is adopted as shown in the following:

$$Score(Ins1, Ins2) = \begin{cases} 0, & \text{if } (Mne1 \mathrel{!=} Mne2) \\ 2 + ForEach\ (Operand)\ \{\ Same\ ?\ 1\ (or\ 3):\ 0\ \} \end{cases}.$$

(8.1)

We know that mnemonic represents the low-level operation of CPU. If two instructions have different mnemonics, then most likely they are not performing the same operation. Thus, we give them a score of 0. If they have identical mnemonic, we give them a matching score of 2 and continue to compare their operands. For each matching (normalized) operand, we give them an additional score of 1. A special case is identical immediate values. If two immediate values have the same literal value, we give them a score of 3. This is because immediate values normally come from the source code directly and carry first-hand information about the inner logic. Giving them extra matching score lowers the false positives.

8.2.2   Basic Block Comparison

After the instruction comparison has been established, the nodes of CFGs, namely basic blocks can now be compared. We remind that for string comparison, the longest common subsequence (LCS) can be used to measure the similarity. Suppose we have two strings, $s_1 =$ "ABCAE" and $s_2 =$ "BAE", and we want to find their LCS. Dynamic programming [105] can be applied to solve this problem efficiently. The general idea is to break down the problem into smaller and simpler problems until the answer becomes straightforward. Table 8.1 shows the memoization table when using dynamic programming to calculate the length of the LCS of these two strings. Following the path highlighted in Table 8.1, we can obtain the LCS of these two strings, "BAE," and its length is 3, as denoted in the last cell of the table.

To apply LCS on basic block comparison, we decide to treat each instruction as a letter, and the whole basic block as a string [112]. However, instead of giving a score of 1 to the same letter, we use the scoring strategy introduced in Sect. 8.2.1. Our proposed algorithm for basic block comparison is detailed in Algorithm 1. As shown, the output, always stored in the last cell of the memoization table, provides the largest similarity score that the corresponding node (basic block) pair could achieve. The mapping of instructions can also be obtained by backtracking the memoization table. Those instructions that failed to be matched are considered as "noises" between two basic blocks. Figure 8.5a shows a matching example.

Intuitively, for any given basic block, the highest similarity it can achieve is when every instruction, mnemonic, and operand are exactly matched, for instance, when it is compared with itself (as shown in Fig. 8.5a). We denote that score as the "self" score, and use it to gauge the information that a particular basic block carries. Another example is illustrated in Fig. 8.5b.

Table 8.1 The memoization table when calculating the LCS of two ABCAE and BAE strings

	s_1	A	B	C	A	E
s_2	0	0	0	0	0	0
B	0	←↑ 0	↖ 1	← 1	← 1	← 1
A	0	↖ 1	←↑ 1	←↑ 1	↖ 2	← 2
E	0	↑ 1	←↑ 1	←↑ 1	↑ 2	↖ 3

Highlighted cells show the backtrack path

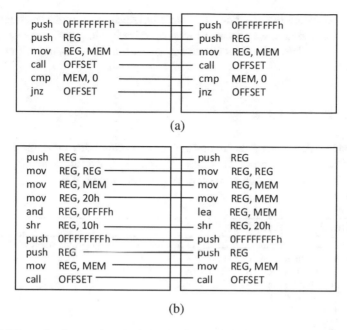

Fig. 8.5 (a) Example of comparing a basic block with itself. (b) Example of instruction alignment. The lines represent the mapping of instructions that gives the highest similarity score

8.2.3 Fuzzy Matching Detection Engine

We have discussed how to compare two basic blocks and obtain a similarity score for them. Since each function can be regarded as a set of basic blocks, the seemingly simplest way is to leverage the Hungarian algorithm [221], to find one to one mapping of all the nodes between functions. However this approach is not efficient since its complexity is $\mathcal{O}(n^3)$ [141]. Moreover, it is prone to mismatching due to the

---

Algorithm 1: Basic block comparison

Input: $BB1$, $BB2$: Two basic blocks with sizes of m and n.
Output: M: Memoization table.

1 **Function** BasicBlockComparison($BB1[1..m]$, $BB2[1..n]$)
2 | M = Array $(0..m, 0..n)$;
3 | **for** $i = 1..m$ **do**
4 | **for** $j = 1..n$ **do**
5 | | M[i, j] = Max (M[i, j-1], M[i-1, j], M[i-1, j-1] + $Score$(BB1[i], BB2[j]));
6 | **end**
7 | **end**
8 | **return** $M[m, n]$;
9 **end**

---

negligence of taking the execution flow and whole structure into consideration. In order to overcome this, we choose to match nodes inside paths, for each path that represents a complete execution. Given any target function, we start with its longest path in CFG.

8.2.3.1 Path Exploration

For the longest path in a target function, path exploration involves finding the most similar path in the reference function. To this end, we adopt an approach that combines breadth first search and dynamic programming [202].

Algorithm 2: Path exploration

Input: P: The longest path from the target function, G: the CFG of the reference function
Output: δ: The memoization table /* σ: the array that stores the largest LCS score for every node in G */

1 **Function** PathExploration($P[1..m],G[1..n]$)
2   δ = Array(0..0, 0..m)
3   σ = Array(1..n)
4   Q = Queue$\{G_{head}\}$
5   **while** $Q.size()! = 0$ **do**
6          $currNode \leftarrow Q.front()$
7   LCS($currNode,P[1..m]$) //compare $currNode$ with every node in P and update the table δ
8   **if** $\sigma(currNode) < \delta(currNode, m)$ **then**
9              $\sigma(currNode) = \delta(currNode, m)$
10   Q.insert(all the successors of currNode)

11   **return** δ

12 **Function** LCS($u,P[1..m]$)
13   **for** $i = 1..m$ **do**
14   **if** $SameDegree(u,p[i])$ **then**
15             $sim = Score(u, p[i])$
16   **else**
17             $sim = 0$
18         $\delta(u, p[i]) = Max(\ \delta(parent(u), parent(p[i])) + sim,$
19                     $\delta(parent(u), p[i]), \delta(u, parent(p[i])))$

Algorithm 2 details the approach. Suppose that P is our longest path from the target function, we always start from the head node of the reference function by putting it into the working queue Q. During each iteration, we pop out the first element from Q as our current node and invoke function LCS to update the memoization table δ. Array σ is used to prune the search space. We only explore the successors of the current node when a larger score has been obtained in the corresponding cell in σ. Otherwise we interrupt the current search and do not explore further its child nodes. After the algorithm terminates, the memoization table δ will be the output.

Similar to obtaining the LCS of two strings, we read out the corresponding matched path by backtracking the memoization table δ. This retrieved path (P_r) in the reference function can achieve the highest similarity score with the longest path (P_t) in the target function using our scoring strategy. However, during our experiments, we found that focusing on only the absolute value of similarity scores sometimes gives undesirable results. We normalize the similarity score by taking the size of both paths into account as follows:

$$NormScore(P_t, P_r) = \frac{similarity\ score}{Score(P_t) + Score(P_r)}. \tag{8.2}$$

Figure 8.6 presents an example. As shown, the target CFG and the reference are similar. However, the reference CFG has two inserted basic blocks (A and B) to perform extra functionality. The longest path ("$1 \rightarrow 2 \rightarrow 3 \rightarrow 4 \rightarrow 5$") in the target CFG is highlighted in black.

At the beginning of the path exploration, we first insert the head node ① of the reference CFG into the working queue Q. Then, node ① is compared with every node in the longest path P and the memoization table is updated accordingly. Since node ① has only one successor, we insert its child Ⓐ in to queue Q and continue the comparison. Since node Ⓐ is newly inserted and there is no matching nodes for it, we update the scores in memoization table but no extra score was obtained. Similarly, we continue to compare node ②, and update the memoization table, but

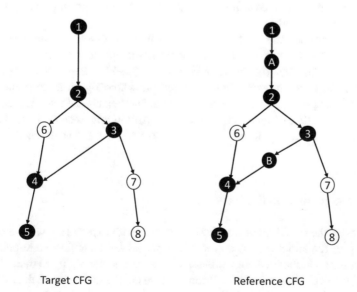

Target CFG   Reference CFG

Fig. 8.6 Two versions of the same function

Fig. 8.7 The memoization table of path exploration

v	Path in Reference CFG	u	1	2	3	4	5
NULL		0	0	0	0	0	0
1	1	0	↖1	←1	←1	←1	←1
A	1→A	0	↑1	↑1	↑1	↑1	↑1
2	1→A→2	0	↑1	↖2	←2	←2	←2
6	1→A→2→6	0	↑1	↑2	↑2	↑2	↑2
3	1→A→2→3	0	↑1	↑2	↖3	←3	←3
4	1→A→2→6→4	0	↑1	↑2	↑2	↖3	←3
B	1→A→2→3→B	0	↑1	↑2	↑3	↑3	↑3
7	1→A→2→3→7	0	↑1	↑2	↑3	↑3	↑3
5	1→A→2→6→4→5	0	↑1	↑2	↑2	↑3	↖4
4	1→A→2→3→B→4	0	↑1	↑2	↑3	↖4	←4
8	1→A→2→3→7→8	0	↑1	↑2	↑3	↑3	↑3
5	1→A→2→3→B→4→5	0	↑1	↑2	↑3	↑4	↖5

this time the obtained score is 2 when node ② is matched to the corresponding node in the longest path. Since node ② has two successors, we assume that the child node ⑥ is visited first. The current partial path will be "1→A→2→6." The other child, node ③ will also be compared after node ⑥, and the corresponding path will be "1→A→2→3." Now the queue Q contains three nodes, node ④, node ⑧, and node ⑦. In the next iteration, all these three nodes will be compared and the memoization table will be updated correspondingly. Node ⑤, node ④, and node ⑧ will be Q's new content. Note that it is the second time for node ④ to be added to Q. We allow the same node to be explored more than once, as long as they represent different execution paths.

In this example, the first path is "1→A→2→6→4," while the latter is "1→A→2→3→B→4." After this iteration, the queue Q has now only one element, node ⑤, and the underlying path is "1→A→2→3→B→4→5." We add a final row to the memoization table and the whole algorithm terminates when Q becomes empty. Table 8.7 shows the final memoization table. We can easily backtrack this table and read out the matching path in reference to the CFG. In this example, the matching path is "1→A→2→3→B→4→5," as denoted in gray in Fig. 8.7.

8.2.3.2 Neighborhood Exploration

At this stage, the initial mapping obtained during path exploration will be extended according to the structure. To this end, we put all the matching node pairs into a priority queue and the elements in the queue are sorted according to their similarity score. At the beginning of each iteration, we pop out the node pair on the front of the queue, which is the pair with the highest similarity score. We then try to match their successors and predecessors. In this process, both in-degrees and out-degrees are also taken into consideration. If there exist multiple possible mappings, Hungarian

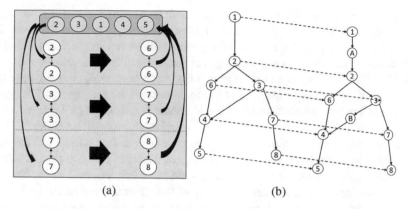

(a)   (b)

Fig. 8.8 An example of neighborhood exploration. (**a**) The priority queue. (**b**) The obtained node matchings

algorithm [221] will be leveraged to find the best one, that is, the mapping giving the highest similarity score. The newly found node pairs will first be checked for consistency with existing mappings. Those inconsistent mappings will be discarded.

The algorithm terminates when the priority queue is empty. The similarity score between the target function and reference function can be calculated as follows:

$$SimilarityScore(f_t, f_r) = \frac{2\sum_{\forall(u,v)\in\gamma} Score(u, v)}{Score(f_t) + Score(f_r)},$$ (8.3)

where γ is the set of all the matching node pairs we obtained during path exploration and neighborhood exploration from target function f_t and reference function f_r.

Figure 8.8 depicts an example of neighborhood exploration. Initially there are five nodes in the priority queue. Each time we pop out an element from the queue and explore its neighborhood. The final obtained matchings are shown in Fig. 8.8b. It is also trivial to calculate the similarity at this stage. For the purpose of simplicity, suppose all the nodes are of the same size and have the same score. The similarity score is calculated according to Eq. 8.3 as follows:

$$Similarity = \frac{2 * 8}{8 + 10} = 88.89\%.$$

8.2.4 Fingerprint-Based Detection Engine

We have previously introduced the proposed fuzzy matching detection engine. In experiments, we found that this technique provides good accuracy. However, the drawback is the scalability. Given a large repository of n functions, finding the possible matches for all the functions, requires to perform the comparison $O(n^n)$ times, which is not efficient.

To mitigate this problem, we designed another fingerprint-based comparison engine, as our initial phase. For any given target function, only those functions that survived the fingerprint-based detection engine will be fed to the fuzzy matching detection engine, to be compared against the target. To this end, we use the normalized instruction set as the fingerprint of a function, while min-hashing [65] and the banding technique [192] are used to process all the fingerprints. Therefore, certain similarity threshold can be imposed. Generally, if we use n hash functions, b bands, r rows, and $n = br$, the imposed Jaccard similarity will be $(1/b)^{1/r}$ [192].

For example, suppose during hashing, we use 210 hash functions. Then for every set, its min-hash signature is a vector whose size equals to 210. We then divide the min-hash signature into 30 bands, where each band consists of 7 rows. Suppose we have two sets with a Jaccard similarity of 0.8. Remember that the probability that their min-hash signature has the same value in certain index equals to the Jaccard similarity of these two sets [192]. Thus, the probability that their min-hash signatures agree in all rows of one particular band is $0.8^7 = 0.2097$, and the probability that the min-hash signature does not agree in at least one row of a particular band is $1 - 0.8^7 = 0.7903$. That is to say, for two sets with a Jaccard similarity of 0.8, in any one band they only have a 20.97% chance of agreeing in all 7 rows, and be selected as a candidate. However, we have 30 bands corresponding to 30 chances to be selected as a candidate. The overall chance that they fail in all the 30 bands is only $(1 - 0.8^7)^{30} = 0.0008$, which means that approximately one in 1200 pairs that has a Jaccard similarity of 0.8 will not be selected as a candidate.

At this phase, it is also trivial to add one more rule based on basic block numbers. In our fuzzy matching graph comparison phase, we are performing a CFG-based fuzzy matching. Thus it does not make much sense to try to match two functions with significantly different number of basic blocks, as this will not produce reasonably good results. So for a target function with n nodes, we only allow functions with size between $n - \gamma$ and $n + \gamma$ to be matched, where γ is a user-defined parameter.

8.3 Evaluation

In this section, we detail our experiments and analysis. All experiments have been performed on a desktop running Microsoft Windows 7 64-bit, with an Intel Xeon E31220 Quad-Core processor, 16 GB of RAM.

8.3.1 Clone Detection

The first experiment involves clone detection from a large repository. In this experiment, different versions of zlib library [17] are used as target libraries. Since zlib is a well-maintained library, the functionality of the same function in different versions should be similar but not exactly identical. Consequently, the same functions between different versions can be regarded as clones. Every time, we try to match functions with their peers in the next version of zlib.

We also introduce two groups of noise functions. The first group represents functions from an assortment of open-source software such as libpng, libjpeg, SQLite, and Firefox. In total it has 2,171,642 assembly functions. The second group represents all the functions of 1701 dynamic library system functions obtained from Microsoft Windows operating system. The total size of these files is around 1 GB and the total number of functions is 2,055,584.

In this experiment, the Jaccard similarity threshold for fingerprint-based detection engine is set to 0.60, 0.65, and 0.70 to study its effect. The tolerance of node number difference is set to 35 throughout the experiment.

8.3.1.1 Open-source Projects

Table 8.2 shows the result of using 2 million functions from open-source projects as noise group. We can see that the average detection time is within seconds and the accuracy is consistently above 90%. The impact of different parameters is also studied. Take zlib 1.2.7 as an example, when we set the Jaccard similarity threshold to 0.60, 0.65, and 0.70, the achieved accuracy is 96.52%, 97.39%, and 98.26%, respectively. The detection time decreased from 3.829 s per function all the way to 1.215 s. The reason is that when we increase the threshold, fewer functions were fed into fuzzy matching engine, resulting in shorter detection time.

8.3.1.2 Dynamic Link Library Files

The second noise group represents all the functions from 1 GB of dynamic link libraries. As can be seen in Table 8.3, compared with open-source project datasets, we end up with a smaller candidate set. That is because this noise group includes

Table 8.2 Clone detection results using open-source projects as noise

zlib Version	Threshold	Overall accuracy	Candidate size	Time (per function)
1.2.5	0.60	95.33%	36,227	3.438 s
	0.65	93.46%	12,481	1.981 s
	0.70	91.59%	4146	1.004 s
1.2.6	0.60	100.00%	41,327	3.965 s
	0.65	100.00%	14,854	2.013 s
	0.70	100.00%	5129	1.129 s
1.2.7	0.60	96.52%	41,117	3.829 s
	0.65	97.39%	14,835	2.081 s
	0.70	98.26%	5121	1.215 s

Table 8.3 Clone detection results using dynamic link libraries as noise

`zlib` Version	Threshold	Overall accuracy	Candidate size	Time (per function)
1.2.5	0.60	96.26%	12,346	2.806 s
	0.65	94.39%	2727	1.468 s
	0.70	91.59%	1911	0.897 s
1.2.6	0.60	100.00%	16,315	2.927 s
	0.65	100.00%	2848	1.558 s
	0.70	100.00%	1989	0.913 s
1.2.7	0.60	96.52%	16,312	2.884 s
	0.65	97.39%	2847	1.572 s
	0.70	98.26%	1988	0.918 s

Table 8.4 Clone detection results between `zlib` and `libpng`

`zlib` Version	Threshold	Overall accuracy	Candidate size	Time (per function)
1.2.8	0.60	92.5%	3526	2.204 s
	0.65	92.5%	751	1.258 s
	0.70	92.5%	242	0.95 s

components from the operating system. Their functionality should be specific and different from the `zlib` library, which is a compression library. As a result, the number of candidate functions that could survive the fingerprint-based detection engine is smaller than that of the last group, but the overall accuracy is still very similar.

8.3.1.3   Clone Detection Between Different Binaries

We also conduct clone detection between two different binaries: `zlib` and `libpng` [8]. As a library for processing PNG image format files, we know that `libpng` is dependent on `zlib` and reuses `zlib` functions. We first compile `zlib` 1.2.8 and `libpng` 1.6.17 with the debugging information attached. By manual analysis of both libraries, we identified *40* clones. We continue to use the two millions functions from Windows operating system as our noise group.

As depicted in Table 8.4, the overall similarity was consistently 92.5% for all similarity thresholds. However, the details were not exactly the same. When the similarity threshold was 0.60, BINSEQUENCE failed to match three functions: `crc32`, `copy_block`, and `inflateReset2`. The `crc32` and `copy_block` were not properly matched because the true matches have different structures with the targets. Consequently, others functions that happen to have similar structures as the targets get wrongly matched. For `inflateReset2` function, its true match failed to survive the fingerprint-based detection engine. When we increase the similarity threshold to 0.65 or 0.70, BINSEQUENCE failed to match `crc32`, inflateReset, and inflateReset2. The copy_block function got correctly matched as the increased threshold ruled out the false matches. At the same time, the true matches for inflateReset and inflateReset2 failed to pass the engine and got wrongly matched.

8.3.2 Compiler Optimization

Compiling the same source code under different compilation environments can also create syntactically different but semantically equivalent functions, namely semantic clones. In this experiment, the compiler MSVC 2013 was used and we continue to use libpng as test library. To introduce mutations, four different optimization levels Od, $O1$, $O2$, and Ox were used. Since Ox is the default optimization level for libpng library, we then use functions compiled with Ox as our target functions. In order to take into consideration of the differences that the compiler optimization might introduce, we set the threshold for the number of basic blocks to 100, and the fingerprint threshold to relatively low values such as 0.25 and 0.40, to prevent the true matches from getting filtered out. We also introduced 1232 noise functions from sqlite.

During the experiment, we found that the accuracy was mainly influenced by three factors: the optimization level, similarity threshold, and the size of target functions. We noticed that the code and structure generated with $O1$, $O2$, and Ox are somewhat similar while Od, however, gives quite different code and structures. As can be seen in Fig. 8.9, the accuracy of Ox vs. $O1$ and Ox vs. $O2$ is consistently above the accuracy of Ox vs. Od. The reason is that nowadays various techniques are being used by compilers to optimize the generated assembly code for increased performance and minimized size. When we choose to compile some source code with optimization disabled (Od), the code is surely very different than the optimized code.

We could also observe from Fig. 8.9 that, using a lower fingerprint threshold could yield higher accuracy. The reason is that when the fingerprint threshold is low, more functions could pass the filter. As a result, the true matches could survive to the next stage. The size of the target functions also has an impact on the accuracy. As shown in Fig. 8.9a, when we consider larger functions, the accuracy also increases. That is because BINSEQUENCE uses both syntactic and structural features to match two functions. When the size of a target function is small, its structure is often trivial or common. As a result, a function with similar structure could be wrongly matched. When the target function has a moderate size, its structure becomes more specific and true matches have more chances of getting matched.

It is worth mentioning that Ox and $O2$ seem to generate identical assembly code in this experiment. Consequently, the accuracy is 100% (Fig. 8.9c), regardless of fingerprint threshold or the size of target function.

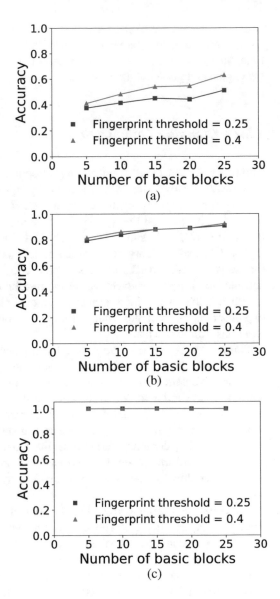

Fig. 8.9 Accuracy of different optimization levels. (a) Ox vs Od. (b) Ox vs O1. (c) Ox vs O2

8.3.3   Code Obfuscation

Note that when experimenting with BINSEQUENCE, we assume that the binary is de-obfuscated. In other words, BINSEQUENCE mainly deals with de-obfuscated code. However, we also conducted an experiment to evaluate the robustness of BINSE-QUENCE on obfuscated code. To this end, we use obfuscator-LLVM [9, 173] as our obfuscator. Obfuscator-LLVM can perform three kinds of obfuscations: bogus control flow, control flow flattening, and instructions substitution. The technique of bogus control flow inserts new basic blocks that contain an opaque predicate and then makes a conditional jump back to the original basic block. At the same time, the original basic block is also cloned and filled up with junk instructions. Control flow flattening can flatten the control flow graph of a program, and instructions substitution replaces standard binary operators with functionally equivalent but more complicated sequences of instructions. We first use obfuscator-LLVM to obfuscate zlib library with these three obfuscation techniques separately, and then use the de-obfuscated functions to match the obfuscated functions. By manually checking the original and obfuscated binary, we identified 83 functions (with at least 5 basic blocks) whose code and structure have been obfuscated. Throughout this experiment, we set the threshold for the number of basic blocks to 100, and the fingerprint threshold to 0.25. We also add 1232 functions from sqlite as noise functions.

As can be seen in Table 8.5, when bogus control flow is enabled, the accuracy of BINSEQUENCE is 53.01%. The main reason is that BINSEQUENCE relies on both syntactic and structural features to match two functions. Inserting new basic blocks with branches will alter the control structure and consequently, decrease the accuracy. However, BINSEQUENCE still succeeds in matching more than 50% of the functions because it can perform a fuzzy structure matching. The second obfuscation technique, control flow flattening seems to pose a problem for BINSEQUENCE. The accuracy is very low in this case. The reason is that control flow flattening can completely change the control flow structure. For instance, the compress2 function has 5 and 28 basic blocks before and after obfuscation, and the deflate function has 260 and 561. So it is very difficult for BINSEQUENCE to match them. For instructions substitution, BINSEQUENCE seems to cope it without problem. Actually substituting instructions with functionally equivalent ones could be looked at upon as some kind of "noises" on the basic block level. Surely the similarity score could decrease; however, our fuzzy matching algorithm can still tolerate these "noises" and easily find the true matches.

Table 8.5 Results for function reuse detection

Obfuscation techniques	Correctly matched	Overall accuracy
Bogus control flow	44	53.01%
Control flow flattening	3	3.61%
Instructions substitution	78	93.98%

8.3.4 Recovering Patch Information

One real-life use case is to use BINSEQUENCE to recover patch information. Thanks to the vulnerability exploiting techniques, more and more code vulnerabilities are being discovered every day. For those closed-source projects, the software developer often provides a patch without disclosing the detailed information regarding the vulnerability. In most cases, the released patch modifies several buggy functions, and leaves the others untouched. By using BINSEQUENCE to compare the before and after patch versions of the same binary, the patched buggy/vulnerable functions can be revealed as their similarity will no longer be 1 after applying the patch. Consequently, the information can be deduced from the way that the bug/vulnerability is patched.

According to Microsoft security bulletin MS15-034, there is a vulnerability in HTTP protocol stack HTTP.sys. When an attacker sends a specially crafted HTTP request, HTTP.sys might improperly parse this request. Consequently, the attacker could execute arbitrary code in the context of the system account. To address this bug, Microsoft released a patch and encouraged its customers to update their systems. By comparing the before and after patch versions of HTTP.sys, BINSEQUENCE identified 11 functions that have been changed. After taking a closer look, we listed 5 functions in Table 8.6 that are related to the bug.

We first take a look at the UlpParseRange function. As shown in Fig. 8.10a, b, both the patched and unpatched versions have 60 basic blocks. BINSEQUENCE successfully matched all the basic blocks. Among all these pairs, 59 pairs have a similarity of 1, which means they remain the same after being patched (after normalization). The only basic block pair highlighted in red in Fig. 8.10a, b shows where the patch took place, basic block number 45.

Figure 8.10c depicts the basic block 45 before and after the patch. We can clearly see that the patched version was calling a function RtlUlongLongAdd, while the unpatched version does not. We can infer that the original function might contain an integer overflow vulnerability. The patched version invokes the RtlULongLongAdd to fix it. Moreover, we can see that the out-degrees of these two basic blocks have been changed. The out-degree of the unpatched version is 1, while that of the patched version is 2. Despite this structure change, our fuzzy structure matching approach still succeed in matching these two basic blocks.

Table 8.6 Patched analysis for HTTP.sys

Function	Similarity
UlpParseRange	0.97
UlpBuildSingleRangeMdlChainFromSlices	0.91
UlpBuildMultiRangeMdlChainFromSlices	0.85
UlpDuplicateChunkRange	0.80
UlAdjustRangesToContentSize	0.50

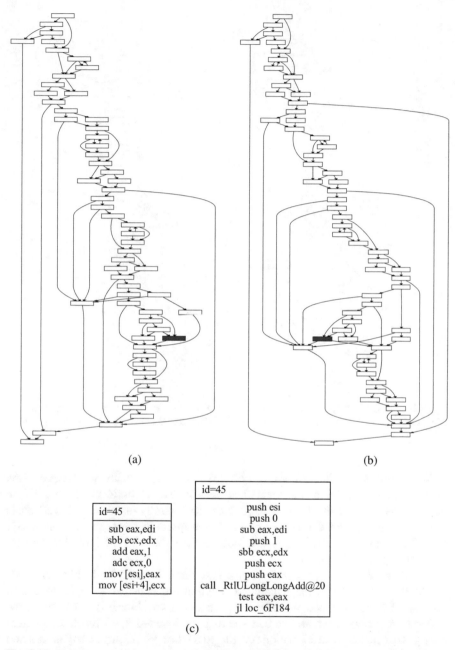

(a)   (b)

id=45
push esi
push 0
sub eax,edi
push 1
sbb ecx,edx
push ecx
push eax
call _RtlULongLongAdd@20
test eax,eax
jl loc_6F184

id=45
sub eax,edi
sbb ecx,edx
add eax,1
adc ecx,0
mov [esi],eax
mov [esi+4],ecx

(c)

Fig. 8.10 The UlpParseRange function before and after patch. (**a**) UlpParseRange function before patch. (**b**) UlpParseRange function after patch. (**c**) Basic block 45 before and after patched (out-degrees are 1 and 2, respectively)

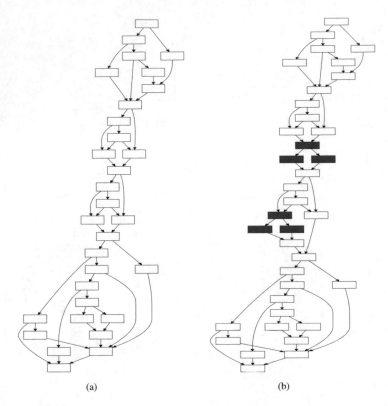

(a)   (b)

Fig. 8.11 The `UlpDuplicateChunkRange` function before and after patch. (**a**) `UlpDuplicateChunkRange` before patch. (**b**) `UlpDuplicateChunkRange` after patch

We continue to inspect the `UlpDuplicateChunkRange` function. As depicted in Fig. 8.11a, b, the unpatched version has 31 basic blocks, while the patched has 37 basic blocks. BINSEQUENCE successfully matched all the 31 basic blocks in the unpatched version to their counterparts in the patched version. Six basic blocks in the patched version are not matched; thus, we can infer that they are inserted to patch the vulnerability.

Figure 8.12 shows the detail of the first three inserted basic blocks. Basic blocks 9, 10, 11, 12 in the unpatched function are matched to basic blocks 9, 10, 11, 15 in the patched function, respectively. Basic blocks 12, 13, 14 in the patched are newly inserted. We can see that the inserted basic block 12 invokes the `RtlULongLongAdd` function (`call_RtlULongLongAdd@20`) as well and makes one conditional jump (`jge loc_5742C`) based on the return value. Our fuzzy matching approach successfully jumped over these inserted basic blocks and matched the rest of the control flow graphs.

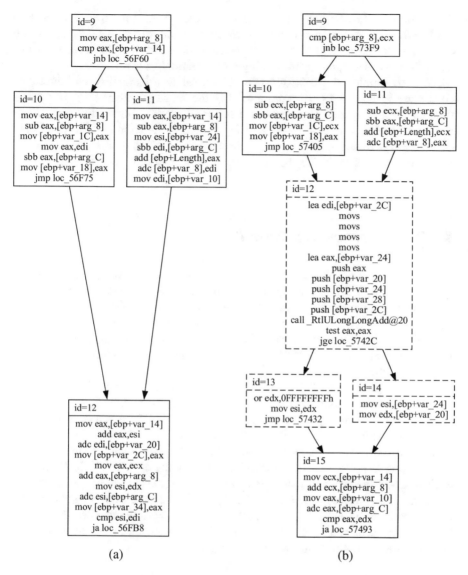

Fig. 8.12 One of the patched parts of the *UlpDuplicateChunkRange* function. (**a**) Before patch. (**b**) After patch

8.3.5 Searching Malware and Vulnerability Functions

One of the most common scenarios where people resort to reverse engineering is malware analysis. Thus, in this experiment, two notorious malware, Citadel and Zeus, have been used. In total there are 557 functions in Zeus. For 67% of them, BINSEQUENCE found an exact match in `Citadel`. Moreover, 92.1% of all the functions in `Zeus` have found a match with similarity above 0.8. This result also confirms the finding of the study performed in [241], which concludes that `Citadel` is based upon `Zeus`, reusing most functions in `Zeus`.

We also employed BINSEQUENCE to recover a vulnerability introduced by code reuse in `Firefox`. According to [15], the `resize_context_buffers` function in `libvpx` library contains a buffer overflow vulnerability that affects `Firefox` before version 40.0.0. By using the buggy function in `libvpx` library as our target, we successfully identified the bug in `Firefox` version 36.0.0 through 39.0.0. For `Firefox` 40.0.0, the patched vulnerable function was returned, with the highest similarity.

8.3.6   Comparison with Other Tools

In this experiment, three other state-of-the-art tools have been employed: DIAPHORA [5], PATCHDIFF2 [10], and BINDIFF [38]. In order to evaluate the tools in terms of robustness, two same family but slightly different compilers have been used, namely MSVC 2010 and MSVC 2013. All the other tools, DIAPHORA, PATCHDIFF2, and BINDIFF, can only perform function matching between two similar binaries. BINSEQUENCE, on the other hand, is not confined to comparing binaries of different versions.

Similar to previous experiments, two test libraries, `zlib` and `libpng`, are used. As can be seen in Table 8.7, for `zlib`, DIAPHORA, PATCHDIFF2, BINDIFF, and BINSEQUENCE correctly matched 105, 110, 130, and 135 functions, respectively. The corresponding accuracy is 72.92%, 76.39%, 90.28%, and 93.75%. It is noteworthy that, aside from the function itself, the first three tools take the call graph of the binary into consideration. BINSEQUENCE, on the other hand, simply queries each function independently. Still BINSEQUENCE achieved the highest accuracy. Similarly, when we use `libpng` as test library, the accuracies for these four tools are respectively 57.37%, 62.48%, 84.28%, and 89.78%. We can see that for all the tools, the achieved accuracy is slightly lower compared to that of `zlib`, and BINSEQUENCE continues to lead in the comparison.

Table 8.7 Comparison with other tools

Library	DIAPHORA	PATCHDIFF2	BINDIFF	BINSEQUENCE
`zlib`	72.92%	76.39%	90.28%	93.75%
`libpng`	57.37%	62.48%	84.28%	89.78%

8.4 Limitations and Concluding Remarks

In this chapter, we presented BINSEQUENCE, a scalable and efficient binary code clone detection engine. Compared with other works, it focuses on fuzzy matching on multiple levels while achieving a balance between scalability and accuracy. We also conducted multiple experiments and discussed different real-world use cases.

During the experiments, we identified the following limitations: (1) Function inlining could be a problem. However, if the target function is large enough, there is a high chance that BINSEQUENCE can still find its match. (2) Equivalent instructions could pose some issues. When different instructions are used to accomplish the same functionality, BINSEQUENCE will not be able to match them. Introducing instruction categorization could overcome this. (3) Currently the approach relies on the longest path. A short path does not carry much structural information and can lead to mismatch. Future enhancements of BINSEQUENCE could take more paths into account, or leverage other different techniques to generate additional starting points more efficiently.

Chapter 9
Authorship Attribution

Binary authorship attribution refers to the process of discovering information related to the author(s) of anonymous binary code on the basis of stylometric characteristics extracted from the code. However, in practice, authorship attribution for binary code still requires considerable manual and error-prone reverse engineering analysis, which can be a daunting task given the sheer volume and complexity of today's malware. In this chapter, we propose BINAUTHOR, a novel and the first compiler-agnostic method for identifying the authors of program binaries. Having filtered out unrelated functions (compiler and library) to detect user-related functions, it converts user-related functions into a canonical form to eliminate compiler/compilation effects. Then, it leverages a set of features based on collections of authors' programming choices made during coding. These features capture an author's coding habits.

This chapter is organized as follows. Section 9.1 introduces an overview of the proposed method. The authorship attribution technique is presented in Sect. 9.2, followed by the evaluation results in Sect. 9.3. Then, we discuss the limitations and draw the chapter conclusions in Sect. 9.4.

9.1 Approach Overview

Authorship attribution is especially relevant to security applications, such as digital forensic analysis of malicious code [229] and copyright infringement detection [258] because the source code is seldom available in these cases. Although significant efforts have been made to develop automated approaches for authorship attribution for source code [90, 183, 270], such techniques typically rely on features that are likely to be lost in the binary code after the compilation process, for example, variable and function naming, original control and data flow structures, comments, and space layout. Nonetheless, at a BlackHat conference [205], the

© Springer Nature Switzerland AG 2020
S. Alrabaee et al., *Binary Code Fingerprinting for Cybersecurity*, Advances in
Information Security 78, https://doi.org/10.1007/978-3-030-34238-8_9

feasibility of authorship attribution for malware binaries was confirmed though the process still requires considerable human intervention.

Most existing approaches to binary authorship attribution employ machine learning methods to extract unique features for each author and subsequently match the features of a given binary to identify the authors [59, 90, 251]. These approaches were studied and analyzed in [60], which uncovered several issues that affect the abovementioned approaches. Notably, a considerable percentage of the extracted features are related to compiler functions rather than to author styles, which causes a high false positive rate. Moreover, the extracted features are not resilient to code transformation methods, refactoring techniques, changes in the compilation settings, and the use of different compilers. We implemented BINAUTHOR that improves the accuracy obtained by Caliskan et al. [90] in attributing 600 authors from 83% to 90%, and then we scaled the results to 86% accuracy for 1500 authors.

We present BINAUTHOR, a system designed to recognize author *coding habits* by extracting author's coding choices from binary code. BINAUTHOR[1] performs a series of steps in order to capture coding habits. First, it filters unrelated functions such as compiler-related functions by proposing a method that is discussed in Sect. 9.2.1. Second, it labels library-related functions and free open-source related functions using our previous works, BinShape [264] (Chap. 4), SIGMA [61] (Chap. 5), and FOSSIL [62] (Chap. 7), respectively. The results of the filtering process represent a set of user-related functions. Third, to eliminate the effects of changes in the compiler or the compilation settings, code transformation, and refactoring tools, BINAUTHOR converts the code into a canonical form that is robust against heavy obfuscation [280]. However, the conversion is time consuming so we apply it only to the set of user-related functions remaining after filtering. Then we collect a set of author choices frequently made during coding (e.g., preferring to use either `memcopy` or `bcopy`). In order to capture the choices, we examined a large collection of source code and the corresponding assembly instructions to determine which coding habits may be preserved in the binary. Next, we designed features based on these habits and integrated them into BINAUTHOR. To verify that the features capture coding habits, we investigated the ground truth source code in a controlled experiment (using debug information) to determine if the choices are based on functionality or habit.

9.2   Authorship Attribution

We propose a system encompassing different components, each of which is meant to achieve a particular purpose, as illustrated in Fig. 9.1. The first component (*Filtering*) isolates user functions from compiler functions, library functions, and open-source software packages. For this purpose, we employ BINSHAPE, and FOSSIL (previously discussed in Chap. 4 and Chap. 7) beside the proposed method

---

[1]https://github.com/g4hsean/BinAuthor.

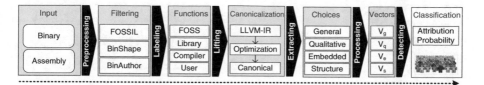

Fig. 9.1 BINAUTHOR architecture

to identify compiler functions. Hence, an additional outcome of the *Filtering* component could be considered as a choice (e.g., the preference in using specific compiler or open-source software packages). The second component (*Canonicalization*) adapts the existing framework ANGR [265] for function lifting into LLVM-IR, then optimizes the lifted LLVM-IR, and finally converts the optimized intermediate representation (IR) into a canonical form. The third component (*Choices*) analyzes user-related functions to extract possible features that represent stylistic choices and then converts the extracted choices into vectors. The vector of choices are used by the attribution probability function in the last component (*Classification*). The aforementioned components are explained in depth in the remainder of this section.

9.2.1 Filtering

An important initial step in most reverse engineering tasks is to distinguish between user functions and library/compiler functions. This step saves considerable time and helps shifting the focus to more relevant functions. The filtering process consists of three steps. First, BINSHAPE [264] (Chap. 4) is used to label library functions. Second, FOSSIL [62] (Chap. 7) is leveraged to label the functions that are related to specific FOSS libraries, such as `libpng`, `zlib`, and `openssl`. The last step filters compiler-related functions, for which the details are given below.

The idea is based on the hypothesis that compiler/helper functions can be identified through a collection of static signatures that are created in the training phase (e.g., opcode frequencies). We analyze a number of programs with different functionalities, ranging from a simple "Hello World!" program to programs fulfilling complex tasks. Through the intersection of these functions combined with manual analysis, we collect about 240 functions as compiler/helper functions related to two compilers, namely GCC and VS. The opcode frequencies are extracted from these functions, after which the mean and variance of each opcode are calculated.

More specifically, each disassembled program P, after passing through the IDA PRO disassembler [45], consists of n functions $\{f_1, \cdots, f_n\}$. Each function f_k is represented as a set of m opcodes associated with the (mean, variance) pair of their frequency of occurrence in function f_k. In this context, each opcode $o_i \in O$ has a pair of values (μ_i, ν_i), which represents the mean and variance values of that specific opcode. We compute μ_i and ν_i as follows:

Table 9.1 An example of
computing (μ_i, ν_i)

Opcode	push	mov	lea	pop
Frequency	19	31	13	7
μ	0.271	0.442	0.186	0.100
ν	0.563	45.563	5.063	27.563

$$\mu_i = \frac{x_i}{\sum_{j=1}^{m} x_j} \tag{9.1}$$

$$\nu_i = \frac{(x_i - \bar{x})^2}{n}, \tag{9.2}$$

where x_i represents the frequency of opcode o_i, m is the number of opcodes, and $\bar{x}$ represents the average of frequencies.

Example: We introduce an example in Table 9.1 to show how we compute (μ_i, ν_i) for each opcode. For instance, suppose a compiler function has the following opcodes and corresponding frequencies: push(19), mov(31), lea(13), and pop(7). We compute μ_i and ν_i as shown in the table, for instance, μ for push is $19/(19 + 31 + 13 + 7) = 0.271$, and ν_i is $(19 - 17.5)^2/4 = 0.563$.

Dissimilarity measurement $D_{i,j}$ is performed based on the distance between the target function f_j and the training function f_i as per the following equation [287]:

$$D_{i,j} = \frac{(\mu_i - \mu_j)^2}{\left(v_i^2 + v_j^2\right)}, \tag{9.3}$$

where (μ_i, ν_i) and (μ_j, ν_j) represent the opcode mean and variance of the training function f_i and target function f_j, respectively.

Each opcode o_i in the target function is measured against the same opcode of all compiler functions in the training set. If the distance $D_{i,j}$ is less than a predefined threshold value $\alpha = 0.005$, the opcode is considered as a match. This dissimilarity metric detects functions, which are closer to each other in terms of types of opcodes. For instance, logical opcodes are not available in *compiler-related* functions.

Finally, a function is labelled as *compiler-related* if the number of matched opcodes over the total number of opcodes (m) is greater than a predefined threshold value obtained from experiments to be $\gamma = 0.75$. Otherwise, the target function is labelled as *user-related*.

9.2.2   Canonicalization

We use a strategy similar to that applied in the recent work by David et al. [111] when lifting the resulting user-related functions.

Lifting Binaries to Intermediate Representation (IR): We adopt the existing framework ANGR [265] for lifting functions into LLVM-IR. We first convert the disassembled binary to the VEX-IR [224] using ANGR, and then implement a translator to convert the VEX-IR to LLVM-IR. This IR representation is beneficial since: (1) it is architecture-agnostic, and (2) the LLVM-IR format is well documented and well maintained and has a plethora of tools for creation, translation, and manipulation.

Optimizing Intermediate Representation: To achieve this goal, we employ the extended version of PEGGY tool [280] to optimize LLVM-IR. PEGGY performs the following tasks: dead code elimination, global value numbering, partial redundancy elimination, sparse conditional constant propagation, loop-invariant code motion, loop deletion, loop unswitching, and basic block placement. In this way, we prevent such changes from affecting our extracted coding choices. For more details on PEGGY, we refer the reader to [280].

Canonical Form: Canonicalization offers several benefits [111]. Lifting the instructions according to LLVM may impose changes such as redundant loads, but these changes will now be reverted. Moreover, in the case of writing dependencies, canonicalization of the expression makes it possible to perform the addition with the constant first, and the result is put in the register before the subtraction is performed. Furthermore, with canonicalization, the comparison becomes simple addition with a positive constant, instead of subtraction with a negative. Note that this last step serves to re-optimize code which might not have been previously optimized [111].

9.2.3   Choice Categorization

Determining a set of characteristics that remain constant for a significant portion of a program written by a particular author is analogous to discovering human characteristics that can later be used to identify an individual. Accordingly, our aim is to automate the identification of program characteristics, but with a reasonable computational cost. To capture coding habits at different levels of abstraction, we consider a spectrum of habits, assuming that an author's habits can be reflected in a preference for choosing certain keywords or compilers, a reliance on the main function, or the use of an object-oriented programming paradigm. The manner in which the code is organized may also reflect the author's habits. All possible choices are stored as a template in this step. We provide a detailed description of each category of author choices in the following subsections, and further present how each feature vector related to each choice is generated.

9.2.3.1   General Choices

General choices are designed to capture an author's general programming preferences, for example, preferences in organizing the code, terminating a function, the use of particular keywords, or the use of specific resources.

(1) Code organization: We capture the way that the code is organized by measuring the reliance on the `main` function using statistical features, since it is considered a starting part for managing user functions. We define a set of ratios, shown in Table 9.2, which can be used to measure the actions used in the `main` function. We thus capture the percentage usage of keywords, local variables, API calls, and calling user functions, as well as the ratio of the number of basic blocks in the `main` function to the number of basic blocks in other user functions. These percentages are computed relative to the length of the `main` function, where the length signifies the number of instructions in the function. The results are represented as a vector of ratios, which is used by the detection component.

(2) Function termination: BINAUTHOR captures the way in which an author terminates a function. This could help identify an author since programmers may favor specific ways of terminating a function. BINAUTHOR considers not just the last statement of a function as the terminating instruction; rather, it identifies the last basic block of the function with its predecessor as the terminating part. This is a realistic approach since various actions may be required before a function terminates. With this aspect taken into account, BINAUTHOR not only considers the usual terminating instructions, such as `return` and `exit`, but also captures related actions that are taken prior to termination. For instance, a function may be terminated with a display of messages, a call to another function, the release of resources, or a network communication. Table 9.3 shows examples of what is captured in relation to

Table 9.2 Features extracted from the `main` function

Ratio equation	Description
#push / l	Ratio of accessing the stack to length
#push / #lea	Ratio of accessing the stack to local variables
#lea / l	Ratio of local variables to length
#calls / l	Ratio of function calls to length
#callees / l	Ratio of the calls to `main` function to length
#indirect calls / l	Ratio of API calls to length
#BBs / total # all BBs	Ratio of the number of basic blocks of the `main` function to that of other user functions
#calls / #user functions	Ratio of function calls to the number of user functions

length(l) represents number of instructions in the `main` function

Table 9.3 Examples of actions taken in terminating a function

Features	
Printing results to memory	Printing results to file
Using system ("pause")	User action such as `cin`
Calling user functions	Calling API functions
Closing files	Closing resources
Freeing memory	Flushing buffer
Using network communication	Printing clock time
Releasing semaphores or locks	Printing errors

function termination. Such features could be captured by extracting the strings and opcodes. Each feature is set to 1 if it is used to terminate a function; otherwise, it is set to 0. The output of this component is a bit vector that is used by the detection component.

(3) *Keyword and resource preferences:* BINAUTHOR captures an author's preferences in the use of keywords or resources. We consider only groups of preferences with equivalent or similar functionality to avoid functionality-dependent features. These include keyword type preferences for inputs (e.g., using `cin`, `scanf`), preferences for particular resources or a specific compiler (we identify the compiler by using PEiD[2]) operation system (e.g., Linux), CPU architecture (e.g., ARM), and the manner in which certain keywords are used, which can serve as further indications of an author's habits. Some of these features are identified through binary string matching, which tracks the strings annotated to `call` and `mov` instructions. For instance, excessive use of `fflush` will cause the string "`fflush`" to appear frequently in the resulting binary.

9.2.3.2 Feature Vector of General Choices

To consider the reliance on the `main` function, a vector v_{g1}, representing related features, is constructed according to the equations shown in Table 9.2. These equations indicate the author's reliance on the `main` function as well as the actions performed by the author. *Function termination* is represented as a bit vector (v_{g2}), which is determined by the absence or existence of a set of features for function termination. *Keyword and resource preferences* are identified through binary string matching. We extract a collection of strings from all user functions of a particular author, then intersect these strings in order to derive a persistent vector (v_{g3}) for that author. Consequently, for each author, a set of vectors representing the author's signature is stored in our repository.

Given a target binary, BINAUTHOR constructs the vectors from the target and measures the distance/similarity between these vectors and those in our repository. The v_{g1} vector is compared using Euclidean distance, whereas v_{g2} vector is compared using the Jaccard similarity. For v_{g3}, the similarity is computed through inexact string matching. Finally, the three derived similarity values are averaged in order to obtain λ_g, which is later used in Sect. 9.2.4 for author classification.

9.2.3.3 Qualitative Choices

We investigate code quality in terms of compliance with C/C++ coding standards and security concerns. The literature has established that code quality can be measured using different indicators, such as testability, flexibility, and adaptability [242].

---

[2]https://www.aldeid.com/wiki/PEiD.

BINAUTHOR defines rules for capturing code that exhibits either relatively low or high quality. For any code that cannot be matched using such rules, the code is labelled as having regular quality, which indicates that the code quality feature is not applicable. Such rules are extracted by defining a set of signatures (sequence of instructions) for each choice.

Examples of low-quality coding styles include reopening already opened files, leaving files open when they are no longer in use, attempting to modify constants through pointers, using float variables as loop counters, and declaring variables inside a switch statement. Such declarations, which can be captured through the structure matching of code, could be considered as a structural choice, possibly resulting in unexpected/undefined behavior due to jumped-over instructions. It is for this reason that we place them in the low-quality category. Examples of high-quality coding styles include handling errors generated by library calls (i.e., examining the value returned by `fclose()`); avoiding reliance on side effects (e.g., the `++` operator) within calls such as `sizeof` or `_Alignof`; avoiding particular calls to some environments or using them with protective measures (since invoking the `system()` in Linux may lead to shell command injection or privilege escalation, while using `execve()` is indicative of high-quality coding); and the implementation of locks and semaphores around critical sections.

Example of Qualitative Choices:

Listing 9.1   A fragment of assembly code capturing a bad habit of dynamic memory allocation

```
...
call ds:malloc
...
or eax, 0FFFFFFFF  // -1 if text_buffer is Null
...
xor eax, eax // 0 if text_buffer is not Null
```

Listing 9.2   A fragment of assembly code capturing a good habit of dynamic memory allocation

```
...
call ds:malloc
...
or eax, 0FFFFFFFF  // -1 if text_buffer is Null
...
push eax       // memory address of text_buffer
call ds:free
...
xor eax, eax // 0 if text_buffer is not Null
```

Consider a template of dynamic memory allocation presented in Listing 9.1. As shown, we have a call to `malloc`, followed by checking whether or not it is Null. It is shown in Listing 9.2 that how the bad habit in Listing 9.1 could be considered as a good habit at the assembly level.

9.2.3.4 Feature Vector of Qualitative Choices

We build a set of idiom templates to describe high- or low-quality habits. Idioms are sequences of instructions with wild-card possibility [182]. We employ the idioms templates in [182] according to the considered qualitative-related choice. In addition, such templates carry a meaningful connection to the qualitative choices. Our experiments demonstrate that such idiom templates may effectively capture quality-related habits. BINAUTHOR uses the Levenshtein distance [296] for this computation due to its efficiency. The similarity is represented by λ_q as follows:

$$\lambda_q = 1 - \frac{L(C_i, C_j)}{max(|C_i|, |C_j|)}, \tag{9.4}$$

where $L(C_i, C_j)$ is the Levenshtein distance between the qualitative-related choices C_i (sequence of instructions) and C_j, and $max(|C_i|, |C_j|)$ returns the maximum length between two choices C_i and C_j in terms of characters.

9.2.3.5 Embedded Choices

We define embedded choices as actions that are related to coding habits present in the source code, which are not easily captured at the binary level by traditional features such as strings or graphs. Examples are initializing member variables in constructors and dynamically deleting allocated resources in destructors. Since it is not feasible to list all possible features, BINAUTHOR relies on the fact that opcodes reveal actions, expertise, habits, knowledge, and other author's characteristics, and then analyzes the distribution of opcode frequencies. Our experiments showed that this distribution can effectively capture the manner in which an author manages the code. Since every functionality can affect the opcode frequencies, BINAUTHOR targets embedded choices by capturing the distribution of opcode frequencies.

9.2.3.6 Feature Vector of Embedded Choices

The Mahalanobis distance [204] is used to measure the dissimilarity of opcode distributions among different user functions, which is represented by λ_e. The Mahalanobis distance is chosen because it can capture the correlation between opcode frequency distributions.

9.2.3.7   Structural Choices

Programmers usually develop their own structural design habits. They may prefer
to use a fully object-oriented design, or they may be more accustomed to procedural
programming. Structural choices can serve as features for author identification.
To avoid taking into account the program functionality, we consider the common
subgraphs for each user function and then intersect them among different user
functions to identify those subgraphs that are unique and those that are common.
These types of subgraphs are defined as k-graphs, where k is the number of nodes.
The common k-graphs form the author's signatures since they always appear,
regardless of the program functionality. In addition, we consider the longest path in
each user function because it reflects the way in which an author tends to use deep
or nested loops. An author may organize classes either ad hoc or hierarchically by
designing a driver class to contain several manager classes, where each manager is
responsible for different processes (collections of threads running in parallel). Both
ad hoc and hierarchical systems of organization can create a common structure in
the programs coded by the same author.

9.2.3.8   Feature Vector of Structural Choices

BINAUTHOR uses subgraphs of size k in order to capture structural choices ($k =$
4, 5, and 6 through our experiments). Given a k-graph, the graph is transformed
into strings using the Bliss open-source toolkit [174]. Then, a similarity measurement is performed over these strings using the normalized compression distance
(NCD) [102]. The reason of our choice for NCD is threefold: (1) it enhances the
search performance; (2) it allows to concatenate all the common subgraphs that
appear in author's programs; and (3) it allows to perform inexact matching between
the target subgraphs and the training subgraphs. BINAUTHOR generates a signature
based on these strings. The similarity obtained from structural choices is represented
by λ_s.

9.2.4   Classification

As previously described, BINAUTHOR extracts different types of choices to characterize different aspects of an author coding habits. Such choices do not equally
contribute to the attribution process, since the significance of these indicators
is not identical. Consequently, a weight is assigned to each choice by applying
logistic regression on each of them in order to predict class probabilities (e.g., the
probability of identifying an author). For this purpose, we use the dataset introduced

Table 9.4 Logistic regression weights for choices

Choice	Probability(P_i)	$P_i/(P_s = 0.39)$	Weight (w_i)
General	0.83	2.128205	0.35
Qualitative	0.63	1.615385	0.27
Structural	0.52	1.333333	0.22
Embedded	0.39	1	0.16
		$\sum_{i=1}^{4}(p_i/p_s) = 6.076923$	

in Sect. 9.3.2. To prevent the overfitting, we test each dataset separately and then compute the average of weights. The weights are calculated as follows:

$$w_i = rnd\left((p_i/p_s)/\sum_{i=1}^{4}(p_i/p_s)\right), \tag{9.5}$$

where p_s is the smallest probability value (e.g., 0.39 in Table 9.4), p_i is the probability outcome from logistic regression of each choice, and the *rnd* function rounds the final value. The probability outcomes of logistic regression prediction are illustrated in Table 9.4.

After extracting the features, we define a probability value P based on the obtained weights. The author attribution probability is defined as follows:

$$P(\Lambda) = \sum_{i=1}^{4} w_i * \lambda_i, \tag{9.6}$$

where w_i represents the weight assigned to each choice, as shown in Table 9.4, and λ_i is the distance metric value obtained from each choice (λ_g, λ_q, λ_e, and λ_s) as described in Sect. 9.2.3. We normalize the probabilities of all authors, and if $P \geq \zeta$, where ζ represents predefined threshold values, then the author is labelled as a matched author. Through our experiments, we find that the best value of ζ is 0.87. If more than one author has a probability larger than the threshold value, then BINAUTHOR returns the set of those authors.

9.3 Evaluation

In this section, we present first the experimental setup, the dataset, and the evaluation results. Then, we illustrate the accuracy and the efficiency of BINAUTHOR as well as the impact of different code transformation techniques. Finally, we apply BINAUTHOR to real malware samples.

9.3.1   Experimental Setup

The described stylistic choices are implemented using separate Python scripts for modularity purposes, which altogether form our analytical system. A subset of the python scripts in the BINAUTHOR system is used in tandem with IDA Pro disassembler. The final set of the framework scripts perform the bulk of the choice analysis functions that compute and display critical information about an author's coding style. With the analysis framework completed, a graph database is utilized to perform complex graph operations such as k-graph extraction. The graph database chosen for this task is *Neo4j*. *Gephi* [25] is employed for all graph analysis functions, which are not provided by Neo4j. *MongoDB* database is used to store our features for efficiency and scalability purposes.

9.3.2   Dataset

Our dataset consists of several C/C++ applications from different sources, as follows: (1) GitHub [19]; (2) Google Code Jam [18], an international programming competition; (3) Planet Source Code [28]; and (4) Graduate Student Projects at CIISE/Concordia University. Statistics about the dataset are provided in Table 9.5. In total, we test 800 authors from different sets in which each author has two to five software applications, resulting in a total of 3150 programs. To compile these datasets, we use GNU Compiler Collection (version 4.8.5) with different optimization levels, as well as Microsoft Visual Studio (VS) 2010.

9.3.3   Evaluation Metrics

In our experimental setup, we randomly split the collected program binaries into ten sets, reserving one as a testing set and using the remaining nine sets for training. We repeat this process 100 times. In order to evaluate BINAUTHOR and to compare it with existing methods, the precision (P) and recall (R) metrics are employed as follows:

Table 9.5 Statistics about the dataset used in the evaluation of BINAUTHOR

Source	# of authors	# of programs	# of functions
GitHub	150	600	110,000
Google Code Jam	500	2000	23,650
Planet Source Code	100	300	12,080
Graduate Student Projects	50	250	9823

$$Precision = \frac{TP}{TP + FP} \tag{9.7}$$

$$Recall = \frac{TP}{TP + FN}, \tag{9.8}$$

where the true positive (TP) indicates number of relevant authors that are correctly retrieved; true negative (TN) returns the number of irrelevant authors that are not detected; false positive (FP) indicates the number of irrelevant authors that are incorrectly detected; and false negative (FN) presents the number of relevant authors that are not detected.

9.3.4 Accuracy

The main purpose of this experiment is to evaluate the accuracy of author identification in binaries. The evaluation of BINAUTHOR is conducted using the datasets described in Sect. 9.3.2.

Results Comparison: We compare BINAUTHOR with three other existing authorship attribution methods [59, 90, 251]. We reuse the source code and dataset of our previous work, OBA2 [59], which performs authorship attribution on a small scale of 5 authors with 10 programs for each. The source code of the two other approaches presented by Caliskan-Islam et al. [90] and Rosenblum et al. [251] can be found in [29] and [20], respectively. Both Caliskan-Islam et al. and Rosenblum et al. present a largest-scale evaluation of binary authorship attribution, which contains 600 authors with 8 training programs per author, and 190 authors with at least 8 training programs, respectively. However, as the corresponding datasets are not available, we compare BINAUTHOR with these methods using the datasets listed in Table 9.5.

Figure 9.2 details the results of comparing the precision between BINAUTHOR and the aforementioned methods. It shows the relationship between the precision and the number of authors present in all datasets, where the precision decreases as the size of author population increases. The results show that BINAUTHOR achieves better precision in determining the author of binaries. Taking all four approaches into consideration, the highest precision of authorship attribution is close to 99% on the Google Code Jam with less than 150 authors, while the lowest precision is 17% when 800 authors are involved on all datasets together. We believe that the reason behind Caliskan-Islam et al. approach that achieves high precision on Google Jam Code is that this dataset is simple and can be easily decompiled to source code. BINAUTHOR also identifies the authors of Github dataset with an average precision of 92%. The main reason for this relates to the fact that the authors of projects in Github have no restrictions when developing projects. In addition, the advanced programmers of such projects usually design their own class or template to be used

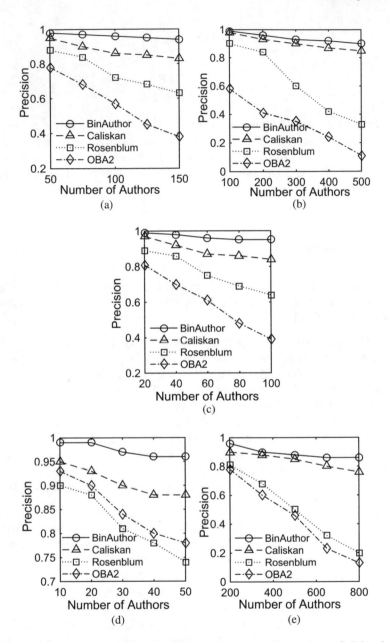

Fig. 9.2 Precision results of authorship attribution obtained by BINAUTHOR, Caliskan-Islam et al., Rosenblum et al., and OBA2. (**a**) Github. (**b**) Google Code Jam. (**c**) Planet Source Code. (**d**) Graduate Student Projects. (**e**) All datasets

in the projects. The lowest precision obtained by BINAUTHOR is approximately 86% on all datasets together. We have observed that BINAUTHOR achieves lower precision when it is applied on Graduate Student Projects. When the number of authors is 400 on the mixed dataset, the precision of Rosenblum et al. and OBA2 approaches drop rapidly to 40% on all datasets, whereas our system's precision remains greater than 86% while Caliskan-Islam et al. approach remains greater than 73%. This provides evidence for the robustness of using coding habits in identifying authors. In total, the different categories of choices achieve an average precision of 98% for ten distinct authors and 86% when discriminating among 800 authors. These results indicate that the author habits may survive the compilation process.

Observations. In the context of the carried out experiments, we made the following observations:

1. *Feature Pre-processing.* We have encountered situations in the existing methods, where the top-ranked features are related to the compiler (e.g., stack frame setup operation). It is thus necessary to filter irrelevant functions (e.g., compiler functions) in order to better identify the author-related portions of code. To this end, we utilize a more elaborate method for filtering to eliminate the compiler effects and to label library, compiler, and open-source software related functions. Successful distinction between these functions leads to considerable time savings and helps shifting the focus of analysis to more relevant functions.
2. *Source of Features.* Existing methods use disassembler and decompilers to extract features from binaries. Caliskan-Islam et al. use a decompiler to translate the program into C-like pseudo code via Hex-Ray [44]. They pass the code to a fuzzy parser for C, thus obtaining an abstract syntax tree from which features can be extracted. In addition to Hex-Ray limitations [44], the C-like pseudo code is different from the original code to the extent that the variables, branches, and keywords are different. For instance, we find that a function in the source code consists of the following keywords: (`1-do`, `1-switch`, `3-case`, `3-break`, `2-while`, `1-if`) and the number of variables is 2. Once we check the same function after decompiling its binary, we find that the function consists of the following keywords: (`1-do`, `1-else/if`, `2-goto`, `2-while`, `4-if`) and the number of variables is 4. This will evidently lead to misleading features, thus increasing the rate of false positives.

9.3.5 Scalability

Security analysts or reverse engineers may be interested in performing large-scale author identification, and in the case of malware, an analyst may deal with an extremely large number of new samples on a daily basis. With this in mind, we evaluate how well BINAUTHOR scales. In order to prepare the large dataset required for large-scale authorship attribution, we obtained sample programs from three sources: Google Code Jam, GitHub, and Planet Source Code. We eliminated

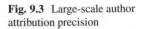

Fig. 9.3 Large-scale author
attribution precision

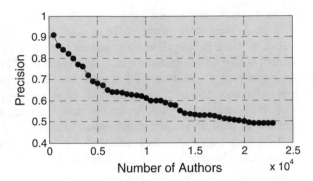

from the experiment programs that could not be compiled because they contain
compilation errors and those written by authors who contributed only one or two
programs. The resulting dataset comprised 103,800 programs by 23,000 authors:
60% from Google Code Jam, 25% from Planet Source Code, and 15% from GitHub.
We modified the script[3] used in [90] to download all the code submitted to the
Google Code Jam competition. The programs from the other two sources were
downloaded manually. All the programs were compiled with the Visual Studio and
GCC compilers, using the same settings as those in our previous investigations. The
performed experiments demonstrates how well the top-weighted choices capture
author habits.

The large-scale author identification results are shown in Fig. 9.3. It shows the
precision with which BINAUTHOR identifies the author, and its satisfactory scaling
behavior as the number of authors increases. Among almost 4000 authors, an author
is identified with 72% precision. When the number of authors is doubled to 8000,
the precision is close to 65%, and it remains nearly constant (49%) after the number
of authors reaches 19,000. Additionally, we test BINAUTHOR on the programs
obtained from each of the sources. The precision was high for samples from the
GitHub dataset (88%) and also for samples from the Planet dataset (82%); however,
it was low for samples from Google Code Jam (51%). The results suggest that it is
easier to perform attribution for authors who wrote code for difficult tasks than for
those addressing easier tasks.

9.3.6 Impact of Code Transformation Techniques

Refactoring Techniques. We consider a random set of 50 files from our dataset
which we use for the C++ refactoring process [30, 41]. We ignore the variable
renaming since it will have no effect in binary code, and we consider the following
techniques: (1) moving a method from a superclass to its subclasses, and (2)

---

[3]https://github.com/calaylin/CodeStylometry/tree/master.

extracting a few statements and placing them into a new method. We obtain a precision of 91.5% in correctly classifying authors, which is only a mild drop in comparison to the 95% precision observed without applying refactoring techniques.

9.3.7 Impact of Obfuscation

We are interested in determining how BINAUTHOR handles simple binary obfuscation techniques intended for evading detection, as implemented by tools such as obfuscator-LLVM [173]. Such obfuscators replace instructions by other semantically equivalent instructions, introduce bogus control flow, and can even completely flatten control flow graphs. Obfuscation techniques implemented by obfuscator-LLVM are applied to the samples prior to classifying the authors. We proceed to extract features from obfuscated samples. We obtain a precision of 92.9% in correctly classifying authors, which is only a slight drop in comparison to the 95% precision observed without obfuscation.

9.3.8 Impact of Compilers and Compilation Settings

We are further interested to study the impact of different compilers and compilation settings on the precision of our proposed system. We perform the following tasks: (1) testing the ability of BINAUTHOR when identifying the author from binaries compiled with the same compiler, but different compiler optimization levels. Specifically, we use binaries that were compiled with GCC/VS on x86 architecture using optimization levels $O2$ and $O3$. In this test, the precision remains same (95%). (2) We use a different configuration to identify the authors of programs compiled with both a different compiler and different compiler optimization levels. Specifically, we use programs compiled for x86 with VS $-O2$ and GCC $-O3$. In this test, the precision slightly drops to 93.9%. We also redo the test for the same binaries compiled with ICC and Clang compilers. The precision remains almost the same 93.8%. This stability in the accuracy is due to the canonicalization process.

9.3.9 Applying BINAUTHOR to Real Malware Binaries

The malware binary authorship attribution is very challenging due to the following main reason: the lack of ground truth concerning the attribution of authorship due to the nature of malware. Such limitation explains the fact that few research efforts have been seen on manual malware authorship attribution. In fact, to the best of our knowledge, BINAUTHOR is the first attempt to apply automated authorship attribution to real malware. We describe the application of BINAUTHOR to some well-known malware binaries. Details of the malware dataset are shown in Table 9.6. Given a set of functions, BINAUTHOR clusters them based on the number of common choices.

A. Applying BINAUTHOR to Bunny and Babar: We apply BINAUTHOR to Bunny and Babar malware samples and cluster the functions based on the choices. BINAUTHOR is able to find the following coding habits automatically: the preference for using Visual Studio 2008 and the use of a common approach to managing functions (general choices); the use of one variable over a long chain (structural choices); the choice of methods for accessing freed memory, dynamically deallocating allocated resources, and reopening resources more than once in the same function (qualitative choices). As shown in Table 9.7, BINAUTHOR found functions common to Bunny and Babar that share the aforementioned coding habits: 494 functions share qualitative choices; 450 functions share embedded choices; 372 functions share general choices; and 127 functions share structural choices. Among these, BINAUTHOR found 340 functions that share 4 choices, 478 functions that share 3 choices, 150 functions that share 2 choices, and 290 functions that share 1 choice. Considering the 854 and 1025 functions in Bunny and Babar, respectively, BINAUTHOR found that 44% $((340 + 478)/(854 + 1025))$ are likely to have been written by a single author (same common choices), and 23% are likely to have been written by multiple authors (contradictive different choices inside the same function). No common choices were identified in the remaining 33%, likely

Table 9.6 Characteristics of malware dataset

Malware	Packed	Obfuscated	Source code	Binary code	Type	#Binary functions	Source of sample
Zeus	✗	✗	✓	✓	PE	557	Our security lab
Citadel	✗	✗	✓	✓	PE	794	Our security lab
Flame	✗	✓	✗	✓	ELF	1434	Contagio [4]
Stuxnet	✗	✓	✗	✓	ELF	2154	Contagio [4]
Bunny	✓	✗	✗	✓	PE	854	VirusSign [14]
Babar	✓	✗	✗	✓	PE	1025	VirusSign [14]

Table 9.7 Statistics of applying BINAUTHOR to malware binaries

Malware	Number of functions with common choices				Number of common functions with			
	General	Qualitative	Structural	Embedded	1 choice	2 choices	3 choices	4 choices
Bunny and Babar	372	494	127	450	290	150	478	340
Stuxnet and Flame	725	528	189	300	689	515	294	180
Zeus and Citadel	655	452	289	370	600	588	194	258

because different segments or code lines within the same function were written by different authors, a common practice in writing complex software.

B. Applying BINAUTHOR to Stuxnet and Flame: BINAUTHOR found the following coding habits automatically: the use of global variables, Lua scripting language, a specific open-source package SQLite, and heap sort rather than other sorting methods (general choices); the choice of opening and terminating processes (qualitative choices); the presence of recursion patterns and the use of POSIX socket API rather than BSD socket API (structural choices); and the use of functions that are close in terms of the Mahalanobis distance, with distance close to 0.1. As shown in Table 9.7, BINAUTHOR identified functions common to Stuxnet and Flame that share the aforementioned coding habits. BINAUTHOR clustered the functions and found that 13% ((180 + 294)/(1434 + 2154)) were written by one author, while 34% ((515 + 689)/(1434 + 2154)) were written by multiple authors. No common choices were found in the remaining 53% of the functions. The fact that these malware packages follow the same rules and set the same targets suggests that Stuxnet and Flame are written by an organization.

C. Applying BINAUTHOR to Zeus and Citadel: BINAUTHOR identified the following coding habits: the use of network resources rather than file resources, creating configurations using mostly config files, the use of specific packages such as webph and ultraVNC (general choices); the use of switch statements rather than if statements (structural choices); the use of semaphores and locks (qualitative choices); and the presence of functions that are close in terms of the Mahalanobis distance, with distance = 0.0004 (embedded choices). As listed in Table 9.7, BINAUTHOR found functions common to Zeus and Citadel that share the aforementioned coding habits. After BINAUTHOR clustered the functions, it appears that 33% were written by a single author, while 53% were written by the same team of multiple authors. No common choices were found for the remaining 14% of the functions. Our findings clearly support the common belief that Zeus and Citadel were written by the same team of authors.

D. Comparison with Technical Reports: We compare BINAUTHOR's findings with those made by human experts in technical reports.

- For Bunny and Babar, our results match the technical report published by the Citizen Lab [205], which demonstrates that both malware packages were written by a set of authors according to common implementation traits (general and qualitative choices) and infrastructure usage (general choices). The correspondence between the BINAUTHOR findings and those in the technical report is the following: 60% of the choices matched those mentioned in the report, and 40% did not; 10% of the choices found in the technical report were not flagged by BINAUTHOR as they require dynamic extraction of features, while BINAUTHOR uses a static process.
- For Stuxnet and Flame, our results corroborate the technical report published by Kaspersky [186], which shows that both malware packages use similar infrastructure (e.g., Lua) and are associated with an organization. In addition,

BINAUTHOR's findings suggest that both malware packages originated from the same organization. The frequent use of particular qualitative choices, such as the way the code is secured, indicates the use of certain programming standards and strict adherence to the same rules. Moreover, BINAUTHOR's findings provide much more information concerning the authorship of these malware packages. The correspondence between BINAUTHOR's findings and those in the technical report is as follows: all the choices found in the report [186] were found by BINAUTHOR, but they represent only 10% of our findings. The remaining 90% of BINAUTHOR's findings were not flagged by the report.

- For Zeus and Citadel, our results match the findings of the technical report published by McAfee [21], indicating that Zeus and Citadel were written by the same team of authors. The correspondence between the findings of BINAUTHOR and those of McAfee are as follows: 45% of the choices matched those in the report, while 55% did not, and 8% of the technical report findings were not flagged by BINAUTHOR.

9.4   Limitations and Concluding Remarks

To conclude, we have presented the first known effort on decoupling coding habits from functionality. Previous research initiatives employ machine learning techniques to extract stylometry styles and can distinguish between 5–50 authors, whereas we can handle up to 150 authors. In addition, existing works have only employed artificial datasets, whereas we utilized more realistic datasets. Our findings indicated that the precision of these techniques drops dramatically to approximately 45% at a scale of more than 50 authors. We also applied our system to known malware samples (e.g., Zeus and Citadel) as a case study. We discovered that authors with advanced expertise are easier to attribute than authors who have less expertise. Authors from the realistic datasets are easier to attribute than authors of artificial datasets. Specifically, in the GitHub dataset, the authors of a program sample can be identified with greater than 90% precision. In summary, the proposed system demonstrates superior results on more realistic datasets.

However, BINAUTHOR has a few important limitations. (1) *Advanced Obfuscation*: The proposed tool must be further developed to handle most of the advanced obfuscation techniques, such as virtualization and jitting, given that it does not deal with bytecode. (2) *Intermediate Representation (IR)*: Through our experiments, we notice that optimizing IR would remove some author styles, e.g., loop deletion. This issue represents a subject of future work. (3) *Functionality*: There are some choices that appear when an author implements a specific functionality. For instance, if the functionality does not have a multiple-branch logic, there is no choice between if and switch.

Chapter 10
Conclusion

The proliferation of malware attacks reported by business organizations and anti-virus vendors provided a strong motivation for security researchers to investigate and propose new efficient and scalable methodologies that can streamline ongoing countermeasure efforts for a multitude of security applications, such as vulnerability detection, patch analysis, reverse engineering, digital forensics, malware detection, and authorship attribution. In this context, this book detailed an array of automated solutions for understanding the behavior of malware binaries.

In this book, we have reviewed the motivations and the background on binary code fingerprinting. In addition, we have presented a comparative study of the most prominent state-of-the-art proposals in this area. Besides, we have addressed different code fingerprinting problems and proposed automated, efficient, and scalable solutions to them. We demonstrated that static and dynamic analyses of binary code, combined with machine learning, can help in identifying compiler provenance, reused functions, third-party libraries such as free open-source packages, and providing insightful answers on authorship attribution.

In Chap. 2, we reviewed existing approaches to binary code fingerprinting. Thus, we systematized the area of binary code fingerprinting according to its most significant dimensions: the applications that motivate its importance, the employed approaches, and the aspects of the framework fingerprints. This important step involved the investigation of different aspects of binary code in order to provide important insights into malware binary analysis and to define new perspectives related to malware research.

In Chap. 3, we presented BINCOMP, a technique which allows to accurately and automatically recover the compiler provenance of program binaries using syntactical, semantic, and structural features to capture compiler behavior. We have shown how BINCOMP can extract specific features from program binaries, which allows to build representative and meaningful features that can be used to describe each compiler characteristics. The obtained results show that compiler provenance can be extracted accurately. Moreover, the results indicate that the approach is

© Springer Nature Switzerland AG 2020
S. Alrabaee et al., *Binary Code Fingerprinting for Cybersecurity*, Advances in
Information Security 78, https://doi.org/10.1007/978-3-030-34238-8_10

efficient in terms of resource use and computing time requirements, and could thus be considered as a practical approach for real-world binary analysis.

In Chap. 4, we investigated the possibility of representing a function based on its shape. We proposed a robust signature for each library function based on diverse collection of heterogeneous features, including control flow graphs, instruction-level characteristics, statistical features, and function-call graphs. In addition, we have designed an innovative data structure, which leverages B^+ tree, in order to efficiently support an accurate and scalable detection. The obtained experimental results demonstrate the usefulness of the presented approach.

In Chap. 5, we proposed an approach called SIGMA that can be employed to effectively identify reused functions in binary code. Instead of relying on one source of information, the proposed approach combines multiple representations into one joint data structure called *SIG*. In addition, SIGMA supports both exact and inexact matching based on *SIG* traces, which allows to handle function fragments. Obtained experimental results demonstrate the effectiveness of this method.

In Chap. 6, we presented an efficient, accurate, and scalable binary function fingerprinting technique called BINSIGN. The fingerprint generation methodology combines different syntactic, semantic, and structural features from the control flow graph of a function. The structure of a control flow graph is captured by decomposing it into partial execution traces. We evaluated BINSIGN's accuracy, performance, and scalability in several experimental setups.

In Chap. 7, we introduced FOSSIL, a system for identifying free open-source software packages. FOSSIL incorporates three components to extract syntactical features, structural, and statistical features, and then applies different methods in order to identify FOSS functions. These components are integrated using a Bayesian network model, which synthesizes the obtained results from each component to determine FOSS functions. This approach facilitates the tedious and often error-prone task of manual malware reverse engineering and exhibits a stronger resilience to code obfuscation. The experimental evaluation of FOSSIL demonstrate that it yields highly accurate results.

In Chap. 8, we presented a fast, accurate, and scalable binary code reuse detection system named BINSEQUENCE. The novelty of this system lies in its focus on fuzzy matching operating at instruction level, basic block level and control flow graph level. In order to enable the use of BINSEQUENCE on large datasets, we designed two filters that allow to reduce the analysis effort by ruling out functions that are not likely to be matched. The experiments conducted involved a large volume of binary code. The obtained results strongly indicate the competitiveness of BINSEQUENCE, which can achieve high accuracy function matching.

In Chap. 9, we proposed BINAUTHOR, a system capable of decoupling program functionality from authors' coding habits in binary code. It leverages a set of features that are based on collections of functionality-independent choices made by authors during coding. Our evaluation shows that BINAUTHOR outperforms existing methods in several aspects, including accuracy, efficiency, and robustness.

Although a great deal of interest has been expressed on the design and implementation of code fingerprinting algorithms to address various reverse engineering and cybersecurity applications, it remains that this research area is at its infancy. The present crucial needs in terms of vulnerability research, automated malware analysis, and reverse engineering combined with recent advancement in artificial intelligence and machine learning will definitely open new avenues and propel further the research and development in this strategic field. In this regard, there are numerous interesting and challenging problems that are worth exploring such as supporting multiple architectures, handling code obfuscation, addressing function inlining in binary executables, detecting unknown vulnerabilities, etc.

References

1. Advanced Message Queuing Protocol (AMQP). https://www.amqp.org/. Accessed: January 2017.
2. Apache Cassandra Web site. http://cassandra.apache.org/. Accessed: January 2017.
3. BinSourcerer. https://github.com/BinSigma/BinSourcerer. Accessed: April, 2015.
4. Contagio: malware dump. http://contagiodump.blogspot.ca. Accessed: February, 2018.
5. Diaphora: A Program Diffing Plugin for IDA Pro. https://github.com/joxeankoret/diaphora. Accessed: January 2019.
6. GNU GCC Internals—Machine Descriptions and Instruction Patterns. https://gcc.gnu.org/onlinedocs/gccint/Machine-Desc.html. Accessed: October 2017.
7. Internet Security Threat Report 2016. https://www.symantec.com/content/dam/symantec/docs/reports/istr-21-2016-en.pdf. Accessed: January 2017.
8. Libpng library. http://www.libpng.org/.
9. Obfuscator-LLVM. https://github.com/obfuscator-llvm/obfuscator/wiki. Accessed: January 2017.
10. PatchDiff2: Binary Diffing Plugin for IDA. https://code.google.com/p/patchdiff2/. Accessed: January 2019.
11. RabbitMQ Web site. https://www.rabbitmq.com/. Accessed: January 2017.
12. The Reactive Extensions for Python. https://github.com/ReactiveX/RxPY. Accessed: January 2017.
13. Thicket Family of Source Code Obfuscators. http://www.semdesigns.com/Products/Obfuscators/. Accessed: January 2017.
14. VirusSign: Malware Research & Data Center, Virus Free. http://www.virussign.com/. Accessed: February, 2017.
15. Vulnerability Details: CVE-2015-4485. http://www.cvedetails.com/cve/CVE-2015-4485/. Accessed: January 2019.
16. Weka: Machine Learning Software. https://weka.wikispaces.com/. Accessed: January 2017.
17. Zlib library. http://www.zlib.net/.
18. Google Code Jam Contest Dataset. http://code.google.com/codejam/, 2008–2017. Accessed: February, 2018.
19. GitHub-Build software better. https://github.com/, 2011. Accessed: May, 2019.
20. Materials supplement for the paper "Who Wrote This Code? Identifying the Authors of Program Binaries". http://pages.cs.wisc.edu/~nater/esorics-supp/, 2011. Accessed: May, 2017.
21. Mcafee: Technical report. www.mcafee.com/ca/resources/wp-citadel-trojan-summary.pdf, 2011. Accessed: Mar, 2017.

© Springer Nature Switzerland AG 2020
S. Alrabaee et al., *Binary Code Fingerprinting for Cybersecurity*, Advances in Information Security 78, https://doi.org/10.1007/978-3-030-34238-8

22. The C Language Library, Cplusplus website. http://www.cplusplus.com/reference/clibrary/, 2011. Accessed: May, 2017.
23. Full Analysis of Flame's Command & Control servers. https://securelist.com/full-analysis-of-flames-command-control-servers/34216/, 2012. Accessed: July 2019.
24. NIST/SEMATECH e-Handbook of Statistical Methods. http://www.itl.nist.gov/div898/handbook/, 2013. Accessed: 2015.
25. Gephi plugin for nneo4j. https://marketplace.gephi.org/plugin/neo4j-graph-database-support/, 2015. Accessed: February, 2016.
26. Malheur: Automatic Analysis of Malware Behavior. http://www.mlsec.org/malheur/, 2015.
27. MongoDB. https://www.mongodb.com/, 2015. Accessed: 2015.
28. Planet source code. http://www.planet-source-code.com/vb/default.asp?lngWId=3\#ContentWinners, 2015. Accessed: March, 2017.
29. Programmer De-anonymization from Binary Executables. https://github.com/calaylin/bda, 2015. Accessed: January, 2017.
30. C++ refactoring tools for visual studio. http://www.wholetomato.com/, 2016. Accessed: February 2016.
31. GAS-Obfuscation. https://github.com/defuse/gas-obfuscation, 2016. Accessed: March, 2017.
32. GNU software repository. www.gnu.org/software/software.html, 2016. Accessed: February, 2016.
33. PELock is a software security solution designed for protection of any 32 bit Windows applications. https://www.pelock.com/, 2016. Accessed: January, 2016.
34. Sourceforge. http://sourceforge.net, 2016. Accessed: February, 2019.
35. The Codeproject repository. http://www.codeproject.com/, 2016. Accessed: July 2019.
36. The Z table. http://www.stat.ufl.edu/athienit/Tables/Ztable.pdf, 2016. Accessed: February 2017.
37. Tracelet system. https://github.com/Yanivmd/TRACY, 2016. Accessed: February, 2018.
38. BinDiff tool: Zynamics bindiff. http://www.zynamics.com/bindiff.html, 2017. Accessed: February, 2016.
39. Nynaeve: Adventure in Windows debugging and reverse enigineering. http://www.nynaeve.net/, 2017. Accessed: March, 2017.
40. The PEiD tool. Available from:. http://www.woodmann.com/collaborative/tools/index.php/PEiD, 2017. Accessed: May, 2016.
41. Refactoring tool. https://www.devexpress.com/Products/CodeRush/, 2018. Accessed: February 2018.
42. DARPA: Cyber Grand Challenge. https://cgc.darpa.mil/, 2019. Accessed: June 2019.
43. EXEINFO PE. http://exeinfo.atwebpages.com/, 2019. Accessed: June 2019.
44. Hex-Rays Decompiler. https://www.hex-rays.com/products/decompiler/, 2019. Accessed: June 2019.
45. Hex-Rays IDA Pro. https://www.hex-rays.com/products/ida/, 2019. Accessed: June 2019.
46. HexRays: IDA Pro. https://www.hex-rays.com/products/ida/, 2019. Accessed: January 2019.
47. OllyDbg, a 32-bit Assembler Level Analysing Debugger for Microsoft Windows. http://ollydbg.de/, 2019. Accessed: June 2019.
48. PEfile. http://code.google.com/p/pefile/, 2019. Accessed: June 2019.
49. RDG_Packer_Detector. http://www.rdgsoft.net/, 2019. Accessed: June 2019.
50. The Paradyn Project. http://www.paradyn.org/html/dyninst9.0.0-features.html, 2019. Accessed: June 2019.
51. PlanetMath. Symmetric Difference. https://planetmath.org/symmetricdifference, 2019. Accessed: 2019.
52. Tigress, a Diversifying Virtualizer/Obfuscator for the C language. http://tigress.cs.arizona.edu/, 2019. Accessed: June 2019.
53. Zynamics, BinNavi: Binary Code Reverse Engineering Tool. http://www.zynamics.com/binnavi.html, 2019. Accessed: June 2019.
54. Laksono Adhianto, Sinchan Banerjee, Mike Fagan, Mark Krentel, Gabriel Marin, John Mellor-Crummey, and Nathan R Tallent. HPCToolkit: Tools for performance analysis of

optimized parallel programs. *Concurrency and Computation: Practice and Experience*, 22(6):685–701, 2010.

55. Hiralal Agrawal and Joseph R Horgan. Dynamic program slicing. In *ACM SIGPLAN Notices*, volume 25, pages 246–256. ACM, 1990.

56. Agrawal, Parag and Arasu, Arvind and Kaushik, Raghav. On indexing error-tolerant set containment. In *Proceedings of the 2010 ACM SIGMOD International Conference on Management of Data*, pages 927–938, 2010.

57. Shahid Alam, R Nigel Horspool, Issa Traore, and Ibrahim Sogukpinar. A framework for metamorphic malware analysis and real-time detection. *Computers & Security*, 48:212–233, 2015.

58. Shahinur Alam, R Nigel Horspool, and Issa Traore. MARD: a framework for metamorphic malware analysis and real-time detection. In *The 28th International Conference on Advanced Information Networking and Applications (AINA)*, pages 480–489. IEEE, 2014.

59. Saed Alrabaee, Noman Saleem, Stere Preda, Lingyu Wang, and Mourad Debbabi. OBA2: an onion approach to binary code authorship attribution. *Digital Investigation*, 11:S94–S103, 2014.

60. Saed Alrabaee, Paria Shirani, Mourad Debbabi, and Lingyu Wang. On the feasibility of malware authorship attribution. In *International Symposium on Foundations and Practice of Security*, pages 256–272. Springer, 2016.

61. Saed Alrabaee, Paria Shirani, Lingyu Wang, and Mourad Debbabi. SIGMA: a semantic integrated graph matching approach for identifying reused functions in binary code. *Digital Investigation*, 12:S61–S71, 2015.

62. Saed Alrabaee, Paria Shirani, Lingyu Wang, and Mourad Debbabi. FOSSIL: a resilient and efficient system for identifying FOSS functions in malware binaries. *ACM Transactions on Privacy and Security (TOPS)*, 21(2):8, 2018.

63. Saed Alrabaee, Paria Shirani, Lingyu Wang, Mourad Debbabi, and Aiman Hanna. On Leveraging Coding Habits for Effective Binary Authorship Attribution. In *European Symposium on Research in Computer Security (ESORICS)*, pages 26–47. Springer, 2018.

64. Saed Alrabaee, Lingyu Wang, and Mourad Debbabi. BinGold: Towards robust binary analysis by extracting the semantics of binary code as semantic flow graphs (SFGs). *Digital Investigation*, 18:S11–S22, 2016.

65. Alexandr Andoni and Piotr Indyk. Near-optimal hashing algorithms for approximate nearest neighbor in high dimensions. In *47th Annual IEEE Symposium on Foundations of Computer Science (FOCS'06).*, pages 459–468. IEEE, 2006.

66. Dorian C Arnold, Dong H Ahn, Bronis R De Supinski, Gregory L Lee, Barton P Miller, and Martin Schulz. Stack trace analysis for large scale debugging. In *IEEE International on Parallel and Distributed Processing Symposium (IPDPS)*, pages 1–10. IEEE, 2007.

67. Thanassis Avgerinos, Sang Kil Cha, Alexandre Rebert, Edward J Schwartz, Maverick Woo, and David Brumley. Automatic exploit generation. *Communications of the ACM*, 57(2):74–84, 2014.

68. Gogul Balakrishnan, Radu Gruian, Thomas Reps, and Tim Teitelbaum. CodeSurfer/x86—A platform for analyzing x86 executables. In *Compiler Construction*, pages 250–254. Springer, 2005.

69. Gogul Balakrishnan and Thomas Reps. WYSINWYX: What you see is not what you eXecute. *ACM Transactions on Programming Languages and Systems (TOPLAS)*, 32(6):23, 2010.

70. Musard Balliu, Mads Dam, and Roberto Guanciale. Automating information flow analysis of low level code. In *Proceedings of the 2014 ACM SIGSAC Conference on Computer and Communications Security (CCS)*, pages 1080–1091. ACM, 2014.

71. Piotr Bania. Generic unpacking of self-modifying, aggressive, packed binary programs. *arXiv preprint arXiv:0905.4581*, 2009.

72. Tiffany Bao, Jonathan Burket, Maverick Woo, Rafael Turner, and David Brumley. BYTEWEIGHT: Learning to Recognize Functions in Binary Code. In *23rd USENIX Security Symposium (USENIX Security 14)*, pages 845–860, 2014.

73. Sébastien Bardin, Philippe Herrmann, Jérôme Leroux, Olivier Ly, Sighireanu M., R. Tabary, T. Touili, and Aymeric Vincent. Description of the BINCOA Model. In *Deliverable J1.1 part 2 of ANR Project BINCOA*, 2009.
74. Sébastien Bardin, Philippe Herrmann, Jérôme Leroux, Olivier Ly, Renaud Tabary, and Aymeric Vincent. The BINCOA framework for binary code analysis. In *International Conference on Computer Aided Verification*, pages 165–170. Springer, 2011.
75. Mayank Bawa, Tyson Condie, and Prasanna Ganesan. LSH forest: self-tuning indexes for similarity search. In *Proceedings of the 14th international conference on World Wide Web*, pages 651–660. ACM, 2005.
76. Ulrich Bayer, Engin Kirda, and Christopher Kruegel. Improving the efficiency of dynamic malware analysis. In *Proceedings of the 2010 ACM Symposium on Applied Computing*, pages 1871–1878. ACM, March 2010.
77. Chandan Kumar Behera and D Lalitha Bhaskari. Different obfuscation techniques for code protection. *Procedia Computer Science*, 70:757–763, 2015.
78. Laszlo A. Belady and Meir M Lehman. A model of large program development. *IBM Systems journal*, 15(3):225–252, 1976.
79. Boldizsár Bencsáth. Duqu, Flame, Gauss: Followers of Stuxnet, 2012.
80. Boldizsár Bencsáth, Gábor Pék, Levente Buttyán, and Mark Felegyhazi. The cousins of stuxnet: Duqu, flame, and gauss. *Future Internet*, 4(4):971–1003, 2012.
81. Bencsáth, B and Buttyán, L and Félegyházi, M. sKyWIper (aka Flame aka Flamer): A Complex Malware for Targeted Attacks. Technical report, Laboratory of Cryptography and System Security (CrySyS Lab), Department of Telecommunications, Budapest University of Technology and Economics, 2012.
82. Daniel Bilar. Opcodes as predictor for malware. *International Journal of Electronic Security and Digital Forensics*, 1(2):156–168, 2007.
83. Hamad Binsalleeh, Thomas Ormerod, Amine Boukhtouta, Prosenjit Sinha, Amr Youssef, Mourad Debbabi, and Lingyu Wang. On the Analysis of the Zeus Botnet Crimeware Toolkit. In *Proceedings of the 8th Annual International Conference on Privacy, Security and Trust (PST)*, pages 31–38. IEEE Press, 2010.
84. Martial Bourquin, Andy King, and Edward Robbins. BinSlayer: accurate comparison of binary executables. In *Proceedings of the 2nd ACM SIGPLAN Program Protection and Reverse Engineering Workshop*, page 4. ACM, 2013.
85. Morton B Brown and Wilfrid Joseph Dixon. *BMDP statistical software*. Univ. of California Press, 1983.
86. David Brumley, Ivan Jager, Thanassis Avgerinos, and Edward J Schwartz. BAP: A binary analysis platform. In *International Conference on Computer Aided Verification*, pages 463–469. Springer, 2011.
87. Danilo Bruschi, Lorenzo Martignoni, and Mattia Monga. Code normalization for self-mutating malware. *IEEE Security & Privacy*, (2):46–54, 2007.
88. Juan Caballero, Noah M Johnson, Stephen McCamant, and Dawn Song. Binary code extraction and interface identification for security applications. Technical report, University of California, Berkeley, Dept. of Electrical Engineering and Computer Science, 2009.
89. Cristian Cadar, Daniel Dunbar, and Dawson Engler. KLEE: unassisted and automatic generation of high-coverage tests for complex systems programs. In *Proceedings of the 8th USENIX conference on Operating Systems Design and Implementation*, pages 209–224. USENIX Association, 2008.
90. Aylin Caliskan-Islam, Fabian Yamaguchi, Edwin Dauber, Richard Harang, Konrad Rieck, Rachel Greenstadt, and Arvind Narayanan. When coding style survives compilation: Deanonymizing programmers from executable binaries. *The 25th Annual Network and Distributed System Security Symposium (NDSS)*, pages 255–270, 2018.
91. Joan Calvet, José M Fernandez, and Jean-Yves Marion. Aligot: cryptographic function identification in obfuscated binary programs. In *Proceedings of the 2012 ACM conference on Computer and communications security (CCS)*, pages 169–182. ACM, 2012.

92. Shuang Cang and Derek Partridge. Feature ranking and best feature subset using mutual information. *Neural Computing & Applications*, 13(3):175–184, 2004.
93. Silvio Cesare, Yang Xiang, and Wanlei Zhou. Control flow-based malware variantdetection. *IEEE Transactions on Dependable and Secure Computing (TDSC)*, 11(4):307–317, 2014.
94. Sang Kil Cha, Thanassis Avgerinos, Alexandre Rebert, and David Brumley. Unleashing mayhem on binary code. In *IEEE Symposium on Security and Privacy (S&P)*, pages 380–394. IEEE, 2012.
95. Sang Kil Cha, Maverick Woo, and David Brumley. Program-adaptive mutational fuzzing. In *IEEE Symposium on Security and Privacy (S&P)*, pages 725–741. IEEE, 2015.
96. Sagar Chaki, Cory Cohen, and Arie Gurfinkel. Supervised learning for provenance-similarity of binaries. In *Proceedings of the 17th ACM SIGKDD international conference on Knowledge discovery and data mining*, pages 15–23. ACM, 2011.
97. Chandra, Mahalanobis Prasanta and Others. On the generalised distance in statistics. *Proceedings of the National Institute of Sciences of India*, 2(1):49–55, 1936.
98. Mahinthan Chandramohan, Yinxing Xue, Zhengzi Xu, Yang Liu, Chia Yuan Cho, and Hee Beng Kuan Tan. BinGo: cross-architecture cross-OS binary search. In *Proceedings of the 24th ACM SIGSOFT International Symposium on Foundations of Software Engineering*, pages 678–689. ACM, 2016.
99. Eric Cheng. *Binary Analysis and Symbolic Execution with angr*. PhD thesis, The MITRE Corporation, 2016.
100. Vitaly Chipounov, Volodymyr Kuznetsov, and George Candea. The S2E platform: Design, implementation, and applications. *ACM Transactions on Computer Systems (TOCS)*, 30(1):2, 2012.
101. Young Han Choi, Byoung Jin Han, Byung Chul Bae, Hyung Geun Oh, and Ki Wook Sohn. Toward extracting malware features for classification using static and dynamic analysis. In *The 8th International Conference on Computing and Networking Technology (ICCNT)*, pages 126–129. IEEE, 2012.
102. Rudi Cilibrasi and Paul Vitanyi. Clustering by compression. *IEEE Transactions on Information Theory*, 51(4):1523–1545, 2005.
103. Paolo Milani Comparetti, Guido Salvaneschi, Engin Kirda, Clemens Kolbitsch, Christopher Kruegel, and Stefano Zanero. Identifying dormant functionality in malware programs. In *IEEE Symposium on Security and Privacy (S&P)*, pages 61–76. IEEE, 2010.
104. Kevin Coogan, Saumya Debray, Tasneem Kaochar, and Gregg Townsend. Automatic static unpacking of malware binaries. In *16th Working Conference on Reverse Engineering*, pages 167–176. IEEE, October 2009.
105. Thomas H Cormen. *Introduction to algorithms*. MIT Press, 2009.
106. Christoph Csallner and Yannis Smaragdakis. Check'n'crash: combining static checking and testing. In *Proceedings of the 27th international conference on Software engineering*, pages 422–431. ACM, 2005.
107. Ţăpuş, Cristian and Chung, I-Hsin and Hollingsworth, Jeffrey K and others. Active harmony: Towards automated performance tuning. In *Proceedings of the 2002 ACM/IEEE conference on Supercomputing*, pages 1–11. IEEE Computer Society Press, 2002.
108. Scott A Czepiel. Maximum likelihood estimation of logistic regression models: theory and implementation. *Available at czep. net/stat/mlelr. pdf*, 2002.
109. DataStax. Connection Pooling. http://docs.datastax.com/en/developer/java-driver/2.1/ manual/pooling/. Accessed: January 2017.
110. Yaniv David, Nimrod Partush, and Eran Yahav. Statistical similarity of binaries. In *Proceedings of the 37th ACM SIGPLAN Conference on Programming Language Design and Implementation (PLDI)*, pages 266–280. ACM, 2016.
111. Yaniv David, Nimrod Partush, and Eran Yahav. Similarity of binaries through re-optimization. In *Proceedings of the 38th ACM SIGPLAN Conference on Programming Language Design and Implementation (PLDI)*, pages 79–94. ACM, 2017.
112. Yaniv David and Eran Yahav. Tracelet-based code search in executables. *ACM SIGPLAN Notices*, 49(6):349–360, 2014.

113. Jesse Davis and Mark Goadrich. The relationship between Precision-Recall and ROC curves. In *Proceedings of the 23rd international conference on Machine learning*, pages 233–240. ACM, 2006.

114. José Gaviria de la Puerta, Borja Sanz, Igor Santos, and Pablo García Bringas. Using Dalvik Opcodes for Malware Detection on Android. In *Hybrid Artificial Intelligent Systems*, pages 416–426. Springer, 2015.

115. De Maesschalck, Roy and Jouan-Rimbaud, Delphine, and Massart, Désiré L. The mahalanobis distance. *Chemometrics and Intelligent Laboratory Systems*, 50(1): 1–18, 2000.

116. Leonardo De Moura and Nikolaj Bjørner. Z3: An efficient SMT solver. In *International conference on Tools and Algorithms for the Construction and Analysis of Systems*, pages 337–340. Springer, 2008.

117. Alessandro Di Federico, Mathias Payer, and Giovanni Agosta. REV.NG: a unified binary analysis framework to recover CFGs and function boundaries. In *Proceedings of the 26th International Conference on Compiler Construction*, pages 131–141. ACM, 2017.

118. Steven HH Ding, Benjamin Fung, and Philippe Charland. Kam1n0: Mapreduce-based assembly clone search for reverse engineering. In *Proceedings of the 22nd ACM SIGKDD International Conference on Knowledge Discovery and Data Mining*, pages 461–470. ACM, 2016.

119. Steven H.H. Ding, Benjamin C.M. Fung, and Philippe Charland. Kam1n0: Mapreduce-based assembly clone search for reverse engineering. In *Proceedings of the 22Nd ACM SIGKDD International Conference on Knowledge Discovery and Data Mining*, KDD '16, pages 461–470, New York, NY, USA, 2016. ACM.

120. Adel Djoudi and Sébastien Bardin. BINSEC: Binary Code Analysis with Low-Level Regions. In *Tools and Algorithms for the Construction and Analysis of Systems*, pages 212–217. Springer, 2015.

121. Tudor Dumitraş and Darren Shou. Toward a standard benchmark for computer security research: The Worldwide Intelligence Network Environment (WINE). In *Building Analysis Datasets and Gathering Experience Returns for Security (BADGERS workshop)*, pages 89–96. ACM, 2011.

122. Chris Eagle. *The IDA pro book: the unofficial guide to the world's most popular disassembler*. No Starch Press, 2011. http://www.amazon.ca/The-IDA-Pro-Book-Disassembler/dp/1593272898.

123. Tobias JK Edler von Koch, Björn Franke, Pranav Bhandarkar, and Anshuman Dasgupta. Exploiting function similarity for code size reduction. *ACM SIGPLAN Notices*, 49(5):85–94, 2014.

124. Manuel Egele, Theodoor Scholte, Engin Kirda, and Christopher Kruegel. A survey on automated dynamic malware-analysis techniques and tools. *ACM Computing Surveys (CSUR)*, 44(2):6, 2012.

125. Manuel Egele, Maverick Woo, Peter Chapman, and David Brumley. Blanket execution: Dynamic similarity testing for program binaries and components. In *23rd USENIX Security Symposium (USENIX Security 14)*, pages 303–317, 2014.

126. Eldad Eilam. *Reversing: secrets of reverse engineering*. John Wiley & Sons, 2011.

127. Ammar Ahmed E Elhadi, Mohd Aizaini Maarof, Bazara IA Barry, and Hentabli Hamza. Enhancing the detection of metamorphic malware using call graphs. *Computers & Security*, 46:62–78, 2014.

128. Kimberly L Elmore and Michael B Richman. Euclidean distance as a similarity metric for principal component analysis. *Monthly Weather Review*, 129(3):540–549, 2001.

129. Khaled ElWazeer, Kapil Anand, Aparna Kotha, Matthew Smithson, and Rajeev Barua. Scalable variable and data type detection in a binary rewriter. In *ACM SIGPLAN Notices*, volume 48, pages 51–60. ACM, 2013.

130. Sebastian Eschweiler, Khaled Yakdan, and Elmar Gerhards-Padilla. discovRE: Efficient cross-architecture identification of bugs in binary code. In *Proceedings of the 23rd Symposium on Network and Distributed System Security (NDSS)*, 2016.

131. Rong-En Fan, Kai-Wei Chang, Cho-Jui Hsieh, Xiang-Rui Wang, and Chih-Jen Lin. Liblinear: A library for large linear classification. *Journal of machine learning research*, 9(Aug):1871–1874, 2008.
132. Wenbin Fang, Barton P Miller, and James A Kupsch. Automated tracing and visualization of software security structure and properties. In *Proceedings of the ninth international symposium on visualization for cyber security*, pages 9–16. ACM, 2012.
133. Mohammad Reza Farhadi, Benjamin Fung, Philippe Charland, and Mourad Debbabi. Bin-Clone: detecting code clones in malware. In *Eighth International Conference on Software Security and Reliability (SERE)*, pages 78–87. IEEE, 2014.
134. Mohammad Reza Farhadi, Benjamin CM Fung, Yin Bun Fung, Philippe Charland, Stere Preda, and Mourad Debbabi. Scalable code clone search for malware analysis. *Digital Investigation*, 15:46–60, 2015.
135. Fredrik Farnstrom, James Lewis, and Charles Elkan. Scalability for clustering algorithms revisited. *SIGKDD explorations*, 2(1):51–57, 2000.
136. Qian Feng, Rundong Zhou, Chengcheng Xu, Yao Cheng, Brian Testa, and Heng Yin. Scalable Graph-based Bug Search for Firmware Images. In *Proceedings of the 2016 ACM SIGSAC Conference on Computer and Communications Security (CCS)*, pages 480–491. ACM, 2016.
137. Jeanne Ferrante, Karl J Ottenstein, and Joe D Warren. The program dependence graph and its use in optimization. *ACM Transactions on Programming Languages and Systems (TOPLAS)*, 9(3):319–349, 1987.
138. Eric Filiol and Sébastien Josse. A statistical model for undecidable viral detection. *Journal in Computer Virology*, 3(2):65–74, 2007.
139. Halvar Flake. Graph-based binary analysis. *Blackhat Briefings 2002*, 2002.
140. Martin Fowler. *Refactoring: improving the design of existing code*. Pearson Education India, 1999.
141. András Frank. On kuhn's hungarian method- a tribute from hungary. *Naval Research Logistics (NRL)*, 52(1):2–5, 2005.
142. Eibe Frank, Yong Wang, Stuart Inglis, Geoffrey Holmes, and Ian H Witten. Using model trees for classification. *Machine Learning*, 32(1):63–76, 1998.
143. Junhao Gan, Jianlin Feng, Qiong Fang, and Wilfred Ng. Locality-sensitive hashing scheme based on dynamic collision counting. In *Proceedings of the 2012 ACM SIGMOD International Conference on Management of Data*, pages 541–552. ACM, 2012.
144. Carlos Gañán, Orcun Cetin, and Michel van Eeten. An empirical analysis of Zeus C&C lifetime. In *Proceedings of the 10th ACM Symposium on Information, Computer and Communications Security*, pages 97–108. ACM, 2015.
145. Thomas Gärtner, Peter Flach, and Stefan Wrobel. On graph kernels: Hardness results and efficient alternatives. In *Learning Theory and Kernel Machines*, pages 129–143. Springer, 2003.
146. Hugo Gascon, Fabian Yamaguchi, Daniel Arp, and Konrad Rieck. Structural detection of Android malware using embedded call graphs. In *Proceedings of the 2013 ACM workshop on Artificial intelligence and security*, pages 45–54. ACM, 2013.
147. Patrice Godefroid, Nils Klarlund, and Koushik Sen. DART: directed automated random testing. In *ACM Sigplan Notices*, volume 40, pages 213–223. ACM, 2005.
148. Patrice Godefroid, Michael Y Levin, and David Molnar. SAGE: whitebox fuzzing for security testing. *Communications of the ACM*, 55(3):40–44, 2012.
149. Christopher Griffin. Graph Theory: Penn State Math 485 Lecture Notes, 2012. http://www.personal.psu.edu/cxg286/Math485.pdf.
150. Ilfak Guilfanov. Fast library identification and recognition technology. *Liège, Belgium: DataRescue*, 1997.
151. Ilfak Guilfanov. IDA fast library identification and recognition technology (FLIRT Technology): In-depth. https://www.hex\discretionary-rays.com/products/ida/tech/flirt/in_depth.shtml, 2012.
152. Sumit Gulwani and George C Necula. Precise interprocedural analysis using random interpretation. In *ACM SIGPLAN Notices*, volume 40, pages 324–337. ACM, 2005.

153. Archit Gupta, Pavan Kuppili, Aditya Akella, and Paul Barford. An empirical study of malware evolution. In *First International Communication Systems and Networks and Workshops (COMSNETS)*, pages 1–10. IEEE, 2009.

154. Greg Hamerly and Charles Elkan. Learning the k in k-means. In *Advances in neural information processing systems*, pages 281–288, 2004.

155. Wook-Shin Han, Jinsoo Lee, and Jeong-Hoon Lee. TurboISO: towards ultrafast and robust subgraph isomorphism search in large graph databases. In *Proceedings of the 2013 ACM SIGMOD International Conference on Management of Data*, pages 337–348. ACM, 2013.

156. Sean Heelan. *Automatic generation of control flow hijacking exploits for software vulnerabilities*. PhD thesis, University of Oxford, 2009.

157. Sean Heelan and Agustin Gianni. Augmenting vulnerability analysis of binary code. In *Proceedings of the 28th Annual Computer Security Applications Conference (ACSAC)*, pages 199–208. ACM, 2012.

158. Christian Heitman and Iván Arce. BARF: A multiplatform open source binary analysis and reverse engineering framework. In *XX Congreso Argentino de Ciencias de la Computación (Buenos Aires, 2014)*, 2014.

159. Armijn Hemel, Karl Trygve Kalleberg, Rob Vermaas, and Eelco Dolstra. Finding software license violations through binary code clone detection. In *Proceedings of the 8th Working Conference on Mining Software Repositories*, pages 63–72. ACM, 2011.

160. Shohei Hido and Hisashi Kashima. A linear-time graph kernel. In *Ninth IEEE International Conference on Data Mining (ICDM'09)*, pages 179–188. IEEE, 2009.

161. Susan Horwitz, Thomas Reps, and David Binkley. Interprocedural slicing using dependence graphs. *ACM Transactions on Programming Languages and Systems (TOPLAS)*, 12(1):26–60, 1990.

162. Xin Hu, Tzi-cker Chiueh, and Kang G Shin. Large-scale malware indexing using function-call graphs. In *Proceedings of the 16th ACM conference on Computer and communications security (CCS)*, pages 611–620. ACM, 2009.

163. He Huang, Amr M Youssef, and Mourad Debbabi. Binsequence: fast, accurate and scalable binary code reuse detection. In *Proceedings of the 2017 ACM on Asia Conference on Computer and Communications Security*, pages 155–166. ACM, 2017.

164. Emily R Jacobson, Andrew R Bernat, William R Williams, and Barton P Miller. Detecting code reuse attacks with a model of conformant program execution. In *Engineering Secure Software and Systems*, pages 1–18. Springer, 2014.

165. Emily R Jacobson, Nathan Rosenblum, and Barton P Miller. Labeling library functions in stripped binaries. In *Proceedings of the 10th ACM SIGPLAN-SIGSOFT workshop on Program analysis for software tools (PASTE)*, pages 1–8. ACM, 2011.

166. Anil K Jain. Data clustering: 50 years beyond k-means. *Pattern recognition letters*, 31(8):651–666, 2010.

167. Jiyong Jang, Abeer Agrawal, and David Brumley. ReDeBug: finding unpatched code clones in entire os distributions. In *IEEE Symposium on Security and Privacy (S&P)*, pages 48–62. IEEE, 2012.

168. Jiyong Jang and David Brumley. Bitshred: Fast, scalable code reuse detection in binary code. *CMU-CyLab-10-006*, 16, 2009.

169. Jiyong Jang, Maverick Woo, and David Brumley. Towards automatic software lineage inference. In *USENIX Security Symposium (USENIX Security 13)*, pages 81–96, 2013.

170. Yoon-Chan Jhi, Xinran Wang, Xiaoqi Jia, Sencun Zhu, Peng Liu, and Dinghao Wu. Value-based program characterization and its application to software plagiarism detection. In *Proceedings of the 33rd International Conference on Software Engineering*, pages 756–765. ACM, 2011.

171. Weiwei Jin, Sagar Chaki, Cory Cohen, Arie Gurfinkel, Jeffrey Havrilla, Charles Hines, and Priya Narasimhan. Binary function clustering using semantic hashes. In *The 11th International Conference on Machine Learning and Applications (ICMLA)*, volume 1, pages 386–391. IEEE, 2012.

172. Jousselme, Anne-Laure and Maupin, Patrick. Distances in evidence theory: Comprehensive survey and generalizations. *International Journal of Approximate Reasoning*, 53(2), 118–145, 2012.

173. Pascal Junod, Julien Rinaldini, Johan Wehrli, and Julie Michielin. Obfuscator-LLVM: software protection for the masses. In *Proceedings of the 1st International Workshop on Software PROtection (SPRO)*, pages 3–9. IEEE Press, 2015.

174. Tommi A Junttila and Petteri Kaski. Engineering an efficient canonical labeling tool for large and sparse graphs. In *Proceedings of the Ninth Workshop on Algorithm Engineering and Experiments (ALENEX)*, volume 7, pages 135–149. SIAM, 2007.

175. Min Gyung Kang, Pongsin Poosankam, and Heng Yin. Renovo: A hidden code extractor for packed executables. In *Proceedings of the 2007 ACM Workshop on Recurring Malcode (WORM)*, pages 46–53. ACM, 2007.

176. Asha Gowda Karegowda, AS Manjunath, and MA Jayaram. Comparative study of attribute selection using gain ratio and correlation based feature selection. *International Journal of Information Technology and Knowledge Management*, 2(2):271–277, 2010.

177. Md Enamul Karim, Andrew Walenstein, Arun Lakhotia, and Laxmi Parida. Malware phylogeny generation using permutations of code. *Journal in Computer Virology*, 1(1-2):13–23, 2005.

178. Wei Ming Khoo. Decompilation as search. Technical report, University of Cambridge, Computer Laboratory, 2013.

179. Wei Ming Khoo, Alan Mycroft, and Ross Anderson. Rendezvous: a search engine for binary code. In *Proceedings of the 10th Working Conference on Mining Software Repositories*, pages 329–338. IEEE Press, 2013.

180. Johannes Kinder. *Static analysis of x86 executables*. PhD thesis, Technische Universität Darmstadt, 2010.

181. Johannes Kinder and Helmut Veith. Jakstab: A static analysis platform for binaries. In *International Conference on Computer Aided Verification*, pages 423–427. Springer, 2008.

182. Donald E Knuth. Backus normal form vs. backus naur form. *Communications of the ACM*, 7(12):735–736, 1964.

183. Ivan Krsul and Eugene H Spafford. Authorship analysis: Identifying the author of a program. *Computers & Security*, 16(3):233–257, 1997.

184. Christopher Kruegel, Engin Kirda, Darren Mutz, William Robertson, and Giovanni Vigna. Polymorphic worm detection using structural information of executables. In *International Workshop on Recent Advances in Intrusion Detection (RAID)*, pages 207–226. Springer, 2005.

185. Jonghoon Kwon and Heejo Lee. Bingraph: Discovering mutant malware using hierarchical semantic signatures. In *Malicious and Unwanted Software (MALWARE), 2012 7th International Conference on*, pages 104–111. IEEE, 2012.

186. Kaspersky Lab. Resource 207: Kaspersky Lab Research proves that Stuxnet and Flame developers are connected. http://newsroom.kaspersky.eu/fileadmin/user_upload/en/Images/Lifestyle/20120611_Kaspersky_Lab_Press_Release_Flame_Stuxnet_cooperation_final_-_UK.pdf, 2012. Accessed: February, 2018.

187. Shuvendu K Lahiri, Chris Hawblitzel, Ming Kawaguchi, and Henrique Rebêlo. Symdiff: A language-agnostic semantic diff tool for imperative programs. In *International Conference on Computer Aided Verification*, pages 712–717. Springer, 2012.

188. Arun Lakhotia, Mila Dalla Preda, and Roberto Giacobazzi. Fast location of similar code fragments using semantic 'juice'. In *Proceedings of the 2nd ACM SIGPLAN Program Protection and Reverse Engineering Workshop*, page 5. ACM, 2013.

189. Andrea Lanzi, Davide Balzarotti, Christopher Kruegel, Mihai Christodorescu, and Engin Kirda. Accessminer: using system-centric models for malware protection. In *Proceedings of the 17th ACM conference on Computer and communications security (CCS)*, pages 399–412. ACM, 2010.

190. Tímea László and Ákos Kiss. Obfuscating C++ programs via control flow flattening. *Annales Universitatis Scientarum Budapestinensis de Rolando Eötvös Nominatae, Sectio Computatorica*, 30:3–19, 2009.

191. Meir M Lehman and Juan F Ramil. Rules and tools for software evolution planning and management. *Annals of software engineering*, 11(1):15–44, 2001.
192. Jure Leskovec, Anand Rajaraman, and Jeffrey David Ullman. *Mining of massive datasets*. Cambridge University Press, 2014.
193. Pierre Lestringant, Frédéric Guihéry, and Pierre-Alain Fouque. Automated identification of cryptographic primitives in binary code with data flow graph isomorphism. In *Proceedings of the 10th ACM Symposium on Information, Computer and Communications Security*, pages 203–214. ACM, 2015.
194. Yuping Li, Sathya Chandran Sundaramurthy, Alexandru G Bardas, Xinming Ou, Doina Caragea, Xin Hu, and Jiyong Jang. Experimental study of fuzzy hashing in malware clustering analysis. In *8th Workshop on Cyber Security Experimentation and Test (CSET 15)*, 2015.
195. Michael Ligh, Steven Adair, Blake Hartstein, and Matthew Richard. *Malware analyst's cookbook and DVD: tools and techniques for fighting malicious code*. Wiley Publishing, 2010.
196. Da Lin and Mark Stamp. Hunting for undetectable metamorphic viruses. *Journal in computer virology*, 7(3):201–214, 2011.
197. Zhiqiang Lin, Xiangyu Zhang, and Dongyan Xu. Automatic reverse engineering of data structures from binary execution. In *Proceedings of the 11th Annual Information Security Symposium*, page 5. CERIAS-Purdue University, 2010.
198. Martina Lindorfer, Alessandro Di Federico, Federico Maggi, Paolo Milani Comparetti, and Stefano Zanero. Lines of malicious code: insights into the malicious software industry. In *Proceedings of the 28th Annual Computer Security Applications Conference (ACSAC)*, pages 349–358. ACM, 2012.
199. Yingfan Liu, Jiangtao Cui, Zi Huang, Hui Li, and Heng Tao Shen. Sk-lsh: An efficient index structure for approximate nearest neighbor search. *Proceedings of the VLDB Endowment*, 7(9):745–756, 2014.
200. Lorenzo Livi and Antonello Rizzi. The graph matching problem. *Pattern Analysis and Applications*, 16(3):253–283, 2013.
201. Fan Long, Stelios Sidiroglou-Douskos, and Martin Rinard. Automatic runtime error repair and containment via recovery shepherding. In *ACM SIGPLAN Notices*, volume 49, pages 227–238. ACM, 2014.
202. Lannan Luo, Jiang Ming, Dinghao Wu, Peng Liu, and Sencun Zhu. Semantics-based obfuscation-resilient binary code similarity comparison with applications to software plagiarism detection. In *Proceedings of the 22nd ACM SIGSOFT International Symposium on Foundations of Software Engineering*, pages 389–400. ACM, 2014.
203. Matias Madou, Bertrand Anckaert, Bjorn De Sutter, and Koen De Bosschere. Hybrid static-dynamic attacks against software protection mechanisms. In *Proceedings of the 5th ACM workshop on Digital rights management*, pages 75–82. ACM, 2005.
204. Prasanta Chandra Mahalanobis. On the generalized distance in statistics. *Proceedings of the National Institute of Sciences (Calcutta)*, 2:49–55, 1936.
205. Marion Marschalek. Big Game Hunting: Nation-state malware research, BlackHat. https://www.blackhat.com/docs/webcast/08202015-big-game-hunting.pdf/, 2015. Accessed: February, 2018.
206. Lorenzo Martignoni, Mihai Christodorescu, and Somesh Jha. Omniunpack: Fast, generic, and safe unpacking of malware. In *Twenty-Third Annual Computer Security Applications Conference (ACSAC)*, pages 431–441. IEEE, 2007.
207. Lorenzo Martignoni, Stephen McCamant, Pongsin Poosankam, Dawn Song, and Petros Maniatis. Path-exploration lifting: Hi-fi tests for lo-fi emulators. In *ACM SIGARCH Computer Architecture News*, volume 40, pages 337–348. ACM, 2012.
208. Sven Mattsen, Arne Wichmann, and Sibylle Schupp. A non-convex abstract domain for the value analysis of binaries. In *2015 IEEE 22nd International Conference on Software Analysis, Evolution, and Reengineering (SANER)*, pages 271–280. IEEE, 2015.
209. Ryan McDonald and Fernando Pereira. Identifying gene and protein mentions in text using conditional random fields. *BMC bioinformatics*, 6(1):1, 2005.

210. Eitan Menahem, Asaf Shabtai, Lior Rokach, and Yuval Elovici. Improving malware detection by applying multi-inducer ensemble. *Computational Statistics & Data Analysis*, 53(4):1483–1494, 2009.

211. Charith Mendis, Jeffrey Bosboom, Kevin Wu, Shoaib Kamil, Jonathan Ragan-Kelley, Sylvain Paris, Qin Zhao, and Saman Amarasinghe. Helium: lifting high-performance stencil kernels from stripped x86 binaries to halide dsl code. In *Proceedings of the 36th ACM SIGPLAN Conference on Programming Language Design and Implementation*, pages 391–402. ACM, 2015.

212. Xiaozhu Meng. Fine-grained binary code authorship identification. In *Proceedings of the 2016 24th ACM SIGSOFT International Symposium on Foundations of Software Engineering*, pages 1097–1099. ACM, 2016.

213. Xiaozhu Meng, Barton P Miller, and Kwang-Sung Jun. Identifying multiple authors in a binary program. In *European Symposium on Research in Computer Security (ESORICS)*, pages 286–304. Springer, 2017.

214. Barton P Miller, Mark D Callaghan, Jonathan M Cargille, Jeffrey K Hollingsworth, R Bruce Irvin, Karen L Karavanic, Krishna Kunchithapadam, and Tia Newhall. The paradyn parallel performance measurement tool. *Computer*, 28(11):37–46, 1995.

215. Jason Milletary. Citadel trojan malware analysis. *Dell SecureWorks Counter Threat Unit Intelligence Services*, pages 10–18, 2012.

216. Jiang Ming, Meng Pan, and Debin Gao. iBinHunt: binary hunting with inter-procedural control flow. In *Information Security and Cryptology–ICISC 2012*, pages 92–109. Springer, 2012.

217. Audris Mockus. Large-scale code reuse in open source software. In *First International Workshop on Emerging Trends in FLOSS Research and Development (FLOSS'07: ICSE Workshops 2007)*, pages 7–7. IEEE, 2007.

218. Mondaini, Rubem P. *BIOMAT 2012: International Symposium on Mathematical and Computational Biology, Tempe, Arizona, USA, 6-10 November 2012*. World Scientific, 2013.

219. Ned Moran and James Bennett. *Supply Chain Analysis: From Quartermaster to Sun-shop*, volume 11. FireEye Labs, 2013.

220. Andreas Moser, Christopher Kruegel, and Engin Kirda. Exploring multiple execution paths for malware analysis. In *IEEE Symposium on Security and Privacy (S&P)*, pages 231–245. IEEE, May 2007.

221. James Munkres. Algorithms for the assignment and transportation problems. *Journal of the Society for Industrial and Applied Mathematics*, 5(1):32–38, 1957.

222. Ginger Myles and Christian Collberg. K-gram based software birthmarks. In *Proceedings of the 2005 ACM symposium on Applied computing*, pages 314–318. ACM, 2005.

223. Lakshmanan Nataraj, Dhilung Kirat, BS Manjunath, and Giovanni Vigna. SARVAM: Search and retrieval of malware. In *Worshop on Next Generation Malware Attacks and Defense (NGMAD)*, 2013.

224. Nicholas Nethercote and Julian Seward. Valgrind: a framework for heavyweight dynamic binary instrumentation. In *ACM Sigplan notices*, volume 42, pages 89–100. ACM, 2007.

225. Beng Heng Ng and Aravind Prakash. Exposé: discovering potential binary code re-use. In *IEEE 37th Annual Computer Software and Applications Conference (COMPSAC)*, pages 492–501. IEEE, 2013.

226. Lina Nouh, Ashkan Rahimian, Djedjiga Mouheb, Mourad Debbabi, and Aiman Hanna. BinSign: fingerprinting binary functions to support automated analysis of code executables. In *IFIP International Conference on ICT Systems Security and Privacy Protection*, pages 341–355. Springer, 2017.

227. Pádraig OáSullivan, Kapil Anand, Aparna Kotha, Matthew Smithson, Rajeev Barua, and Angelos D Keromytis. Retrofitting security in cots software with binary rewriting. In *Future Challenges in Security and Privacy for Academia and Industry*, pages 154–172. Springer, 2011.

228. Karl J Ottenstein and Linda M Ottenstein. The program dependence graph in a software development environment. In *ACM Sigplan Notices*, volume 19, pages 177–184. ACM, 1984.

229. Gary Palmer et al. A road map for digital forensic research. In *First Digital Forensic Research Workshop*, pages 27–30, 2001.
230. Hanchuan Peng, Fuhui Long, and Chris Ding. Feature selection based on mutual information criteria of max-dependency, max-relevance, and min-redundancy. *IEEE Transactions on Pattern Analysis and Machine Intelligence (TPAMI)*, 27(8):1226–1238, 2005.
231. Jannik Pewny, Behrad Garmany, Robert Gawlik, Christian Rossow, and Thorsten Holz. Cross-architecture bug search in binary executables. In *IEEE Symposium on Security and Privacy (S&P)*, pages 709–724. IEEE, 2015.
232. Jannik Pewny, Felix Schuster, Lukas Bernhard, Thorsten Holz, and Christian Rossow. Leveraging semantic signatures for bug search in binary programs. In *Proceedings of the 30th Annual Computer Security Applications Conference (ACSAC)*, pages 406–415. ACM, 2014.
233. Van-Thuan Pham, Wei Boon Ng, Konstantin Rubinov, and Abhik Roychoudhury. Hercules: reproducing crashes in real-world application binaries. In *Proceedings of the 37th International Conference on Software Engineering-Volume 1*, pages 891–901. IEEE Press, 2015.
234. Marius Popa. Techniques of program code obfuscation for secure software. *Journal of Mobile, Embedded and Distributed Systems*, 3(4):205–219, 2011.
235. Jing Qiu, Xiaohong Su, and Peijun Ma. Library functions identification in binary code by using graph isomorphism testings. In *2015 IEEE 22nd International Conference on Software Analysis, Evolution, and Reengineering (SANER)*, pages 261–270. IEEE, 2015.
236. Jing Qiu, Xiaohong Su, and Peijun Ma. Using reduced execution flow graph to identify library functions in binary code. *IEEE Transactions on Software Engineering (TSE)*, 42(2):187–202, 2016.
237. Babak Bashari Rad, Maslin Masrom, and Suahimi Ibrahim. Opcodes histogram for classifying metamorphic portable executables malware. In *e-Learning and e-Technologies in Education (ICEEE), 2012 International Conference on*, pages 209–213. IEEE, 2012.
238. Jonathan Ragan-Kelley, Connelly Barnes, Andrew Adams, Sylvain Paris, Frédo Durand, and Saman Amarasinghe. Halide: a language and compiler for optimizing parallelism, locality, and recomputation in image processing pipelines. *ACM SIGPLAN Notices*, 48(6):519–530, 2013.
239. Ashkan Rahimian, Philippe Charland, Stere Preda, and Mourad Debbabi. RESource: a framework for online matching of assembly with open source code. In *International Symposium on Foundations and Practice of Security*, pages 211–226. Springer, 2012.
240. Ashkan Rahimian, Paria Shirani, Saed Alrbaee, Lingyu Wang, and Mourad Debbabi. Bincomp: A stratified approach to compiler provenance attribution. *Digital Investigation*, 14:S146–S155, 2015.
241. Ashkan Rahimian, Raha Ziarati, Stere Preda, and Mourad Debbabi. On the Reverse Engineering of the Citadel Botnet. In *International Symposium on Foundations and Practice of Security*, pages 408–425. Springer, 2013.
242. Václav Rajlich. Software evolution and maintenance. In *Proceedings of the Future of Software Engineering*, pages 133–144. ACM, 2014.
243. M Ramaswami and R Bhaskaran. A study on feature selection techniques in educational data mining. *arXiv preprint arXiv:0912.3924*, 2009.
244. David A Ramos and Dawson Engler. Under-constrained symbolic execution: correctness checking for real code. In *24th USENIX Security Symposium (USENIX Security 15)*, pages 49–64, 2015.
245. Alexandre Rebert, Sang Kil Cha, Thanassis Avgerinos, Jonathan Foote, David Warren, Gustavo Grieco, and David Brumley. Optimizing seed selection for fuzzing. In *23rd USENIX Security Symposium (USENIX Security 14)*, pages 861–875, 2014.
246. Konrad Rieck, Philipp Trinius, Carsten Willems, and Thorsten Holz. Automatic analysis of malware behavior using machine learning. *Journal of Computer Security*, 19(4):639–668, 2011.
247. Kaspar Riesen, Xiaoyi Jiang, and Horst Bunke. Exact and inexact graph matching: Methodology and applications. *Managing and Mining Graph Data*, pages 217–247, 2010.

248. Danny Roobaert, Grigoris Karakoulas, and Nitesh V Chawla. Information Gain, Correlation and Support Vector Machines. In *Feature Extraction*, pages 463–470. Springer, 2006.
249. Roman, Steven. *Coding and Information Theory*, vol. 134, Springer Science & Business Media, 1992.
250. Nathan Rosenblum, Barton P Miller, and Xiaojin Zhu. Recovering the toolchain provenance of binary code. In *Proceedings of the International Symposium on Software Testing and Analysis*, pages 100–110. ACM, 2011.
251. Nathan Rosenblum, Xiaojin Zhu, and Barton P Miller. Who wrote this code? identifying the authors of program binaries. In *European Symposium on Research in Computer Security (ESORICS)*, pages 172–189. Springer, 2011.
252. Nathan E Rosenblum, Barton P Miller, and Xiaojin Zhu. Extracting compiler provenance from program binaries. In *Proceedings of the 9th ACM SIGPLAN-SIGSOFT workshop on Program analysis for software tools and engineering*, pages 21–28. ACM, 2010.
253. Kevin A Roundy and Barton P Miller. Hybrid analysis and control of malware. In *Recent Advances in Intrusion Detection (RAID)*, pages 317–338. Springer, 2010.
254. Chanchal K Roy, James R Cordy, and Rainer Koschke. Comparison and evaluation of code clone detection techniques and tools: A qualitative approach. *Science of Computer Programming*, 74(7):470–495, 2009.
255. Brian Ruttenberg, Craig Miles, Lee Kellogg, Vivek Notani, Michael Howard, Charles LeDoux, Arun Lakhotia, and Avi Pfeffer. Identifying shared software components to support malware forensics. In *International Conference on Detection of Intrusions and Malware, and Vulnerability Assessment (DIMVA)*, pages 21–40. Springer, 2014.
256. Andreas Sæbjørnsen, Jeremiah Willcock, Thomas Panas, Daniel Quinlan, and Zhendong Su. Detecting code clones in binary executables. In *Proceedings of the eighteenth international symposium on Software testing and analysis*, pages 117–128. ACM, 2009.
257. Hassen Saïdi, V Yegneswaran, and P Porras. Experiences in malware binary deobfuscation. *Virus Bulletin*, 2010.
258. Saul Schleimer, Daniel S Wilkerson, and Alex Aiken. Winnowing: local algorithms for document fingerprinting. In *Proceedings of the 2003 ACM SIGMOD international conference on Management of data*, pages 76–85. ACM, 2003.
259. Matthew G Schultz, Eleazar Eskin, Erez Zadok, and Salvatore J Stolfo. Data mining methods for detection of new malicious executables. In *IEEE Symposium on Security and Privacy (S&P)*, pages 38–49. IEEE, 2001.
260. Farrukh Shahzad and Muddassar Farooq. ELF-Miner: using structural knowledge and data mining methods to detect new (Linux) malicious executables. *Knowledge and information systems*, 30(3):589–612, 2012.
261. Marc Shapiro and Susan Horwitz. The effects of the precision of pointer analysis. In *Static Analysis*, pages 16–34. Springer, 1997.
262. Eui Chul Richard Shin, Dawn Song, and Reza Moazzezi. Recognizing functions in binaries with neural networks. In *24th USENIX Security Symposium (USENIX Security 15)*, pages 611–626, 2015.
263. Paria Shirani, Leo Collard, Basile L Agba, Bernard Lebel, Mourad Debbabi, Lingyu Wang, and Aiman Hanna. BinARM: Scalable and efficient detection of vulnerabilities in firmware images of intelligent electronic devices. In *International Conference on Detection of Intrusions and Malware, and Vulnerability Assessment (DIMVA)*, pages 114–138. Springer, 2018.
264. Paria Shirani, Lingyu Wang, and Mourad Debbabi. BinShape: Scalable and robust binary library function identification using function shape. In *International Conference on Detection of Intrusions and Malware, and Vulnerability Assessment (DIMVA)*, pages 301–324. Springer, 2017.
265. Yan Shoshitaishvili, Ruoyu Wang, Christopher Salls, Nick Stephens, Mario Polino, Andrew Dutcher, John Grosen, Siji Feng, Christophe Hauser, Christopher Kruegel, et al. Sok:(state of) the art of war: Offensive techniques in binary analysis. In *IEEE Symposium on Security and Privacy (SP)*, pages 138–157. IEEE, 2016.

266. Ramandeep Singh. A review of reverse engineering theories and tools. *International Journal of Engineering Science Invention*, 2(1):35–38, 2013.

267. Asia Slowinska, Traian Stancescu, and Herbert Bos. Howard: A dynamic excavator for reverse engineering data structures. In *NDSS*. Citeseer, 2011.

268. Manuel Sojer and Joachim Henkel. Code reuse in open source software development: Quantitative evidence, drivers, and impediments. *Journal of the Association for Information Systems*, 11(12):868–901, 2010.

269. Dawn Song, David Brumley, Heng Yin, Juan Caballero, Ivan Jager, Min Gyung Kang, Zhenkai Liang, James Newsome, Pongsin Poosankam, and Prateek Saxena. Bitblaze: A new approach to computer security via binary analysis. In *Information systems security*, pages 1–25. Springer, 2008.

270. Eugene H Spafford and Stephen A Weeber. Software forensics: Can we track code to its authors? *Computers & Security*, 12(6):585–595, 1993.

271. Mark Stamp. A revealing introduction to hidden markov models. *Department of Computer Science San Jose State University*, 2004.

272. Saša Stojanović, Zaharije Radivojević, and Miloš Cvetanović. Approach for estimating similarity between procedures in differently compiled binaries. *Information and Software Technology*, 58:259–271, 2015.

273. Guillermo Suarez-Tangil, Juan E Tapiador, Pedro Peris-Lopez, and Arturo Ribagorda. Evolution, detection and analysis of malware for smart devices. *IEEE Communications Surveys & Tutorials*, 16(2):961–987, 2014.

274. Zhao Sun, Hongzhi Wang, Haixun Wang, Bin Shao, and Jianzhong Li. Efficient subgraph matching on billion node graphs. *Proceedings of the VLDB Endowment*, 5(9):788–799, 2012.

275. Johan AK Suykens and Joos Vandewalle. Least squares support vector machine classifiers. *Neural processing letters*, 9(3):293–300, 1999.

276. Yufei Tao, Ke Yi, Cheng Sheng, and Panos Kalnis. Quality and efficiency in high dimensional nearest neighbor search. In *Proceedings of the 2009 ACM SIGMOD International Conference on Management of data*, pages 563–576. ACM, 2009.

277. Yufei Tao, Ke Yi, Cheng Sheng, and Panos Kalnis. Efficient and accurate nearest neighbor and closest pair search in high-dimensional space. *ACM Transactions on Database Systems (TODS)*, 35(3):20, 2010.

278. Annie H Toderici and Mark Stamp. Chi-squared distance and metamorphic virus detection. *Journal of Computer Virology and Hacking Techniques*, 9(1):1–14, 2013.

279. Christoph Treude, Fernando Figueira Filho, Margaret Anne Storey, and Martin Salois. An exploratory study of software reverse engineering in a security context. In *2011 18th Working Conference on Reverse Engineering*, pages 184–188. IEEE, October 2011.

280. Jean-Baptiste Tristan, Paul Govereau, and Greg Morrisett. Evaluating value-graph translation validation for llvm. *ACM Sigplan Notices*, 46(6):295–305, 2011.

281. Sharath K Udupa, Saumya K Debray, and Matias Madou. Deobfuscation: Reverse engineering obfuscated code. In *12th Working Conference on Reverse Engineering (WCRE'05)*, pages 10–pp. IEEE, November 2005.

282. Julian R Ullmann. An algorithm for subgraph isomorphism. *Journal of the ACM (JACM)*, 23(1):31–42, 1976.

283. Maarten Van Emmerik. Identifying library functions in executable file using patterns. In *Software Engineering Conference, 1998. Proceedings. 1998 Australian*, pages 90–97. IEEE, 1998.

284. S Vichy N Vishwanathan, Nicol N Schraudolph, Risi Kondor, and Karsten M Borgwardt. Graph kernels. *The Journal of Machine Learning Research*, 11:1201–1242, 2010.

285. William M Waite and Gerhard Goos. *Compiler construction*. Springer Science & Business Media, 2012.

286. Andrew Walenstein, Michael Venable, Matthew Hayes, Christopher Thompson, and Arun Lakhotia. Exploiting similarity between variants to defeat malware. In *Proc. BlackHat DC Conf*, 2007.

287. Jason Tsong-Li Wang, Qicheng Ma, Dennis Shasha, and Cathy H. Wu. New techniques for extracting features from protein sequences. *IBM Systems Journal*, 40(2):426–441, 2001.
288. Xinran Wang, Chi-Chun Pan, Peng Liu, and Sencun Zhu. Sigfree: A signature-free buffer overflow attack blocker. *Dependable and Secure Computing, IEEE Transactions on*, 7(1):65–79, 2010.
289. Zheng Wang, Ken Pierce, and Scott McFarling. Bmat-a binary matching tool for stale profile propagation. *The Journal of Instruction-Level Parallelism*, 2:1–20, 2000.
290. Daniel Weise, Roger F Crew, Michael Ernst, and Bjarne Steensgaard. Value dependence graphs: Representation without taxation. In *Proceedings of the 21st ACM SIGPLAN-SIGACT symposium on Principles of programming languages*, pages 297–310. ACM, 1994.
291. Tao Xie, Darko Marinov, Wolfram Schulte, and David Notkin. Symstra: A framework for generating object-oriented unit tests using symbolic execution. In *Tools and Algorithms for the Construction and Analysis of Systems*, pages 365–381. Springer, 2005.
292. Fabian Yamaguchi, Nico Golde, Daniel Arp, and Konrad Rieck. Modeling and discovering vulnerabilities with code property graphs. In *IEEE Symposium on Security and Privacy (SP)*, pages 590–604. IEEE, 2014.
293. Fabian Yamaguchi, Alwin Maier, Hugo Gascon, and Konrad Rieck. Automatic inference of search patterns for taint-style vulnerabilities. In *IEEE Symposium on Security and Privacy*, pages 797–812. IEEE, 2015.
294. Chaitanya Yavvari, Arnur Tokhtabayev, Huzefa Rangwala, and Angelos Stavrou. Malware characterization using behavioral components. In *International Conference on Mathematical Methods, Models, and Architectures for Computer Network Security*, pages 226–239. Springer, 2012.
295. Yanfang Ye, Tao Li, Yong Chen, and Qingshan Jiang. Automatic malware categorization using cluster ensemble. In *Proceedings of the 16th ACM SIGKDD international conference on Knowledge discovery and data mining*, pages 95–104. ACM, 2010.
296. Li Yujian and Liu Bo. A normalized levenshtein distance metric. *IEEE Transactions on Pattern Analysis and Machine Intelligence*, 29(6):1091–1095, 2007.
297. Syarif Yusirwan, Yudi Prayudi, and Imam Riadi. Implementation of malware analysis using static and dynamic analysis method. *International Journal of Computer Applications*, 117(6), 2015.
298. Junyuan Zeng, Yangchun Fu, Kenneth A Miller, Zhiqiang Lin, Xiangyu Zhang, and Dongyan Xu. Obfuscation resilient binary code reuse through trace-oriented programming. In *Proceedings of the 2013 ACM SIGSAC Conference on Computer & Communications Security (CCS)*, pages 487–498. ACM, 2013.
299. Yijia Zhang, Hongfei Lin, Zhihao Yang, and Yanpeng Li. Neighborhood hash graph kernel for protein–protein interaction extraction. *Journal of biomedical informatics*, 44(6):1086–1092, 2011.
300. Yijia Zhang, Hongfei Lin, Zhihao Yang, Jian Wang, and Yanpeng Li. Hash subgraph pairwise kernel for protein-protein interaction extraction. *IEEE/ACM Transactions on Computational Biology and Bioinformatics (TCBB)*, 9(4):1190–1202, 2012.
301. Eric R Ziegel. Probability and Statistics for Engineering and the Sciences. *Technometrics*, 2012.
302. Viviane Zwanger and Felix C Freiling. Kernel mode API spectroscopy for incident response and digital forensics. In *Proceedings of the 2nd ACM SIGPLAN Program Protection and Reverse Engineering Workshop*, page 3. ACM, 2013.